Doug Van
Volkenburgh

About New York

About New York

FRANCIS X. CLINES

McGRAW-HILL BOOK COMPANY

New York
St. Louis
San Francisco

Printed in the United States of America.

1 2 3 4 5 6 7 8 9 0 BP BP 8 7 6 5 4 3 2 1 0

LIBRARY OF CONGRESS CATALOGING IN PUBLICATION DATA
Clines, Francis X.
About New York.
1. New York (City)—Social life and customs—
Collected works. 2. New York (City)—Description—
1951-   —Collected works. I. Title.
F128.52.C52   974.7′1   80-16080
ISBN 0-07-011384-X

Book design by Roberta Rezk

This Is Kathy's Book

Preface

For three years, *The New York Times* had me roam its richest story—the city itself—and file reports three times a week on whatever I pleased. Sometimes I would drop in on the Mayor, or a tunnel cop. I would hang around with a blind beggar for a while or go to the race track with a rich landlord, or spend a night watching prostitutes or just listening to the sounds after closing time at the Bronx Zoo.

The editors who had me do this, Abe Rosenthal and Syd Schanberg, set no limits because they wanted the story of the quality of the city that defies the usual categories of journalism. This is the story of the city's ordinary people, how they come to live and die in the city and make peace with it or not.

More than any other beat, this is a story of time and place. It is a narrative story more than an analytical one. It would be enough, I thought, to aim for a point years hence and simply try to describe what life looked like and felt like for this instant, to document the obvious truth that each human being is precious in his or her slot of time.

While much of the newspaper necessarily watched the headline events, I had the smaller story of plain individuals, the story that, as the photographer August Sander has explained, gets at a larger truth: "The individual does not make the history of his time; he both impresses himself on it and expresses its meaning."

Such a job would be a privilege anywhere, but in New York it was grand fun and frightening opportunity: watching peerless individuals and staring at facets of a gem.

There was no set method to this job. I have certain prejudices that were indulged: Having been born in Brooklyn of a woman born in Hell's Kitchen, I have an outer-borough curiosity, and a suspicion that the affluent and the privileged have entrée enough to the daily prints. Then again, the finest people turned up on West 72nd Street in Manhattan as fatefully as on 81st Street in Bay Ridge, and the memories of certain blocks and buildings and individuals can never be fully recounted.

The city is such a sight that it strikes deep into a witness and summons up all sorts of storytelling ways. For me, these ways go back to places like Noone's Tavern in Bay Ridge thirty years ago when I was a silent youngster trailing my father, on Saturdays, privileged to listen and watch ordinary people searching for a smile in life. These storytelling ways plagiarize the gifts of countless others, particularly the wit and cynicism of newspaper people like Jerry Allan at the *Buffalo Evening News* and Sheldon Binn at the *Times*. And these ways are rooted in the splendid love of words and life displayed by the truest New Yorkers such as Bill Farrell at the *Times*.

I have a new assignment now—new people in a different place—but New York will never be done with me. It will outlive all the people I love and all the stories I loved to tell, and it will survive as a memorial to us all, to all the ordinary people at its heart.

Washington, D.C.   F. X. C.
June 1980

1

Street Smarts

Oh-All Right!

Every morning people have no choice but to arise and emerge from the apartment buildings of the Upper West Side and face the sun-red trauma of a new day. The lucky ones hear the word of Jacob, who is running around in knickers and long striped socks, splashing and gunning automobiles to life as if they were people. "Everythin's gonna be oh-all right," he insists in the cold streets, again and again.

Darting and declaiming, Jacob, whose real name is Herbert Jacobs, resembles another East Side author of another West Side best-seller on the Weltanschauung of jogging. But he is far more original: He parks and moves residents' cars all day in the local streets, threading a living through the outrageous fortunes of the city's alternate-side-of-the-street parking regulations.

Begun in the dim past as a street-cleaning measure, these regulations exist now basically as a premise for clawing fresh revenues into the city's towaway program, at the rate of $90 a violation. In his role, therefore, Jacob, with his little black bag containing monastery-size rings of keys to dozens of customers' cars, is as vital to the peace of this quintessentially harassed and blessed Manhattan hamlet as any three eager young lawyers on the rent control/reform club/pro bono make.

"Y'got to know what yo're up to ou'chere, else the tow truck beat you, and that's the name of that," Jacob says in his Carolina drawl, popping open the hood of a mustard Oldsmobile and inserting a ballpoint pen just right to hold the carburetor open.

"You watch me," the lean, nimble street genius says, getting into the car. And, boom, there is ignition. Jacob retrieves the pen, closes the hood and says, "We're gone."

•

He drives a block up West End Avenue to 84th Street, where he already has marshaled a long, neat morning row of double-parked cars which are his holding pattern on the cusp of the 8 A.M.-to-11 A.M. subsection of the parking regulations.

He jogs with his bag of keys to the next car and the next, getting into them, firing them in the stone-cold city, moving them to the schizoid spirit of the law. "We're gone," he says with each. And always, as a neighbor goes by: "Everythin's gonna be oh-all right."

After fifty-three years of life and twenty-five years of moving cars back and forth from one curbside to the other in an eight-block swath north of 80th Street and west of Broadway, Jacob seems as pastoral as a shepherd, tending his metallic flock seven days a week. Customers can leave their cars at night anywhere in his territory, and they will be parked somewhere close the next morning out of the way of the towaway man.

Some West Siders don't use their cars for weeks at a time and don't know where they are exactly, except that they are in Jacob's calloused hands. The locomotion is relentless, but Jacob doesn't seem world-weary as he moves about in his winter outfit (the all-season knickers and striped socks plus three stocking hats, ten undershirts, three sweaters, five pair of long johns, a jacket and boots).

He wears no gloves, handling all those keys. But his black bag contains a bottle of spiked egg nog, and on any block he seems able to disappear into a building for an instant and to return with a bucket of steaming boiler water to drench open frozen locks.

•

"It's comin'," Jacob says, staring down West 83rd Street, vapor-voiced as a prophet. He is speaking not of Judgment Day but of a snowfall heavy enough to force the suspension of parking regulations and thus give him a day off. "I heard the man say 8 inches on the radio. When it comes, I rests. There were fifty-two snow days last winter. Very fine."

One client claims Jacob helps her find herself as much as her car every morning. And Jacob is so confident on his streets that he stops a courtly man with a cane by saying, "And here's our best doctor." And the physician, A. O. Sternberg, nods and says, "And you, Jacob, are our best car parker."

"I knows the people who have the strong hand," Jacob explains. "Now, over at the *po*-lice house," he says, emphasizing the special syllable of authority, "they have the strong hand, and I knows the man there and wax his Mercedes-Benz all nice for free."

•

With private garage rates running to $110 a month, Jacob's service is a bargain. He won't talk prices, but one customer pays $30 a month and stresses that Jacob offers to work off a violation if the towaway man beats him. He enlists auxiliary services, too. "There's Pedro, mah mechanic on 82d, and Sol Singer, mah tire and battery man on Amsterdam."

He uses the same tone about professionals in his clientele who, he says gratefully, do favors for him. "There are mah doctors," he says, backing down a full block at full speed. "There's mah feet doctor who helps mah feet, and there's mah Cuban dentist who pulls mah teeth for free, and up there's Dr. Mark-a-which."

A psychiatrist? Jacob uses a psychiatrist? "Well, y' see one day I was acting up in the street, talking to m'self and I says I better see that man. And he says even tho' mah wife lives uptown and I'm down, she was on mah mind. Get this—I loved her and had jealousy."

Truly, such a free consultation could only accrue to a car parker on the Upper West Side, a happily humanist neighborhood where even the cars seem part of a vibrant world of contentious ideas and ever evolving self-revelations. (That

Volvo, for example, outside the building of the famous social critic actually is a mint-new, four-door 1979 Angst with shtik shift. And the sad MG outside the tired writer's place is a dented 1959 Libido.)

In this case, the doctor was wise enough to prescribe Jacob to Jacob. "He says, that's all right. Don't worry. Everythin's gonna be oh-all right."

[1/16/79]

Virtuoso

The Stradivarius is in pieces, stripped and gutless and an anxious sight. And the news that this unglued creation truly is a Stradivarius is startling, like being told that a man found weeping on a psychiatrist's couch is Plato.

The hands of Jacques Français move the pieces with tender authority, making them look like a violin again, pointing out the dents and cracks of time that his master craftsmen are expunging, confidently promising to restore to life the rare sound of this instrument and in the process turn Mr. Français's $30,000 auction "steal" into a $100,000-plus resale.

"It is not the money, it is the hunt—the pleasure of discovering a sleeper and bringing it back," says Mr. Français in his thirteenth-floor office on West 57th Street near Carnegie Hall.

Here is a combination of hearth and shop with a dozen fresh roses on the monsieur's desk and customers arriving like rich and wretched law clients, carrying their hopes and broken loves to him in velvet-lined cases and in sacks of chamois and of mundane plastic.

•

Mr. Français receives customers as a gentle host, greeting them in a towering room before a fireplace that stands cold on a sunny day, a room that resembles an estate dining hall, highlighted by the earthy and caramel tones of violins and cellos grouped in the shadows like dinner guests mellowed by brandy.

He is a special sort of businessman who heals the

occasional wounds of violins possessed by such friends and concert artists as Isaac Stern. And he performs instant critiques on thousands of anonymous fiddles every year as a fifty-three-year-old broker of rare violins and, closer to his soul, as a searcher for extraordinary values veiled by grime and ignorance.

Mr. Français receives so many inquiries from people throughout the nation who think they possess violin treasures that he has a form letter he sends advising them that unless they have some encouraging documentation they should not make the trip because they are most likely wrong.

"Still they come—with junk," says Mr. Français with a thrust of his Gallic profile. "Quite often someone dies and the family finds a violin in the estate and they troop in together like ducks in a row, with lawyers, and no one trusting the rest." He describes how he has them put the violin on the red-clothed table by the fireplace and step away. "I approach the case. I open it. I look down. I say, 'No.' And I walk out."

He laughs at his strut from the internecine frustration, stressing that when he is badgered into viewing such unpromising violins he always does so without accepting a consultation fee. "Then I am free to tell them that my opinion is final, and they can not ask questions."

The other day, Mr. Français spoke French when telling a delicate dowager-looking woman that her cherished fiddle, which she had slowly unwrapped for him like a secret in the confessional, was not a treasure and not worth the price of repair at his shop. "It is nothing for me, Madame," he said politely.

The vivid beauty of his business is in his repair shop, where a master, René Morel, reigns as a vice president of the concern. Dressed in a blue smock, he directs the restoration of instruments worth $300,000 and more, boldly taking them apart and applying some methods that are centuries old and others of his own devising that are as finely wrought as neural surgery, with precise clamps and tools of his own design.

Mr. Morel, who like Mr. Français is descended from eighteenth-century violin makers in Mirecourt, France, restores the shape of tired treasures by making exact corrected casts with orthodontal plaster and zinc and using bags of hot sand to soften the wood and reshape it. To get at cracks and dents, he and his assistants carefully sand down an area of the violin panel from the underside with a caressing level of friction until a vaporous opening is produced. An exact replacement piece is shaped from stores of valuable wood, carefully matching grain for grain.

A restoration can cost $5,000 at Jacques Français, and there is a waiting list of up to three years for some jobs. The wood—maple and spruce—is very special and is usually purchased from old European violin makers whom Mr. Français knows and tracks as they prepare to retire.

•

Restoring varnish tones is an art in itself. The pigments and tones are increasingly difficult to obtain, with Mr. Français's sometimes buying a decade's supply of special vegetable-based colors from a French concern.

"And rasps!" he says, taking up one of these hand tools as if it, too, were a Strad. He uses only extremely precise rasps made by hand by a Frenchman who is a temperamental craftsman.

"He only makes them once every ten years or so—about a hundred at a time," Mr. Français says, "and I must wait for the miracle of getting ten and hoarding them."

Mr. Morel is the sort who can work day after day in the most detailed scale and still put in 530 hours of spare time at home, as he did over a recent period of months, restoring a $300,000 Guarneri cello.

The six craftsmen in his shop began, of course, with prodigious talents, he says. But, like violinists, they must develop through long experience. "You have to see great art in order to make great art," he says.

There is an enormous inspiration for this purpose in the shop of Jacques Français—most particularly a steel safe of twelve shelves containing a treasure of rare violins—Amati, Stradivari, Guarneri—the names soar forth. Facing them can be a moment of fine tension, like the surface quiver on the bowl of water resting on the bottom shelf for protective humidity. Atop this wealth of wood rests a bust of Beethoven, who seems appropriately transfixed in a swoon of genius.

[2/22/77]

Openers

The old pro was in the locker room at Yankee Stadium, granting an interview in his striped uniform before the opening day game, wondering how strong his legs would be in his twenty-third season of rounding the corner from the distribution room and hustling to the upper deck with the trays of cold beer, and pivoting and squatting and going to his right and left to snag the coins thrown by customers.

There was a nervousness in the air, still winter-dead under the left-field stands where the vendors' locker rooms are, as Ken Spinner, thirty-seven years old and a career hawker (currently Yankee and Shea Stadiums, Madison Square Garden and the Nassau Coliseum), tied on his blue apron with the deep change pockets. "I like my job, the money and the competition," he said. "My legs are tired but the new crop of kids keeps me thinking young."

The Yankees' 250-vendor lineup this year ranges from Mr. Spinner, a kind of Satchel Paige of hawking who began at Ebbets Field with 15-cent frosticks, to such promising young rookies as Mary Nestor, a fourteen-year-old who draped her red ponytail over her right shoulder as she sold peanuts ("Hey, peanuts! Peanuts!" she piped) in the field level No. 11 section near home plate.

Mary showed a beautiful move in the opening game, keeping her back to the field and going to her nickel and dime pockets cleanly to continue making change at the moment Jim Wynn hit the first Yankee homer and her clientele jumped up and burst into screams.

There is a comeback vendor in the lineup, too, thirty-year-old Steve Smith, a stadium hawker ten years ago and a school teacher now with a pregnant wife. He still has the major-league forearms for hoisting beer trays and frankfurter baskets overhead in a tight spot, and he's back for the money, not love of the game.

He seemed a bit guilty as he admitted how time had changed his motives, in contrast to the younger generation of vendors who, just like their fellow businessmen out on the field playing with bats and balls and gloves, talk a candid line of entrepreneurial goals. In fact, Jeff Williams, an eighteen-year-old Haaren High student in his fifth season, might have made George Steinbrenner, the free-spending Yankee owner, weep with joy as he stood for a moment by the leather-popping sounds of the left-field bullpen and presented the business overview.

"The big deal, of course, is we got Reggie," Jeff said, referring to Reggie Jackson, the crowd-pleasing slugger crassly obtained by the Yankees on the open market like a consignment of diamonds and coffee. "The way I figure, the fans are going to come out past two million. Do that, and I got a chance of going over $3,000 for the season."

He made a beautiful smile and a right fist gesture toward the green, green grass of the field: pride of the new Yankees.

•

The vendors' roster has life's full variety of good people. There are Renaissance men passing happily through on the way to bigger things, such as Ed Julie, a medical student, and Warren Merguerian, a dental student, two close friends who began vending back when they were students at the Bronx High School of Science. There is the lean, scrappy, Eddie Stanky type of hawker—Paul Weber, who took a punch in the eye one day when he spilled some of his beer tray onto a big guy in upper deck 17.

And, of course, no lineup is complete without a free-thinking hustler, a Jim Bouton-type who openly analyzes life as he looks for its angles. Dave Goode, smiling tall and curly haired at age twenty-one, plays this position. In his eighth season, Mr. Goode is reputed to be one of the $100-a-day hawkers. (The average range, based on 16 percent commissions, is $30 to $50.) But he slides off that subject by telling why he prefers the Yankee customer to the Met fan at Shea, where he also hawks.

"The Shea fan is a stiff, a family guy who has to watch his money," Dave said. "Here at the stadium you can do maybe 25 percent better with the Archie Bunker types who want their beer through the game."

For sheer, lucrative thirst, he attests, there is nothing like a Red Sox game, preferably on a hot night with the park full of shouting gamblers and rowdies.

"Hell, the Boston crowds are great drinkers even on a cold day," Dave said. "And the worst job is peanuts in the bleachers on a Memorial Day doubleheader with an expansion team."

•

At 12:55 P.M. on opening day, two hours after the vendors had shaped up beyond the outfield wall, Gary Cohen, a former Yankee vendor dressed in a three-piece mauve suit who is the chief executive of the vendors now in behalf of Canteen Corporation, nodded to his field manager, Sal Luigi, a short, quietly watchful man whose assistant herded all 250 vendors into the right-field bleachers for the pregame pep talk.

There was a buzz of talk (watch out for the "bug juice" jobs of selling orange drink, and for the "Con Ed kids"— slum children admitted free to the bleachers, some of whom pick the vendors' pockets). But then they were shushed, and Sal Luigi, bathed in sunshine and straining over the organ music to be heard in the honest, now antediluvian accent of Ebbets Field, where he began in this game, declared:

"O.K., guys, let's stay together. This is a family deal. Yiz wanna make a buck?—I'll see yiz make a buck. Let's get to our areas and keep the stuff moving!"

A charming, greedy roar—the first real one, predating the paying customers—was the response Sal got, and the pin-striped hawkers went forth with jingling pockets to get their merchandise and play the game.

[4/9/77]

The Good Life

Some days life as a homosexual can seem pretty good. Fresh orange juice in the penthouse. ("To heck with Anita Bryant.") A compliment from the maid as she arrives drenched from a gray Manhattan rain. "Saw your picture in the paper. Looked handsome." A batch of telegrams and letters from friends offering congratulations on being chosen as the first publicly identified homosexual to be appointed to the city's Commission on Human Rights.

"And I've been getting great telephone calls," said the appointee, Robert L. Livingston. "Including three classmates from Yale who admitted they were gay."

Actually, life as a homosexual can often seem good, Mr. Livingston says, once the decision is made to abandon the wearying practices of forced lying that begin as a teen-ager. However, current law does not encourage such candor and even permits discrimination where it is chanced, he says. So he feels there is more than enough homosexual cause left in the city, with moments of unfair trial every day for some of the half million men and women homosexuals that he estimates live in the city.

•

Mr. Livingston hardly rattles chains in your face as he sits in his penthouse. In fact, several times he says that in claiming full standing in society homosexuals should not overlook telling the news that they can be as happy as anybody else.

"People don't realize it's fun being gay," says Mr. Livingston, a forty-five-year-old man who uses personal

15

candor as a civic wedge. "I have a wonderful life—good friends, a lover. I wouldn't have missed this for money. Being active and being involved is fun. I am not unhappy with my life."

Neither is the Beame administration unhappy with his life, apparently. The remarkable fact that a seventy-one-year-old Mayor whose behavior range goes all the way from conservative to shy should proclaim the appointment of a homosexual activist in an election year is clear proof that politicians now discern some sort of positive edge in a minority cause that used to be dismissed with a snicker.

Not too many years ago the homosexual debate among city politicians focused on such questions as whether intrusive demonstrators deserved a macho punch in the nose.

Now, however, Mr. Livingston is talking of "the only closet that really counts, the ballot box." If this smacks of the sort of "give a damn" conventionality and sloganeering that eventually washes over every moderately successful cause, Mr. Livingston is delighted.

"I am conventional," he says. "I believe in the system. Most gay people are conventional." Some are extortionists like those in the Samuel Bronfman case, he said, some win Nobel prizes. "But most are plain and want the same things as everybody else."

But the rub for some heterosexuals is the suspicion that this particular movement wants not just full civil-rights protection under the law, but some sort of positive social approbation, an imprimatur of "normalcy."

•

Mr. Livingston says no, he is not interested in other people's moral judgments or of the use of such a highly relative term as "normalcy." You cannot legislate social acceptance, he agreed. "The problem is a gay person is accepted if he laughs at all the 'fag' jokes everybody makes and if he goes around the office like a black man saying, 'I'm not black.' "

While Mr. Livingston has been receiving messages of

16

enthusiasm from the city's homosexual community, he has had to point out that the Commission on Human Rights has no jurisdiction over some of their alleged grievances, particularly in the employment area. The City Council has several times rejected an extension of the antidiscrimination statute to job opportunities for homosexuals, and Mr. Livingston says this is one issue he will be pursuing from his new post.

Of course, there are businesses in this city that do not discriminate against homosexuals in hiring, he agrees. The more subtle problem is that homosexuals sense, rightly or wrongly, that various concerns and industries are intolerant and, knowing there is no law to assure protection, homosexuals do not risk applying.

It is a "nagging" kind of problem, he says, less obvious than such federal issues as less-than-honorable discharges for homosexuals in the military, and such state issues as "moral character" standards for certain kinds of licensing that prove inhibiting.

•

"Did you ever wonder why there are so few gay activist stockbrokers?" he asks, contending it is the licensing fear, not a paucity of homosexual stockbrokers.

Mr. Livingston is not hailing his appointment as any kind of a victory, merely an opportunity to educate the public. A wealthy man who has dabbled in publishing and politics, he says he will organize a voter registration drive in this mayoral election to maintain his special constituency's new edge in public life.

"By being vocal we have dragged a Trojan horse into the city—they think we have power," he said. "Now we must deliver."

He doesn't much care if some people resent his oath of public service this morning. He is prepared for familiar questions and will answer that no, the public's sons are not in danger of seduction; no, homosexuals do not have special ways of recognizing each other; and no, it is not catching.

[3/24/77]

17

Tough Talk

Abraham D. Beame was speaking in re-membrance of crises past. Once, hanging around outside the poolroom on Stanton Street, young Abe Beame stuck up for his childhood friend, Nervo, when an interloper from a neighboring gang gave insult. "I kicked him in the behind," Mr. Beame said.

Oh come on. That 1973 campaign stuff about "Spunky" Beame is true? The Mayor gave a look as if the questioner had just insulted Nervo all over again on the steamy Lower East Side.

"See this?" He had removed his eyeglasses and was showing a scar near his left eye. "Did I fight? We used to have block fights. People back then thought that was the ultimate in street crime and disruption. We'd throw bottles and milk cans from the roofs. I got hit and knocked down and cut my head—here."

The magistrate of the Big Apple smiled, as if just touching the long-ago blemish could change his mood. "I remember going to Kohler's drug store and standing on a chair as the druggist sewed it up."

•

Abraham D. Beame was speaking in remembrance of crisis present. "What do you mean?" he said. "I can get mad."

But nothing like Nervo and the kick in the pants, right? What about the nights in Albany two years ago when the legislative leaders got their hands on the fiscal crisis and got rough with the Mayor? Mr. Beame said, "Oh I dealt with Warren Anderson."

He referred to a vile personal instruction the Mayor, furious and frustrated, offered Mr. Anderson, the upstate Republican who is Senate majority leader, as the two men were seated with other leading politicians in the Governor's office and negotiating the crimping of the city government.

The instruction, Chaucerian in tone if not originality, is a commonplace vulgarity, but in Albany it is still recalled by witnesses as sounding historic on the lips of the quiet, gray, internalized man who is Mayor, a man who finally got angry and redeemed his claim to humanity. "Listen, if I didn't get mad sometimes, you could put me in the cemetery."

•

Abraham D. Beame was ignoring the obvious, the editorialists' adieus and the polls of political rivals crazed enough, perhaps by the withering winter, to want to succeed him. The polls say he is no more than third choice of ordinary people forced to face the laundry-list of aspirants beginning to pop out at us lately like tired ingénues.

Third place? "Ah, it doesn't bother me. A poll is good the day it happens, that's all."

He remembers a day in 1965, right after he won the Democratic primary to be mayoral candidate.

"Oh, I was riding high. I remember Teddy White was interviewing me—we were sitting on the lawn of some big estate somewhere—and my P.R. man interrupted." The candidate's media strategist had a big smile and great news about the first Beame-versus-Lindsay poll.

"The guy said, 'Beame 48 percent, Lindsay 34—it's all over.'" The following election day, of course, Mr. Beame lost to the incumbent Mayor, John V. Lindsay.

Mayor Beame smiled like a fleet, tattered fox: "We took a poll. There's your poll."

•

Does he dare to eat a peach? That is the kind of question tempted by the cryptic presence of Abraham D. Beame, 5-feet-2-inches tall and five fathoms deep, a man who never surrenders his full impressions, according to close advisers. His style has a matte finish and his idea of playing the game of politics is not to raise the stakes dramatically and ruffle the deck, but rather to quietly memorize the discards.

One potential city appointee—a more-than-self-confident man known to be well composed and witty at parties of the city's striving social elite—thought his appointment was all but secured when he went in to see Mr. Beame.

"My God, the Mayor chose not to say anything beyond hello. Suddenly I had the burden of carrying on a monologue, sweat pouring down my sides, and he just sat there like this sweet Jewish doll! It was harrowing."

This sort of passiveness, unnerving to strangers, was a wily trademark of an earlier Mayor, Robert F. Wagner. Mr. Beame has put a new glaze on it, a Dresden élan that lets him watch and listen. He is a vortex disguised as a smudge.

How could a man who was one of the best buttonholing district captains ever among Brooklyn Democrats seem passive or shy?

"When it came to those things I wasn't shy. I always enjoyed the street work more than giving speeches. That's politics; that's public service."

•

Abraham D. Beame was wearing his night work suit, the tuxedo, and, seated among hundreds of fellow politicians over the dregs of banquet filet mignon, had to look up and watch a movie that showed Abraham D. Beame thirty years ago, a handsome phantom that drew "ah's" from the audience, then applause. A little surprise for him at a political dinner.

What did he think at the sight of that man whose hair seemed black as the ink of that thirty-year-gone budget conference? "When I looked at that I thought, 'I got older.' "

[4/12/77]

20

Gospel Pride

The Rev. Baybie Hoover could smell the newsstand, so she knew exactly where to reach and touch the building corner where she sings with her tin cup amid the heavy crowds across from Bloomingdale's. She took the tin cup from her wraithlike layers of clothing and felt it, discovering it was battered and pinched shut.

"I guess it got squeezed in the cab door again," Baybie Hoover said, smiling upward at herself. She bent the cup right, put her cane at her side carefully, speaking to the cane: "Cane, stay right there." She held the cup out like a maestro tapping the music stand, and began singing in a very plain and pretty voice filled with the tones of her Kansas church roots: "What a Friend We Have in Jesus."

Quickly, a pedestrian dropped a coin in the blind woman's cup and Baybie got the sound and vibration of it at once and interrupted her song: "God bless you. Thank you." Her street song resumed: ". . . All our sins and grief to bear."

The day was the kind when the sun starts to stand up to the tired winter cold and bring color back to town. Some in the crowds flowing by the intersection of Lexington Avenue and East 59th Street were obviously pleased to see Baybie back at her corner, singing like a plump urban robin.

Baybie—this is the name she most prefers, the name she adopted for herself eight years ago—has been singing Christian gospel songs on the city's streets, beating out the rhythm with the coins in her cup, for twenty-six years. She and her best friend, Virginia Brown, had been two blind

21

street singers for years in Wichita when their director, Reverend Taylor, a man who used to take two of every three dimes dropped into their cup, left them and died. The two women sang their way east through a string of cities, piecing together the bus fare.

"What's Kansas got for me?" Baybie says, explaining the past in terms of the present. "New York is my city. It's so big and everything. It's the first place where I ever was treated like a human being."

She dislikes being treated as a "blind person" who should quietly stay out of the sight of society. She laughs in telling about how some other blind person sometimes will tap right up to her and whisper annoyance that her "begging" is giving a bad impression. "If I just stood there with a cup, that'd be begging," Baybie says. "But I give the people something. I sing my songs for them."

•

Baybie Hoover has memorized hundreds of songs and figures she can sing at least four hours straight without repeating any. She does white gospel songs, including such standards as "The Old Rugged Cross" and "How Beautiful Heaven Must Be," plus radio-Christian songs like "Automobile of Life," and tabloid ballads like "Floyd Collins."

On her strong days—in the past—she could do seven hours a day, and she worked a variety of corners in Manhattan, the Bronx and Queens. "I remember Jackson Heights was always good because there are plenty of Jewish people there and they are generous, even if all I did was stand there and sing about Jesus the livelong day."

Those strong days are over because the sixty-two-year-old woman has arthritis now. But she still tries her singing for shorter periods every week and says she could do more if she had something better than her present walker-cane, something that could be converted to a chair or a perch so she didn't have to keep shifting her heavy weight from one foot to the other.

Her title of "Reverend" comes from her ordination with the Radio Gospel Church and from a fifteen-minute show

22

she does every Sunday morning on WHBI. She sings on the air and does mild preaching: "Dear Jesus, we thank thee for this wonderful opportunity to sing thy praises. . . ."

•

Even the most cynical observer of the city's horde of street mendicants would have a hard time finding a false note about anything Baybie sings or says. It is a secret pleasure at winter's end to watch her in her little capped hat, her face lifted in Jesus-singing satisfaction while all about her sighted people are passing in far greater complication, looking for a certain shop window or face, preoccupied with invisible hope.

"Seven hours a day on the street singing," Baybie says. "I took it like a job. I gave it everything I had. Once someone came up and said, 'You think you have talent?' And I said, 'I haven't thought that much about it, but I always give it everything I have.'"

The first day she was in New York, Baybie remembers, she was so happy she got footloose and fell from a curb. "I skinned my hand and I said, 'Oh good, I've got a whole lot of New York in my hand.' In those days, I'd feel how clean the sidewalks were, scraping my feet along, clean enough to eat off. Now I can feel the garbage and dirt all over the sidewalk."

•

"The people are much tighter now, too. I got knocked flat by someone rushing by the other day. I says, 'Praise the Lord, Baybie, and get yourself up if you can.'"

Of course Baybie got up, treating the incident like another odd song to be remembered. Baybie's own name seems like a song, deliberately misspelled to make it special.

"I changed it because my Grandma, the only person who ever loved me when I was little, called me baby, real slow," she says. "My old name was Nadine, which means hope, but I'm tired of hoping."

Baybie smiles upward and says, "Baybie means new, staying young. It makes me think of love, of approval."

Wrapped in winter woolens and songs, the Rev. Baybie Hoover looks radiant with herself. "Oh, it's a magic name," she says. "I have pleased someone very dear to me." She laughs. "Myself."

[3/20/79]

So What
Do You Think?

Sounds like wall-to-wall white people to me." Marki Marcus, young, black and handsome, and with his cynicism coming into its own in the half-court world of Columbus Avenue, was offering his impression of the city's summer job picture for teen-agers.

Last month, Marki, a fifteen-year-old student, stayed up all night in line for more than twelve hours with hundreds of other teen-agers trying to apply for a summer job, holding on tightly to the required paper work—a statement of depressed income from his family, four photographs of himself, working papers, Social Security number and proof of school enrollment.

This week, Marki heard about Mayor Beame's private list of privileged youngsters slated to be secretly boosted into summer park jobs because they have political patrons watching out for them. No mention of photographs, or income statements or all-night bureaucratic hassles, just the mere wafting of such magic names as "Meade" and "Donny" and the other chief political loyalists of the Mayor.

When the news of this came out, two deputies of the Mayor were forced to play roles resembling the good and bad angels, as if Mr. Beame could be, after all his years in politics, personally innocent of the knowledge of this particular fruit of the patronage tree. The good angel was pronounced victorious, but Marki Marcus wondered about that up at the settlement house playground at 93rd Street and Columbus Avenue.

"I want to know who's behind all this," he said,

properly suspicious of why he had to stand and wait through the night while anonymous privileged teen-agers were, as his friend Saran Kaba put it, "home in bed all warm, with a job waiting for them." Saran, another of the all-night job applicants, was cynical and angry.

"Anything that has to do with government has to be this way," she said in the Goddard-Riverside Community Center, where the warm-weather softball leagues were being beefed up to take in idle youngsters from the streets. "I don't trust government one bit."

The youths at Goddard actually were speaking to the heart of the fiscal crisis as it has been presented to the layman by the Mayor and other politicians—that there must be sacrifices by all. The youngsters were asking where was the equality of sacrifice. Standing amid the playground noise, a visitor witnessed painful spring growth as it dawned on them that some teen-agers might be more equal than others.

"The Nixon business doesn't rub off on them the way this does," said Ruth Messinger, a member of the local school board, No. 3, who stayed up all night with more than 1,000 local teen-agers when they lined up for several hundred jobs as if there were World Series tickets. She recalled one youngster who discovered at 3 A.M. that he needed photos and set off for the coin photo booths of Times Square. She never saw him return.

"This thing at City Hall is a cynical, incredible political caper, and the kids see it," Mrs. Messinger said. "This is their first sight of white-collar crime, the juvenile version of what we know keeps happening down there."

•

Sometimes, though, the cry of criminality can be misapplied to what seems the far more endemic problem of politics, the self-insulation of mediocrity. In this controversy, thankfully, there is more than cynicism in the settlement house world of youth and optimism and industry. While one youth mouthed dated scraps of liberal syllogisms about fewer jobs meaning "more muggings of white people," there were more who were not entirely embittered.

"My father said I was crazy to wait all night," said Mariela Mangual, who is about to graduate from Brandeis High. "But I want work. I went ahead."

Her knowledge of work thus far comes mainly from her parents, who came here from Puerto Rico more than twenty years ago and have held various factory jobs ever since. Mariela did not get a job, because, after waiting all night on the line, she got sick and had to go home.

"I'm still looking for a job—I'm not giving up." She laughed. "Maybe I should call someone at City Hall."

If she did call, she would get a righteous rebuff, because after suffering notoriety, the Mayor's office said it was curtailing its secret role of V.I.P. ombudsman. First it was announced that these special jobs were to be filled with appointees from former years, where possible. This seemed to be a confusing policy that would strain even the traditions of nepotism by having to solicit the favored youths of summers past, some of whom presumably are into more stable and lucrative career patterns of full-time, second-generation patronage jobs.

But the Mayor, back from vacation and preparing for his re-election drive, apparently thought this over, too, and issued an order yesterday that announced a policy of eliminating political favoritism in these City Hall jobs.

•

Whatever the Mayor proclaims, the ambitious teen-agers at Goddard-Riverside already know that the City Hall system is not for them. Their main focus now is waiting to hear the final word from their own Kafkaesque system on whether they have actually received the jobs they need. "They gave out numbers that night, like going to 786, and I got number 36," Saran Kaba said. "So what do you think?"

[5/7/77]

27

Vibrations

It sounds like the long-rumored city apocalypse, but the case of the Tree of Life versus the Urban Development Corporation is actually a struggle for a lively corner in Harlem, where "the vibrations are very heavy," to quote the identical enthusiasms of Brother Ernest and Dr. Moore.

Brother Ernest—a writer and spiritual man named Ernest Collier—is in the basement of the Tree of Life store directing a yajnya, a marathon Sanskrit chant dedicated to eliminating the fear of death, not to mention the notice of eviction received recently from the state's Urban Development Corporation.

Dr. Moore—John E. Moore, a self-proclaimed herbalist extraordinaire who learned his roots and potions from Southern midwives and Northern hobos—is upstairs, telling how he sniffs out cures even in the underbrush of Central Park. He is beaming amid endless packets and jars labeled myrrh and ginseng, chickweed and chaparral, yellow dock and sarsaparilla.

The air in this book, herb and spiritualism store smells as heavy as the advertised vibrations. The air is laced with flute music said to have been recorded recently in the burial chamber of the Great Pyramid. These tattings of sound are soothing and drift out onto 125th Street, which swallows them whole, along with the disco racket thrown out from the Rainbow record store across from Tree of Life and the sheer reassuring sound of people moving through life on Harlem's premier boulevard.

•

The corner at issue is 125th Street's northwest intersection with Lenox Avenue. The corner's relevant dreams are, first, the late Nelson A. Rockefeller's idea to stir up a grand Urban Development Corporation office building and hotel project there in the name of black capitalism, and, second, the determination of the Tree of Life's entrepreneur, Kanya KeKumbha, to hold off the Rockefeller dream in the name of the heavy vibrations within his own lucrative-looking niche of black capitalism.

West of the bookstore, the State Office Building is up and has been open for several years. It seems to tower aloof from the crazy-quilt vibrancy of 125th Street, and what was dreamed back then seems a colonial repository in the sidewalk light of today.

East of this tower, Kanya KeKumbha is a squatter in the tired store that the development agency owns and now intends to tear down to make way for a stretch of fresh retail marts, a parking garage and a cultural center. This is the preliminary phase of the hotel plan that the project's lawyer insists is still feasible despite all the talk of "planned shrinkage" that has become fashionable with politicians now, much the way talk of black capitalism used to be, and despite the disbelief, chanting and mocking laughter in the Tree of Life.

"Who the hell's going to come uptown looking for a luxury hotel here?" Mr. KeKumbha asks. He is speaking not only as a student of "the ancient wisdom" and as proprietor of the Aquarian Science Free Reading room, but also, he says, as a former insurance salesman and stockbroker who foundered when he tried to launch a black mutual fund back in the optimistic days when Mr. Rockefeller was having a piece of Harlem blueprinted.

•

After the bad vibrations of that fling with capitalism, Mr. KeKumbha decided to indulge the spiritual readings that had first engrossed him as a teen-ager when he had encountered such books as "The Prophet" and "Light on the

Path" that are classics on the metaphysical bookstore circuit.

"I started out with a card table and a $75 inventory right out there on the sidewalk—metaphysical items, 50-cent astrology charts, 75-cent self-improvement books," Mr. KeKumbha says, "and it grew and grew."

He speaks with a pride understandable in a man who now does a steady, rent-free volume of sales in scores of book titles all the way up through $50 copies of "Ancient Egypt, Light of the World." Through the Sanskrit chanting and the sweet incense that suffuse the old store on 125th Street, Mr. KeKumbha's optimistic entrepreneurial pride is eerily reminiscent of Mr. Rockefeller, who, a visitor standing in the Tree of Life recalls, had just opened his own store to minister to the masses' spirit with art reproductions when he died.

The Rockefeller spirit marches on in the form of U.D.C. minions.

•

"I was in the Tree of Life the other day," says Jeff L. Greenup, the lawyer for the development agency's Harlem subsidiary who sent Mr. KeKumbha the eviction notice last month. "It seemed to me the man had a viable program going there. He's an articulate businessman. Good sense of PR."

These are crass compliments in comparison with the virtues of "profound personal insights and spiritual development" Mr. KeKumbha describes flowing from the store's wares and lectures in numerology, body ecology, palmistry and tarot-card reading. He cites pages of endorsements from community residents, including a two-year-old proposal from the local planning board to spare the building and let the bookstore stay for rent of $1 a year.

The U.D.C. says it's willing to get another place for the store, either down the block or in the planned retail mart. But Mr. KeKumbha says seven years of "heavy vibrations" have made the building a "power source" in the community's spiritual life.

"Well, I tell him," replies Mr. Greenup, "that my client and myself seem to have more faith than he does in the strength of those vibrations and their ability to withstand a move down the block."

Mr. KeKumbha insists his vibrations will prevail. Mr. Greenup insists the state will have its garage and mart this fall, and the bulldozer's vibrations will be felt very soon through the Tree of Life.

[4/17/79]

Waiting for a Benefactor

There is harmonica music from the watchman's radio sounding through the empty building that was once busy Delafield Hospital, and downstairs eighty-year-old Dr. Anna Goldfeder will not give up her five decades with the mice and mysteries of cancer research.

She bought space heaters to keep her mice alive through the empty winter of the deserted hospital. And even after the city cut off her budget, she managed enough of a federal grant to keep a lab staff of three going through the routine of her various cancer research experiments.

This unseen effort in the tomblike hospital gets at the essence of all problems, survival. Survival on the physical level of studying the floridly living death of carcinoma, and on the spirit level of the woman's fight to keep her long life of special intelligence moving forward.

Moving away from the harmonica music, very proud in her white smock and very precise in her accented discourse, the small woman seems like a finely wrought antimacassar glinting in the dimness of a shuttered mansion. Her heels click in the corridors. In a walk with a stranger to her lab, views of the Hudson cut brilliantly into the corridor dimness of the waterfront building at 164th Street and Fort Washington Avenue.

•

"I'm waiting for a benefactor," she says and the remark is not as hopelessly Pinteresque as it sounds. For while Delafield has been turned into a warehouse in the two years since it closed, Dr. Goldfeder will not be stored away. She has a promise of space from New York University, but needs renovation money, about $60,000, to set up all the cages, microscopes and radiation equipment. "I need money—I would put an appropriate memorial plaque on my new office, of course."

Downstairs, the remaining mice look healthy except for the ones with tiny carefully measured cancers about them. A man washes test tubes. A student peers through a microscope. Everyone is quiet. The X-ray machine looks worn and tired from years of silently burning out life pieces.

The doctor tracks everything. An autobiographical essay she published last year in "Cancer Research" had sixty-four footnotes of documentation of the various phases of her career in a field of diabolical frustrations. "Unfortunately, in cancer research the tendency is to reach a point where you think you have something but then find you can't go forward."

So fifty years can amount to valuable threads in an unfinished fabric. Her latest thread seems particularly cherished because it takes Dr. Goldfeder full cycle from her undergraduate, magna cum laude days in Prague, where her devotion to science was first spun from curiosity about the basic growth, structure and metabolism of the cell.

•

"This is the mystery of life itself," Dr. Goldfeder says in outlining her current isotope research into the kinetics of cellular growth.

Money seems only slightly less a mystery and life force for a cancer-scientist. She recalls the richer days of former Mayor Fiorello H. LaGuardia when any self-respecting branch of government wanted its own separate cancer-research institute, and she became a principal in the city's own. While she no longer has the city budget line, she still has the title of director of the city's Cancer and Radiobiological Research Laboratory, this forgotten outpost at Delafield. For years, the city post gave her Civil Service protection and a salary. That plus helpful grants from the

National Cancer Institute helped her get this far, to the point of fighting to go farther.

"You can't throw living animals in the Hudson," she says of her loss of city financing. "So I stand up and say you can't throw me out." But the city seems to be simply passing her by silently, in its own metabolic ague.

In her resistance, among the first to be protected were thousands of creatures designated X/Gf mice. This is an albino strain the doctor developed for research. They are exceptionally free of spontaneous cancers and so provide a reliable test subject for certain needs. She found a home for this research stock at Columbia University, but only a temporary home, she emphasizes, until that benefactor cuts through the gloom at Delafield.

•

Dr. Goldfeder stays scientific when she discusses herself, offering facts the way she holds the mice—briefly by the tail, between thumb and index finger while she quickly sweeps the underbelly for salient information. As a girl she was proud when the teacher offered several problems to solve and she chose the most difficult. As an old woman, she regrets giving up the violin and her weekly ticket to the opera, but she had to cut back and lives alone directly across from the hospital.

Friends die and it is sad, and she feels "humiliated" moreover, when cancer is the cause and she cannot help them. She goes to the lab mostly seven days a week and the watchman sees her safely across the street. Clearly it is everything. "I am grateful to nature," she says. But more life, if you please. "I always felt life was like a big wave. You either keep swimming or sink to the bottom."

On the way out, there is rock music on the watchman's radio, and the doctor brushes off questions about how many more decades of cancer research will be needed. She repeats that she is willing to put up a plaque for that benefactor.

[3/22/77]

Dynamite
on Broome Street

That's not his last duchess rising there in steel on Broome Street, looking as if she were still alive. It's "Skinny Dynamite," a willowy, hard-edged sculpture inspired by a woman whom Bob Bolles, a welder-artist, says he once so lustily loved that he decided to memorialize her in the middle of Broome Street.

And over from "Skinny Dynamite" as the morning trucks roar by on the way to the Holland Tunnel is a "Bundle of Love," a giant tricycle of a creation welded together by Mr. Bolles from tractor and piledriver scraps.

"Another lady friend, wonderful lady," says Mr. Bolles, whose Bohemian life style, even beyond the women who fire it, is best illustrated by the open traffic island he has filled with seventeen big pieces of his welded works.

"I think it should be called Bolles's National Park," the artist says humbly, surveying his oeuvres in the sun-warmed street and being smiled upon by his friend, a beautiful woman named Anne who has not yet been memorialized in the Broome Street collection.

"I am his assistant," says Anne.

"She is my lover," says the welder, all mustache and grin.

•

The two stand in what is certainly the most public sculpture garden in the city, so public that a driver could collide with it if he was not careful.

"Some drunk plowed his Volkswagen into 'The Chicken,'" Mr. Bolles says, gesturing at a marvelous-looking creature resembling a giant iron rooster, with feet of long skinny wrenches and tailfeathers made from the leaf springs of junked autos. "The Volks was totaled; 'The Chicken' only lost two tailfeathers." He smiles proudly at the concoction, which is dedicated to the live-poultry market it permanently faces.

Mr. Bolles says that creating the pieces is the point of it all, that he has been burning and bending metal with heat for most of his forty-four years. But clearly his ego must not suffer from the never-ending audience that goes by in the traffic crossing West Broadway on the way to the tunnel, of necessity going right past the sculpture in the once-empty traffic triangle.

"The truck guys are great," he says. "Sometimes they remember me and drop off some steel scrap. Or they hire me to weld repairs on the trucks."

Pointing westward toward Thompson Street, the welder says: "I do a lot of simple ironwork in the neighborhood. I mean here, the good old Italian and Portuguese neighborhood, not SoHo over there. SoHo is for the touristas."

The welder is fairly sneering back toward West Broadway, the heart of the SoHo district, which has changed from an old loft industrial area, where there used to be plenty of machinery to be welded, to an artist's squatting grounds and now to an affluent enclave of art galleries and high-priced residential lofts.

That is all mock-Bohemia to the welder, who says the only jobs he gets over there now are demolition cuttings when more old factory spaces are cleared out to make way for the next batch of expensive co-ops.

Mr. Bolles lives on Thompson Street, across from Augie's Cafe, where the artist takes his morning espresso and checks for any phone messages of welding jobs. He also checks at Napoli's Bar on Sullivan Street, where he and his friends like to have a sidewalk drink in the afternoon, a "veranda" way of saluting an ordinary good day, he says.

•

When he is not welding machinery to make food money or working in his basement shop, the artist is often at the

Broome Street Bar. The owner, Kenny Reisdorff, was sick of the sight of the trash-littered traffic triangle and put Mr. Bolles up to occupying it with his creations seven years ago. City officials eventually realized what was happening as the artist welded away to his heart's content on public properties. There was a bureaucratic confrontation, but neighborhood people, some of whom like to park and chain their motorcycles to his creations, backed the artist, according to Mr. Bolles, and so he now has official permission to make and leave his sculptures in the street.

In his work clothes the artist looks like a lean, feisty cowboy, wearing two bandanas and leather pants. He wields his tanks across through traffic and pops a flame on the end of his cutting torch, tuning it like a violinist to a clean point of 6,000 degrees. Goggles in place, he straddles fresh scrap, a 7-foot length of 24-inch pipe lying like a blank block of marble. The half-inch shell yields to the artist's flame, and bright, hot orange bits steadily tumble onto the streets, like specks of the sun. Quickly, a work in progress begins to emerge from the pipe, a flame-shaped, feathery filigree of a pattern.

He pauses and shows how one part of the emerging silhouette has a hint of female figure in it. He smiles at Anne, who is standing by "The Chicken," back from the flame. But this work is not to be Anne in steel. It is to be dedicated to the children of the neighborhood, he says, in honor of the noisy Fourth of July celebrations they have.

It will be a 7-foot-tall column depicting firecracker flames and noise, standing tall with "The Chicken," "Skinny Dynamite," and the rest of the welder's garden on Broome Street.

[3/27/79]

The Morning After

Absolutely and forevermore, the people in the refrigerator had found the end of animation. Indeed, the bearded man rolled out in cold drawer No. 68 had collapsed into death while he was dancing at a discothèque.

"That is not a bad way to die," the Chief Medical Examiner says, looking down at the naked brown body's passive face.

He jokes gently in this stainless-steel staging area of the good night. The medical examiner, Dr. Dominick J. Di-Maio, is on his morning rounds of inspecting people who turned up from life during the night.

It is a place of cold steel, pallid tile, and supine flesh. "Come on, Barbara, we have a flock of cases," he says to Mrs. Gordon, who takes his dictation down on what killed the people in the drawers.

It is hard to say what preserves decorum as the refrigerator doors are opened one after another by Sam Williams and the bodies are wheeled out in all their variety of smashed and punctured or perfectly whole and totally languid repose. Clothes help draw the line between the living and the dead. Dr. DiMaio's blue shirt sleeves are rolled up, his tie is loosened and his thin, dark-rimmed eyeglasses are windows of curiosity. He is bald with a white fringe of hair that seems ceremonial as he peers down at each corpse.

•

His rounds of the dead are repeatedly interrupted by phone calls and other business, and this morning there is a sensitive case involving the murder of a Brazilian citizen in a midtown hotel and a report to the Brazilian consulate.

"Hog-tied," Dr. DiMaio is saying, describing how the murderer pinioned that victim.

Another case is recalled and, right there by the bank of mortuary cabinets with its one open door and outthrust body, the doctor sends for the homicide ligatures of the old and the new "hog-tying" cases. Leather belts were employed in both murders, knotted as bindings. The doctor looks, he pokes. "The knots are different."

Immediately, he hands back the belts and shifts his attention to the body waiting at his elbow, a "well-developed, well-nourished white male," the doctor narrates as he lifts open an eyelid, opens the mouth for a glance, probes the abdomen He looks over attendant paperwork and rules death is from cirrhosis of the liver and massive internal hemorrhage. Sam slides the man back into the bank like a dossier.

There is a small old lady in drawer No. 30 who obviously fell to her death. But the doctor doesn't entirely accept the police report of a drunken accident, no foul play. "Report says window sill was 30 inches up with a 13-inch opening. Look at her. How the hell could she fall out?? Send her up, Sam."

The latter is an order for an autopsy in which a body is taken apart and searched by a forensic pathologist for signs of unnatural, violent death. Not every body sent to the morgue is autopsied. The city doctors do not have the need or the time and budgetary wherewithal to be so totally thorough. Dr. DiMaio makes this point when he is interrupted by a phone call from an anxious private physician who has repeatedly requested a particular autopsy.

•

"Certainly not," Dr. DiMaio finally says into the phone. "She's seventy-three years old, in a nursing home, with a history of heart condition, and you won't sign for her? Can you show foul play?"

The medical examiner's face takes on an extra biting

look as he adds, "Don't worry, doctor, this won't count against your death record, if that's what you're worried about."

He snaps the phone back on the wall and returns to the morning corpses, stepping for a moment onto the large floor-level scale where the bodies are weighed. The arrow bounces up to 187 pounds.

"I ate too much yesterday," he says. Under the circumstances, the remark seems a much-needed celebration of life, particularly since the doctor is entering special mortuary room 24 where partially decomposed bodies are kept. Here death is perversely vivid in surreal colors and odors and even the doctor, after thirty years of this, grimaces and hurries a bit more. He checks two "floaters"—bodies found in the river—and a wizened man who put a pistol to his brain.

"Get me a knife," the doctor says to an aide, and right there he probes for the bullet, a task no more remarkable to the doctor than a bit of first aid, but one that begs a visitor to glance elsewhere—a conversation with Mrs. Gordon, perhaps.

"We take turns making the rounds with him," she says. "I couldn't do it every day." Like other professionals at the morgue, she describes the one certain trial of composure: "I can take anything but a child. When I see a murdered child, that's it."

•

Dr. DiMaio enters the main autopsy room and the place is literally buzzing with surgical saws as five of the eight steel tables are occupied. The bodies face windows of opaque glass that flicker almost theatrically with the shadows of falling snowflakes. Light floods the room as pathologists uncap and open the bodies. It is more mechanical than morbid as parts are catalogued and entities undone.

Dr. DiMaio is to do the autopsy on the Brazilian man, who had been beaten and smothered. An impeccably tailored homicide detective stands by, natty evidence that there is life before death. The doctor makes small talk with him. "We are fifty behind last year, but our busy season is coming," he says as snowflakes flicker past the window.

[12/6/77]

Where a Hundred Flowers Bloom

With all that he held in beauty the other morning—thousands of dollars in multicolored roses fresh from Israel and Holland, crowds of anemones bright as tiddlywinks, gentle pallets of lilies and orchids—Jimmy Portolino's spirit did not blossom much until he could greet and hug Yasmin Moses.

This is understandable. Yasmin Moses is a relief from things botanical. She is beautiful and confident as she arrives at Jimmy's store in the wholesale flower district, strutting past the roses in boots and jeans and charcoal blazer with a fall leaf in her breast pocket. She is brown-eyed, and her hair shines dark against the flower colors. She is excited by this angled flower and that hushed one and the others she is buying in clusters.

"You look beautiful, Doll," Jimmy says with his hug. Yasmin smiles, her lips emphatic and unpainted, her arms in a diplomatic fending position, her gaze slipping back to the flowers with a buyer's intent.

"I'm not sure if I'm trying to get a color scheme going or just picking what I like," Yasmin says, setting up her day like a painter daubing up her palette. She is choosing, dipping among pompom daisies, simple and clean, pausing at something called star of Bethlehem, whitish green and surreal, bending to sniff a lacey white flower.

"Oh God," she says in delight, closing her eyes. "That smells like mortal sin."

All this color and life in petals and stems—not to mention Yasmin Moses herself, a freelance floral designer who makes daily rounds for restaurants and her other clients—flares up in the city's wholesale flower market at dawn every business day. A crop of brilliance stretches down through market shops on the Avenue of the Americas south of 30th Street. The scene grows gray and empty by lunchtime, so most New Yorkers never see it. But Yasmin Moses revels and profits in it like a honey bee.

•

By the time she has her third diplomatically fended hug of the morning, Yasmin says, "I better come to work looking more bedraggled." But surely she understands the feeling: She is more than handsome. She is friendly. She is Greek-American, like most of the wholesalers, and she prefers their earthiness to what she remembers as the ingrown anxieties of couture, a field where she worked designing expensive evening clothes after studying at the Parsons School.

Downstairs in the exotics room at Jimmy's, she asks Irving, another warm greeter, for a calla lily that leans to the left, not the right. "What? You're nuts," says Irving, delighted to meet the request.

Yasmin is just as specific about the red amaryllis around the corner at Pennock's, and Dominic respects this as he waits on her. There is a smell of fresh water and greenery in the store and a commercial buzz in which a wholesaler is haggling prices on the phone: "I'm serious, too, Spiro, I'm not your brother."

At Klamos & Tooker's, Neil Andacht smiles at the sight of Yasmin as she enters. He kisses her cheek. Yasmin is good for the wholesale market, he agrees. She desires his irises, two big bunches. And then on to Major's for background greens: great gobs of Scotch broom, lemon leaf, quince twigs and leather leaf.

Yasmin departs dragging three big boxes filled with close to $150 in flowers. She struggles into a taxi that looks daffodil-yellow in her presence and heads off on this day's rounds—the Wine Bar in SoHo, where she daily replenishes her arrangements; Modern Bride magazine, where she is to do ten flower baskets for a photo display, and a private business luncheon at Dow-Badiche, a textile company on West 40th Street.

•

The buildings drift by and she talks of aiming for a wildflower style. "I don't do 'Fall' arrangements—all that yellow and brown," she says firmly. "I do spring and summer all year, pinks, lily of the valley. The city is never depressing for long when I know where to get a white tulip in December."

In the freight elevator on the way up to the textile office, Yasmin Moses says she has the nicest job, "a luxury job, because flowers are luxury." She gets $75 and up for a large arrangement, considerable flower power for someone twenty-six years old. In the office, designers and secretaries detour from office rounds soon as they notice Yasmin unpacking a score of different flowers in the office kitchen.

"New Yorkers make way for flowers," she says. "They don't do that for many other things."

As she works, Yasmin provides a brief biography, from childhood in Chevy Chase, Md., to a slavish bit of success, as she describes it, in clothing design. "You kill yourself for months for fifteen minutes of glory on a runway. Flowers are more satisfying, any day. Most people benefit from flowers."

Gradually, carefully, Yasmin reaches flower by flower for what she wants for the first vase. Her hands flick across three shades of daisy to a graceful aster maria. She pokes in some Scotch broom, splays in some snapdragons. She steps back, fetches a touch of magenta. Then comes the properly leaning calla lily, a clarion emplacement. The office moves along toward springtime, a touch of iris, a twist of lemon leaf, a sprig of Yasmin Moses.

[11/11/78]

44

2

Stolen Moments

The Battle of Lexington

In the night, the long white frock coat and plantation hat of the tall man gave him a shepherd's bearing as he stood in the light of a coffee shop and kept a proprietor's eye on the women standing on the corners hawking themselves to motorized streams of men.

The taillights of the shoppers' cars became brighter red, flaring in the darkness as if they were Pavlovian gadgets, as the men slowed and stopped, sometimes three to a car, to hear prices quoted by the prostitutes and even to be touched sometimes in a free-sample selling style, the competition among the women being so intense.

There were dozens of women at 4 A.M. last Saturday in a sixteen-block Manhattan grid centering on Lexington Avenue and 26th Street, working the curbs with prancing invitation as cars passed slowly. They jammed the corners of what local residents call the all-night "meat market."

There was a woman called Silky, whose name was shouted like a selling logo, who crossed the shoppers' stream diagonally, smooth and hard as bone in tight white denim, who shouted and leaned into the cars. "Hey, sugar. Here I am." Other women used the passive sell, profiling in the street light.

The predominant uniform of the night was the garish, dated skimpiness of hot pants and in these bright scraps the women flitted deceivingly as glowworms.

•

The man in the white frock coat watched his charges in the company of four other male pimps, black and white together in their own uniform sheen of three-piece suits, glistening shoes and jewelry. Through the windows of the coffee shop at 26th Street and Lexington Avenue, they seemed like dulled airport controllers on the night shift, and on the four corners immediately in front of them there were twenty women selling hard at 4:15.

This was the ultimate convolution of the American drive-in experience of uniformed smiling waitresses gathered in a mercantile chorus of you-deserve-to-have-a-nice-day-sugar—a nightlong commercial of offerings to a glaring, humming chrome-plated line of lechery.

At 4:30, the prostitutes at the intersection saw a police car arrive on the complaint of a man who said his pocket had been picked right in his own car as two prostitutes crowded and distracted him. The man in the white frock coat shooed the women away for a while, and most of them clumped off on platform shoes like a special breed of hobbled, tinted pigeons.

A dozen waited in the coffee shop with the pimps, and the overhead pools of light flattened out the glint of their costumes. A prostitute took the break to order fried eggs and she had to admire a green-and-white ring, ugly as a jungle insect, that was extended for inspection on the fist of one of the pimps.

•

Quick as the Department of Consumer Affairs can say "caveat emptor," the police incident was over and the street business, which had been continuing anyway at most corners, resumed fully at 23rd and Lexington with all the curl and perfume of a netherworld orchid mart.

The view from the driver's seat for a passing innocent could be intimidating, as a creature in hot pants materialized at a red light like a fantasized hood ornament, blocking the way, actually rubbing against the fender. The car's steel shell held and after a terrible stare through the windshield she yielded to a green light.

The sky softened to blue-black after 5 o'clock. A local resident lifted his window and his shade three stories above Eng's laundry just north of 23rd Street. He looked down on the new day, his bald head all pink dome at the window, and there were a half dozen prostitutes all about his front stoop. Two newly returned from transactions exchanged the hand-slap greetings of athletes. The man made no sound and watched.

Across the street, in the shadows of an armory, the uniform of the day appeared. Olive drab, it blended in better than the hot-pants parade. It was worn by weekend Army reservists arriving for a field trip. Four of them were quiet as scouts as they stood and watched the market across the street. "It reminds me of Munich," said a stout sergeant with the name DeBari stenciled cleanly across his shirt-front.

The street scene continued with more troops arriving and the automobiles going by with their special appetites and the women holding the corners. It was a tableau on the doggedness of duty. By 5:30, with the sky turning royal blue, the troops were a loose, gaping crowd.

"Damn!" one very young trooper said loudly and appreciatively toward the women. But the two groups kept their distance and when a beautiful blond prostitute in shorts turned the armory corner and walked past, her legs long and pastel in the first light, she looked down, passing the men in apparent shyness.

"Good morning, sir!" said a private to a gleaming specimen of an officer, a young captain in tightly tailored fatigues. His stenciled name, Witherell, stood out from his chest as he saluted and his shoulder patch proclaimed, "Airborne." He bit his pipe stem tightly and he was ready for this new day.

By 6 A.M., Witherell's men outnumbered the prostitutes. Hungry, the captain eyed the coffee shop and stepped out with an aide, crossing over, his boots shiny in the street. The man in the white frock coat and white plantation hat stood outside the coffee shop, judging what was left of his night. He looked the captain over and stepped aside, two men of natty rank passing in a dawn of shifting bodies.

[6/9/77]

Rolling into
the Dusk

Even between the strolling hookers on Eighth Avenue and the Tenth Avenue variety who cater at corners to slow-driving motorists on carnal prowl, childhood can be a meadow, an asphalt meadow.

Minutes after he gets home from school, fourteen-year-old Brian Mullen suits up in his ragamuffin-eclectic hockey outfit, clambers down in boot roller skates from his fourth-floor tenement apartment and skates past the storefront garage of chestnut and pretzel vending carts and across West 49th Street to get Ralphie, Kenny, Dizzy and the other guys into their daily frenzy of street hockey.

In the early winter nip, it is the fastest game on 49th, faster than the hookers and eternally more innocent. A few hours with Brian as he cuts and checks, feeds and scores, and races back and forth across the schoolyard rink with great whirring strides of joy, is a restorative without equal for anyone wondering lately whether humanity has packaged and peddled itself into a fatally indentured circus.

Brian is a winner—seventy-four goals and thirty-four assists in the Queens league alone last year. He is so good at roller hockey, leading the forward lines of various pickup church and club teams, that he has graduated to ice skates, being the youngest member of the West Siders ice hockey team, a group that makes the Skyrink on West 33rd into a neighborhood shrine on weekends.

With his pumping legs and flicking wrists, Brian is positioning himself to follow in the honored memory of his two older brothers, Tom and Joe, who skated their way from the tenement leagues to the current ice hockey teams at Boston College and American International College in Massachusetts.

·

Every city neighborhood with children has its all-consuming sport. In this case, hockey has dominated for decades. A laid-off cop returned to a neighborhood game recently and told of his own childhood victories, obviously facing some poignant moment in his life, according to Brother Mark Cavanagh, the coach at Sacred Heart parish, which has fielded powerhouse teams for years.

While all about us there is the depressing TV-induced threat of children wasting away as mere sports spectators, Brian and his friends are living the real life of childhood. And his contests feature such refreshing sights as Puerto Rican hockey players, a development roughly akin to developing a line of Jewish jockeys, and one that surely can be engendered only on the streets of New York. (The kids talk reverently of Edgar Alejandro, a tenement alumnus with a great shot who helps coach now at American International College.)

The boys' conversation is routinely raw with sexual denigrations, but Brian seems to pay only half attention, mainly watching the puck and shifting his shoulders and legs fluidly as he stick-handles, somehow keeping the blue hood of his jersey up so he is easy to pick out of the scrapping pack.

Between scrimmages the boys already are building the oral traditions that will comfort them into the future. Ralph Irizarry, Brian's wingmate, expands on the triple overtime victory over College Point a few years ago, and another game where Brian scored two goals in the final thirty-three seconds for a 6 to 5 victory. "Hey, man, we took them apart."

And the Great Wheel Switch when a terrible 12-to-1 drubbing by a Brooklyn team was followed by the decision to switch to composition wheels instead of the steel ones because of the foreign Brooklyn rink. The result? "We won

6 to 5 in double overtime,'' says Brian, slapping the remark home like a puck.

•

The hockey is so intoxicating that it seems to produce extended innocence. "Nah, I gave up drinking," says twenty-two-year-old Kenny Steen, skating alongside Brian and Ralph last week. "I want to keep playing," he continued, his face relaxed and scraggly with the need of a shave. "I even go all the way up to Dyckman Street on weekends—those guys are animals," he says appreciatively.

A week ago, Brian had math, Spanish and English to figure into his tragically short hockey evening, and when Ralph asks about some extended play, Brian says, "Well, I got a lot of homework." Ralph responds in the great groaning, nasal objection that has been universal for New York's street children for decades: "C'mon-n-n-n."

•

Back in the scrimmage, a break-away with Brian up front. He closes on goal guarded by Kenny Byriter, a fourteen-year-old whose missing tooth (lost, like his soul, to hockey) is shielded from view by his moderately ghastly hockey mask. A cross pass to Ralph who seems to let the defense set on him before flicking the puck back to Brian, who is open and scores as Kenny collapses like a skeleton an instant too late for the block.

The score is a great moment on 49th Street, with dusk already in and the sodium street lights backlighting the players. There is a deep, perfect cold, the kind that produces red noses and serenity. The lights are on in Brian's tenement, dinner is on the stove.

"I gotta go," Ralph says, and he skates east on 49th Street, a scuttling, intense figure leaning forward on his wheels, the lighted skyscrapers of midtown looming beyond Eighth Avenue. Brian plays on, with only a few players and very little talk setting the tone for the final chance, the final burst of motion and scheming as chimney smoke drifts above the tenements. Finally, Brian is spent and hungry and he skates across the street and walks four flights up to home, still in his skates.

[11/16/76]

Killing Time

There was a sunny day in Ossining last week that brushed the Hudson blue and billowed the trees with freedom and made for society's perfect revenge. Men who have done society harm saw the Hudson and the trees reel with life. They watched the day run hot and shadowy as the walls of Sing Sing, their prison now known as the "State Correctional Facility at Ossining." If rehabilitation is a dead ideal and punishment is all that's left for motive, then the day was sadistically gorgeous, a thing of righteous beauty.

In the quiet village flanking the prison, you could sense freedom in the simplest things: Three boys roaming wherever they pleased on their bikes along Spring Street bordering the prison. A man selling cut flowers, sitting still and reading in the shade of a big umbrella near the center of the village.

The summer beer sign with icicles drawn on the word "cold," tantalizing passers-by outside Fiore's store. The rattle and hot-tar smell of a train cutting right through Sing Sing on the commuter tracks that bisect the prison grounds.

•

To see and hear and smell all this, to walk freely through the hot sun and buy a cold beer seemed to make the day an instrument in society's satisfaction as a visitor went to the shadowed doorway in the wall.

Inside the old Sing Sing death house, the inmate Jaycees were typing goodwill letters. Old bolt marks were visible on the floor where the electric chair used to be and there was an empty hole where the heavy wiring carried power for electrocutions, below the skylight that vented the scene for the witnesses. Death seemed long gone this sunny day, particularly with the Sing Sing Jaycee chapter operating there, casual against the pale blue walls.

Sing Sing is the reception funnel for the state prison system and about half its 1,150 men are in transit to other prisons. As for the rest, there are only about two to three hours of work available for an inmate each day at best. So life involves great expanses of recreation and idle time, which the superintendent, Stephen Dalscheim, admits is a special worry on a hot, lazy day.

The sun reaches differently into the parts of Sing Sing. East of the tracks, the large red-brick building No. 5 has the maximum-security Big House look of a 1930's movie. The leaves of a houseplant poke out like fingers through the bars of one cell window. A man with a mustache looks out from another window, facing the free, blue Hudson. He looks cranky in his box-room, and the river goes on by.

West of the tracks, the sun hits the dormitory grounds of the more trusted inmates, and a dozen of them are sunbathing on the grass in shorts, rubbing tanning oil on their bodies, relaxing and watching the sky arc over a high barbed fence stretching between them and the Hudson.

While they rest, a man—a laborer hired from outside—is digging a plumbing trench nearby, his head bobbing near ground level as he grunts and shovels up the dirt.

"Imagine what's going on in that guy's head?" a guard asks. "He's in that hot hole working hard and these inmates are stretched out watching." True, the irony is thick as the buzzing heat.

•

David Berkowitz was processed through here a few days before on his way upstate. He was passive, guards say, in his Mona Lisa simper mood. This man, the "Son of Sam" killer, had the power to set off a furious renewal of the age-old debate about crime and punishment. But inside, such questions seem eccentric with all these men waiting out combined centuries of time, like fish frozen in a river.

What do you do with them? How do you punish with idleness? The old liberal-conservative polarities that soon will rattle the hustings seem pale in the Sing Sing sunshine. Would it be liberal or conservative, or merely poetic, to mandate that the thug who messed up a poor old lady trying to sun herself on the Grand Concourse should do his time without benefit of sunbathing himself?

And if you take one of the sunbathers to dig a trench, what do you tell organized labor and the construction industry who claim first call on jobs for the law-abiding?

•

The prison seems crammed with paradox. In one attempt at decency—special ethnic menus for the several family picnic days allowed the inmates each year—prison and charity officials try to meet requests for roast pig or yellow perch or corned beef. During the most recent picnic, a happier Sunday than most, the superintendent worked up in his office on the next zero-growth austerity budget mandated on the prison by state officials.

It is a pleasure to leave the human puzzle of Sing Sing and return to the tree-shaded world surrounding it. On the way outside, the visitors' room is seen to be crowded like a bus terminal waiting room, with women and children clustered by their men and the day shining at the barred window in confusing beauty.

[6/29/78]

Water Music

The lone woman arrived last August in an old barge that was tied up by the eastern foot of the Brooklyn Bridge, and she lived inside it. When she went out she often carried a violin.

The longshoremen alongside on Pier 1 could see that much about the interesting mop-haired newcomer to the Brooklyn river bank. Then came some hellos, and by the time the baby grand piano arrived, Red Noto, the dock boss, took a gang of longshoremen over as neighbors to load the piano gently into the barge, Olga Bloom's barge, which turned out to be beautiful inside, lined with mahogany from an old ferryboat.

Olga had a friend visiting that night, Ruth Vinitsky Antine, and to repay the men the two women sat the dockworkers by the warmth of the fireplace and played three hours of chamber music in the barge.

"A whole program of sonatas—uncompromising music," Olga says. "We played Mozart. We played Beethoven. We played Handel." She pauses at each great name as if challenging the darkly passing river to match strength for strength.

•

Olga Bloom's barge is a big improvement for the city's tired waterfront. Not only is she taming longshoremen (the other day she gave them Brahms in the lunch-hour sun), but all kinds of musicians have come to visit, staring up at the bridge that arches abstractly like music itself, watching the passive gleam of Manhattan across the river, playing music and renewing their spirit by the water.

For Olga, the barge means she is finally free of the past, of investing her music talent playing in back-up groups for the gamut of commercial ventures that keep a typical New York musician anonymously alive—movies, TV jingles, rock music backgrounds. Now she only plays "the uncompromising music" with all the effort and pleasure of her old music school years.

Beyond her deliverance, there is much more. For Olga Bloom has taken the 102-foot-long vessel, which used to haul coffee, and slowly turned it into an invitingly modest music hall, stocking it with a string quartet of bright young Juilliard students who began Sunday concerts for the public a few weeks ago.

•

The whole idea is as frail as it is worthy, built around the neglected treasures of the city's waterfront and its musicians. Olga has put her widow's mite into the barge, hoping to chart a record of public patronage in the next year that will attract the federal or private subsidies needed for survival in this country's cultural market. Barge-music Ltd. is the fancy nonprofit corporate name, but basically it's just Olga Bloom, her barge, and her uncompromising music.

The idea for it occurred to her years ago when her late husband, Tobias Bloom, who was a violinist with Toscanini, used to invite friends over to their home to play chamber music for private enjoyment.

"Many great musicians came to play," Mrs. Bloom recalls. "And I used to think, what a waste—all this fine music and no audience." She chafed as well over the fate of too many graduates of music schools who find no classical market. And even for the luckier ones, she says, a symphony orchestra can present problems of regimentation and no sense of community attachment.

On the very first day that she had friends over for the view and some chamber music, Olga Bloom knew the barge had an audience. As they played, the drop-ins by strangers began. Customers walked over from a barge restaurant a little bit up the river bank. "We invited them in and someone put a fin on my violin," says Mrs. Bloom, who needs all patrons, large and small.

That same day there were some teen-agers from Red Hook knocking around the docks. "Real macho kids with Cuban heels, the whole bit," Mrs. Bloom says. "I told them to keep an open mind about music. They listened and behaved like the best Carnegie audience and one of them even kissed my hand at the end."

And later a romantic-looking couple stopped to listen and the woman, a performer with the Royal Ballet, improvised a dance on the barge while Olga and her friends played their uncompromising music.

•

For all her beautiful solitude by the river, Mrs. Bloom is enmeshed in a community of individuals who assisted when she introduced herself and asked straight out for help with her barge by the bridge.

There are the Rivara brothers at Seaway Marine, who helped find the barge. There is Tony Materra, who volunteered his welding talent; Albert Frank, a music student who did the brick and woodwork; the people at C.L.I.C.K. in the old Brooklyn Navy Yard who helped with code requirements; Florence Barnett, a friend and city cultural official who helped search for a berth; Fred Richmond, the Congressman who, she notes, "assigned an aide to protect my interests across the river" at City Hall, where the politics of culture is an art form; Dean Gideon Waldrop, who got Juilliard deeply involved; Peter Stamford, who gave Mrs. Bloom a free berth behind the National Maritime Historical Museum by the bridge; and of course, Red Noto and the gang from Pier 1.

The four Juilliard students—Joel Pitchon, Dan Smiley, Judith Nelson and Julian Rodescu—come aboard to play every Sunday at 4 P.M., choosing their own program, delighted with the wood-rich acoustics and the gentle surge from the dark river. Olga Bloom pays the musicians the entire gate—a maximum of seventy-five people at $5 a head—and apologizes that it can't be more. She absorbs the costs of the barge herself, including utilities and wine and cheese for the musicales. She sleeps on the barge quite simply on a couch, and her life seems as fine as the uncompromising music.

[4/25/78]

Fellow Traveler

Joe Grimaldi has decided he must move to California because of a bad foot and, naturally, he notified us in his usual way, by getting down on his knees and chalk-printing on the asphalt at Church and Barclay Streets, the intersection where he daily panhandles while his red dog flops and snoozes in the shade.

Now that he's moving on, he can honestly say—in plain print, the way he chalks, but without all the Marxist trappings he loves—that this city has been a real jungle for him. Don't get the man wrong; there isn't a resentful bone in his body. It's just that he is a complex panhandler who wishes Communism on us as a better life, and who sees a hereafter as his own best hope.

For years now, the sunlight has determined his waking hours jungle-style, for he sleeps in a bedroll on the abandoned West Side Highway, finding a cardboard box to retreat into when it snows.

This is unremarkable to him as far as it goes. It took on a jungle quality in his eyes the time his own hemorrhaging awoke him terrified in the middle of the night. Two weeks later, he returned from a charity-ward stomach operation and had to run limping away from two muggers who poked into his winter box and tried to nap in his bedroll.

Never mind that if you want to know about life, Mr. Grimaldi says. Look instead to Communism, which he says is appealing to him because he has been mostly poor and lonely all his life, and look to religion as he has done all his forty-seven years since being raised the son of a Brooklyn cobbler. Contradictions? Not if you think about it the way he does, and compose your thoughts at night and have them ready to be written down every day on the asphalt.

•

Mr. Grimaldi, a splintery rail of a man at 5 feet 6, 140 pounds, looks so mild standing there gray-haired, holding forth his green baseball cap for donations, saying not a word as his red dog sleeps on the shore of the pedestrian stream. He is one of the most interesting loners in a city of loners, and even pedestrians who ignore his cap often stop to read his daily text.

"To destroy your worst enemy, use the truth," Mr. Grimaldi has written. "And if that's not enough, then your worst enemy is the truth."

Passers-by, particularly capitalist bosses, may want to debate some of his blatantly pro-Soviet scrivenings about capitalist bosses, but he just stands there silently with his cap out. A more typical audience reaction is a curbside pause and a smile down at his asphalt comment on President Carter's recent voluntary tax payment: "President Carter pays dollars to Uncle Rich, while 300 millionaires pay nothing, thanks to legal tax loopholes. Better he should have given his gift to the poor."

His cosmic stuff seems to really get them: "Of all living creatures on earth, only man has a knowledge of death. It's man's punishment for being so damn smart."

He's not exactly Thoreau, but the broken West Side Highway isn't Walden Pond, either. He panhandles neatly, nonaggressively, quiet-eyed, with none of the intimidation of the greasy-rag windshield beggars and none of the jagged angles of the classic American assassin profile that we glimpse in crowds every day.

•

He learned panhandling five years ago, after losing his driver's license and job as a school bus driver.

"You're ashamed of panhandling at first," he says. "But you get hardened. I never took welfare money, and people give to a panhandler out of conviction. They're good people."

He is usually alone except for the red dog and for the chess games he seeks out up in Washington Square. He loves chess and he loves mathematics, and some of his beggar's coins are used to maintain subway lockers, where he stores a dozen of his favorite science books.

After panhandling, seated on the steps of St. Peter's Church right there at his intersection, he begins to talk science, belittling some of the theories he has cooked up for laughs at night in his bedroll, like the notion of the earth as a giant flywheel that might be harnessed for power.

Taking pains for a visitor's slowness, he tells how Kirlian photography works—the photography that uses electric charges and gets eerie, animate-looking skeletal impressions of inanimate objects. Suddenly he is off matter-of-factly on a tale out of Graham Greene, in which Mr. Grimaldi decides to put Kirlian photography to the test and so sequesters a communion wafer from church.

"I didn't swallow it. I put it in an envelope and took it back to where I was living then, a flophouse. I got a hold of a car battery and other stuff and put it between two charged plates, but I got no picture. Nothing at all."

•

Ah, now we're getting somewhere with this man and soon will feel confident to dismiss him as mad and, there-fore, ready for California. Except he doesn't sound mad, really, just alone and searching for a large answer in something that for him was a quiet test of faith in a flophouse, not a cosmic meddling. Besides, by his words you know him, and he is too droll to be mad.

"I'm going to California for health reasons in about thirty to sixty days," the panhandler chalked last week. "Donations accepted. The young, good-looking gentleman with the red Communist dog."

[7/1/77]

It Floats

At the edge of the naked city, far from the rent-crazed hordes and strobe-lighted poseurs, lies a place that is the heart of whiteness, a fragrant, monomaniacal place called Port Ivory.

Around the clock, the pulsing machinery of Port Ivory produces three long continuous 2-by-4-inch ribbons of soothing white puttylike material that worms forth endlessly, warm and pliable as taffy.

What we have here in a seventy-two-year-old factory on the west coast of Staten Island is the stuff of Ivory soap, ribbons of Ivory looming into being endlessly like a giant squeeze of toothpaste or a boundless surge of soft vanilla ice cream. Ivory soap is now one hundred years old, a triumph of the ancients in the risky world of American marketing, and the Port Ivory factory is the biggest single producer of the nation's biggest-selling soap.

And, through the one hundred years of Ivory, it floats; oh, does it ever.

Even before the three ribbons move down the line to be sliced, hardened and stamped into various hotel slivers and home-sized bars, Joe Morrazzo swipes a knife expertly at the sinuous whiteness every twenty minutes and drops dumplings of the soap into his three specific-gravity test jars. They are filled with a mixture of kerosene and gasoline, a tougher float test than water.

"Naaahh," Joe says, smiling, when asked whether gongs sound and Port Ivory screeches to a halt when a test dumpling of Ivory sinks. Instead, workers pluck the aberrant stretch of white from the assembly line and adjust the machinery, which operates quite like a giant ice-cream maker in cooling and thickening liquid soap base piped over from the giant kettle storage area of the 135-acre plant.

•

"It's no secret what makes Ivory float," says Dick Antoine, the Ivory operation manager. "It's air. So we fine tune the machines to make sure the proper amount of air is whipped into the mixture."

Floatability is such a mark of Ivory soap's performance that the Port Ivory factory process includes three floatation tests: Joe Morrazzo's incisions three times an hour into the long warm ribbon; a second test of a completed bar every two hours to make sure the logo-stamping machine isn't pounding air from the soap, and unannounced visits by quality control workers who give the soap a final spot-check for appearance and performance.

The Ivory centennial celebration conceivably could have begun last year, not this, one hundred years after a company of Middle West candlemakers, Procter & Gamble, had a chemist develop a product called White Soap in 1878.

But the crucial ingredient did not come until a year later when, according to the company's history, a worker went on his lunch hour and left the soap machine running by mistake. When he returned he found the mix frothier than usual, but he decided no harm was done. Soon after, orders came in mentioning the attractive oddity of "that soap that floats." Eventually the fortunate accident was puzzled out and immediately incorporated into the process, producing a priceless trademark.

If that were not enough serendipity for one American success story, Harley Procter, son of the company's co-founder, was puzzling over what to name the floating white soap and found it in the Bible, according to company history. It was on a Sunday at church and he found the name in a reading of the forty-fifth Psalm: "All thy garments smell of myrrh and aloes and cassia out of ivory palaces whereby they have made thee glad."

By the standards of modern America, that's already

enough success to warrant a Broadway musical entitled "Harley!" with a frothy psalm scene featuring a line of dancers in ivory-white derbies doing the Fosse float.

But there's more. This same Procter ("Harley," Act Two) decided for competitive reasons to have the soap analyzed by chemists and concluded that its impurities amounted to 0.11 percent uncombined soda, 0.28 trace of salt, and 0.17 miscellaneous matter. Simple math and a dash of genius produced, in 1882, the advertising slogan "99 44/100 percent pure," surely one of the tightest and best American slogans since "Jesus saves."

The slogan's virtue was subtlety, and it survived longer than another Ivory tag line with the same message: "Are you certain that the plate you eat on and the cup you drink from has not been washed with soap made from diseased cattle?"

Modern Ivory is made from animal fat, coconut oil, moisture and what the company says are such small amounts of nonsoap ingredients—perfume and color preservatives—that the "99 44/100 percent pure" claim is still warranted.

At Port Ivory, the workers are friendly and smell nice, and plant safety includes eyewash fountains in case a stray squirt catches someone. One fragrant line worker is Ruth Walters, whose very persona, not just career, is casually summarized by a Port Ivory executive: "Ruth is thirty-six years in Ivory miniatures."

Mrs. Walters has worked her years solely in the hotel-sliver half of the plant, where the assortment includes ½-ounce pieces for single-night-stay motels, and 3-ounce pieces for hotels specializing in convention-week bookings.

"I love Ivory," Mrs. Walters declared when asked how she broke away from the purity-racked job at the end of the day.

But surely there are times she can do without the haunting aroma of her labor?

"It's a great smell," Mrs. Walters replied, smiling there on the Ivory miniature packing line. "Why would I want to get away from it? When I'm on vacation I like to go buy packages of Ivory and unwrap them to check the quality."

That's how things are at Port Ivory, although another worker is a sliver less zealous. "It washes off," he said, as the ribbons oozed forth toward a second century.

[9/15/79]

Down These
Mean Streets

The looters scattered, roachlike, in the full morning sunlight, then stopped to watch brazenly when the owner of Joe's candy store showed up and saw his store disemboweled onto the Brownsville sidewalk. He let out a furious howl.

As if blind and wounded, the man went after one edge of the crowd that held his candy bars and cigarettes. The looters skittered off a bit more toward Watkins Street, the children and women in screams and laughter, the teen-aged boys swaggering, like toreadors.

The crowd was discovering after a night of looting that not only could the store-breaking be continued in daylight, but also that the arrival of the owner only heightened the occasion to a mass tease, like the running of the bulls in Pamplona.

"Oh those scum, those bastards, those rotten scum," said Frank Mason, a muscular, bearded man, watching the display. All along Pitkin Avenue, the Brownsville shopping district where Mr. Mason grew up, the texture of the 1977 city blackout was becoming visible.

It was not a matter of genial sing-alongs in East Side bars, although there was that. Or outer borough imitations of British perseverance and Hoosier hospitality, although there was that. Or Everyman become Boy Scout, although there was that, too.

To Mr. Mason and the others in Brownsville the texture of the blackout this time quickly eclipsed any fond remembrances of the 1965 darkness and its sense of friendly survival.

•

The darkness this time was blood on the window shards of Kiddie Bargain Town on Pitkin Avenue, where the looters wadded themselves in, slashing their own vanguard, and popped back out with a ludicrous inventory of baby carriages and strollers and infant paraphernalia.

It was a glittering, slithery carpet of broken glass and hydrant water stretching down the Pitkin strip, cordoned off by the police who witnessed a kind of vague darting, a cyclical frenzy by crowds watching one minute, pushing into the store the next.

"It seems worse than last night," Officer John Somerville of the 73rd Precinct said, standing in the middle of Pitkin. "They're standing around like vultures."

With more than 2,700 looters and vandals arrested, it was one of the largest police roundups in the city's history. But if the ghetto merchants and residents saw the truth, it was a token roundup.

The darkness this time was the act of two little boys initiating themselves into theft, clambering through the charred remains of John's Bargain Store, coming out with school supplies, and almost getting trampled by an old woman protecting an armful of pots.

It was the pathetic rubble of empty boxes and paper bags, marked Deutsche Jewelers, stuck in the glass and water outside the gutted store. "It was like World War III," said Abraham Deutsche, while his uncle fairly moaned in grief and boxed together scraps and records.

•

The Deutsches had rushed over from their home in Borough Park after midnight, too late, and watched through their broken door as other stores were hit. They saw vandals hitch an auto and chain to the steel curtains that sealed off virtually all the Pitkin stores and then yank them out like baby teeth.

"This is a whole different element," said Mr. Mason, alternately consoling merchants and fuming. "They're not native New Yorkers. Being black, I worked twice as hard for what I got rather than be scum on welfare. We fought our way out of Harlem to come out here, and I remember when there was no [protective] gates on the stores. This morning I saw them all waiting by Waldbaum's, waiting for someone to throw the stone and to move in. It's disgraceful."

"Hey, like everything's free," said Albert Figueroa, summarizing the crowd's mood even as he helped his neighbors, the Deutsches, by keeping his leashed German shepherd, King, barking and snarling at the doorway. As Mr. Mason made his rounds on Pitkin Avenue, the scene often was of white, Jewish merchants standing outside their stores in groups watched by crowds of blacks and Hispanics.

"Look, I'm all right," Stan Goodman said. "My Spanish and black help came in and watched the place. I'm all right."

But the "soul brother" cachet of past riots, where black merchants were spared, was not too visible in this blackout. On 125th Street in Harlem, for example, Sonny Robinson, proprietor of a black-owned camera shop known in the area for twenty-four years, watched over a jumble of broken glass and empty display counters.

Like other merchants, he counted differences from the 1965 blackout—chiefly the hot July night this time and the more depressed economic state of the ghetto, compared with the chill November evening and the Vietnam war economy of twelve years ago.

The darkness this time had a feral texture to it that seemed slow in dawning on the quieter parts of the city. For a while, the news of this blackout was measured as something less than 1965 because the rest of the Northeast was not involved.

•

But this blackout, as epic as 1965's was, lasted longer—in 1965 the lights were back on by daylight. At midday yesterday, there were merchants and residents worried that if their neighborhoods hit dusk without electricity restored, the looting would intensify.

"Then you can hang it up, daddy," said Lenron Goode, the head of a private security agency. Mr. Mason wondered whether the mere restoration of electricity would slake the lust for loot. He eyed the sportive groups in sunlight, lugging away boxes of meat and sacks of booty, and thought the festivity could go forward on its own.

This was an interesting point. When the power suddenly was restored to 125th Street in Harlem yesterday morning the main effect appeared to be a sudden, blaring resurrection of hustle music from a record store's sidewalk speaker.

The music was more motif than alarm to a crowd regrouping outside Busch's Jewelers, where the steel protective curtain long since had been bent back like a sardine-can lid. The music throbbed and the kids, then some teen-agers and adults, ducked under and went in, looking for gems missed in the earlier raids, before the blackout lengthened into morning and brought sunlight as a looting aid.

On Pitkin Avenue, Mr. Mason took it all personally. "Animals," he said, moving down toward his own auto repair shop, which had been spared. "This is my roots, where I grew up."

He stopped outside 1707 Pitkin, the Jewel Box, plundered apart. "That's where I got my wife's engagement ring—aw, man," Mr. Mason said. He was a strange sight, looking strong, but sad and standing next to a small boy who was smiling and showing his friend a fine gold chain he had picked up in the daylight.

[7/15/77]

Some Flights of Fancy

There are people who take the A train in the dark, going down from Harlem and points south to the city's ocean coast so they can watch birds stirring about Jamaica Bay in the blue edge of dawn. These city bird watchers walk from the subway's Broad Channel station to the marshes, and they are as quiet and undemanding as the birds they stare at, and as adaptable.

A few years ago, strangers with bows and arrows—extra weird and rarefied as city thugs go—took advantage of the bird watchers' information network. They showed up at another favored vantage place in Pelham Park in the Bronx and trailed the bird watchers to kill some of the last owls seen in that borough.

The bird watchers adapted and now they do not put precise locales in their taped telephone bulletins of rare sightings, such as the pair of peregrine falcons that were swooping about the canyons of lower Manhattan recently, feeding on the crowds of pigeons.

•

"It was a snap for the falcons, like getting on a cafeteria line," says Jim Ash, a construction worker with a gift for watching birds in the city as the rest of us go past blind, and for imagining what they are up to. The first time, ten years ago, he saw a strange bird go by with a long stretched neck and legs and a curved bill. "I said, 'What the hell was that?'" Mr. Ash remembers.

He looked the bird up in a book, discovering that this creature, a glossy ibis, was of a species windblown through history all the way from Egypt. The look and story of this bird got him, and the others, and Mr. Ash found about him a worthy puzzle of pieces flying through the air and perching like new ideas.

Thus was Mr. Ash, born and bred in New York City, to look inward and down, off on a complicated nature adventure in which he doesn't even have to leave the city.

He does roam occasionally—the new frontier lately with city "birders" is to go miles out on charter fishing boats, not with hooks and rods but with simple scopes, to sight some of the species of pelagic, sea-based birds beyond the city horizon. On land, some of the best spots include penthouse gardens, the springtime Ramble in Central Park, oases such as Trinity churchyard, the city's last great canopy forest in Forest Park, Queens, and some of Mr. Ash's own construction sites.

While fellow construction workers huddle over morning coffee, Mr. Ash looks in the nooks of steelwork in migration weather for birds dead, broken and restoring themselves from midflight exhaustion. Looking all through the city, he has built a personal record of sighting 304 different species, excluding certain exotic excesses that can only happen here.

"I was birding in Forest Park and I saw a macaw in a tree," he says. "I stopped dead: a macaw?" The bird had gotten loose from a cargo bay at Kennedy International Airport or from some pet lover's apartment. Such birds, bizarre in their jungle plumage, are about as valuable as purple cows to the urban birder.

•

Soon there will be a great event of birds in the city, one that fits in with the spirit of any number of other seasonal turnings, like the prewinter food gorging of the San Gennaro street festival and the Fifth Avenue shop window couture of new, muted plumage. Scores of species and thousands of individual birds will swoop down the city's coast in great chattering clouds and graceful wedges.

This will be the first mass movement south of the passerines, the many land perching birds. On a clear day after a sudden temperature drop, with a good northwestern wind—the tangy sort of day that signals a citydweller that football is back in prime time—Mr. Ash will go to the empty beaches of Riis Park.

"You wouldn't guess that Riis Park is the créme de la créme of places for watching the great fall migration, but it is," Mr. Ash says. Even the untrained eye will be stunned at the sight of 50,000 blackbirds marshaling themselves for survival, he says, in great curving, nagging sheets. The flocking crowds stretch overhead all day long, like a negative Milky Way, but only a few New Yorkers will watch them and tell them apart.

•

The other day, whorls of tree sparrows nibbled final meals from bayberry clumps in the Jamaica Bay Wildlife Refuge as Mr. Ash wandered by with his scope on a tripod. On the northern horizon, the Manhattan skyline seemed lifeless and in the past. A jetliner ascended well enough east to cause no stir in a rich, motley gathering. There were gulls, egrets, herons, mallards and geese of numerous variety, and plovers and sandpipers and countless others, strutting and standing, staring and feeding.

The twenty-five-year-old refuge is man's contrivance as much as nature's, for it is in considerable part the work of a retired city parks worker, Herb Johnson. The centerpieces of the refuge—two artificially diked fresh water ponds set amid the salt marshes—have thrived because of Mr. Johnson's knowledge of horticulture. He stippled the place with a clever blend of new seed and fruit growth back in the 1950's, knowing how to coax roots into sand.

The resulting unusual mix of fresh- and salt-water birds, side by side, is now one of the key possessions of the new Gateway National Recreation Area. The refuge already seems somewhat abused by the non-birder: The inevitable urban jogger tramps by in a loud outfit. But subtle fall colors of the birds provide immediate relief, and the neighborhood of glinting ponds and wind-bent grasses seems hearty.

74

"It's all free—you just have to look about you," Mr. Ash says. He watches a finch crack open a thistle seed and live.

[9/22/77]

The Funeral of Mr. Yee

The Chinese friends and relatives of Mr. Yee paid their last respects at the money-burning ceremony and they followed his coffin from Bacigalupo's funeral home onto Mulberry Street where Carmine, the band leader, gave a signal with his trombone and concluded a dirge version of "Nearer My God to Thee."

The six-man band, wearing black caps as they sounded forth on the narrow sidewalk, went into an extra slow, deeply drummed rendition of Chopin's funeral march. Carmine played at a near-keening level as the mourners followed the coffin, its coppery skin glinting in the daylight, to the hearse outside Giambone's restaurant.

In the park opposite, a muscular teen-ager stopped dribbling his basketball and watched as the mourners were helped into a half-dozen limousines, which had small signs of Chinese characters identifying the occupants. They slowly left Chinatown, and Carmine respectfully led his gray-haired band around the corner, the gig having ended.

People in the street and a few rubbernecking diners from Giambone's were left wondering about the charm and confusion of having witnessed an old-fashioned Little Italy street band sounding away sadly at a Chinese funeral. Beyond a matter of life and death, the tableau represented a bit of symbiosis in the neighboring cultures of Chinatown and Little Italy thriving tightly about Canal Street in Manhattan.

•

Bacigalupo's—a century-old Little Italy landmark with an endless burial procession from a handsome former bank building on Mulberry—quietly became the Ng Fook Funeral Home last fall when Edward Chan, an experienced undertaker from Hong Kong, bought the establishment. While the old-line business has thinned with the suburban and outer-borough diaspora of Italian-Americans, the Chinese community has increased and, fortunately for Carmine and the other old Italian musicians, the Chinese funeral customs include a preference for live music.

So there was Carmine inside Bacigalupo's, assembling his men in front of Mr. Yee's open coffin and giving a downbeat for such songs as "What a Friend We Have in Jesus," and a gentle, airy tune from the old neighborhood, "Il Tuo Popolo" (Your People). The music seemed to soothe the mourners, who sat on folding chairs and listened and watched through a blur of lighted candles by the bier.

"The other day we had an Italian wake in the back and a Chinese one in the front parlor," said John A. Toomey, who manages the place for Mr. Chan. "When the band started playing, some of the Italians came out of the back and they were saying, 'Oh yeah, we had a band at my grandfather's funeral.'"

But Carmine, who is seventy-four years old, says the Italians rarely use the old band-playing custom at funerals now. The only one he could recall in the last decade or two was an old Italian widow who died in Brooklyn two years ago and, mirroring her husband's sendoff in the 1930's, was laid to rest serenaded at graveside by a twenty-piece band.

Back in Hong Kong, a generous departure might include a thirty-piece orchestra—Chinese musicians, of course—Mr. Chan noted. Here, only rarely does an affluent Chinatown leader require such an expensive accompaniment of homeland dirge, plus the thirty or more limousines to carry it off. Generally, Carmine's band is fine.

"It's not easy to play slow, you know," Carmine said. "And not every musician can play standing up in the street." His band—two trumpets, a bass drum and a snare drum, the trombone and a tuba-like baritone—are all union men, said Carmine, who wants his last name omitted so there are no misunderstandings at the union hall. The musicians are somewhat retired, although three funerals in one week plus some livelier stuff for the recent Times Square antiporn demonstration keeps their toes tapping.

"We've had full careers as musicians," Carmine stressed. "It's not just Chinese funerals, you know. I played at both World's Fairs."

Chinese come from all over the suburbs and the country for Chinatown funerals, and some even fly in from Hong Kong. The bodies or ashes often require intricate shipping arrangements back to the Orient mainland. Mr. Chan and Mr. Toomey seem like a good combination for handling such final traffic.

•

Minutes after Mr. Yee left the other day, a few doors down at the Wah Wing Sang funeral parlor a second Italian street band played the final Chopin escort as another Chinese family marched in the street behind a coffin to a hearse, which blocked off the cross-street traffic. A blond woman in a green Cadillac impatiently beeped her horn, and a funeral attendant quickly went to her car, briefly switched from poker face to near leer and said low and direct: "Take it easy, baby."

The hearse moved out, then the blonde picked up the pace of her own life. Mulberry Street quieted down with the day's funerals over, and an old Italian man came out of Bacigalupo's, set up a striped plastic garden chair by the doorstep under the Ng Fook sign and began watching things.

[5/10/77]

City Hall Lunch

Lunch hour, summer of '78, City Hall Park: A year ago you could be fairly sure at this hour that there was a Mayor at his desk across the way, nibbling a tuna-fish sandwich. But the new Mayor is more adventurous and roams up to Chinatown, crosscutting through the great swirl of midday hunger that is worth an anthropologist's giving up a lunch hour to watch.

Any former child who ever played store with kitchen-cabinet contents or who ventured out from fantasy to open a lemonade stand can slip into a lunch-hour trance watching the Sabrett-wagon man at Park Place as he whisks cold drinks and hot dogs from separate metal compartments. (Childhood is a good lunch-hour retreat in Manhattan.)

This Sabrett man, with a curly black mustache, is very polite and sure-handed, making change and saying, "Thank you, ma'am," just like a merchant-child. Under his striped umbrella, he whips open first the left-hand lid to get a fresh bun, then the right-hand lid to poke a steamed wiener into place, then a quick swipe of the mustard-pot brush, kept at his right hand like a pistol, then a flip of the center lid to lace on some sauerkraut or onions, or both for those who prefer internal roiling on the lunch hour.

On the square block heading west from this wagon, the industry of feeding is moving along with all of the pouring and stacking and flaming of a foundry. At the Treat Deli in the middle of the block, countermen are patching together sandwiches, wielding knife, garnish and wrapping with rapid dexterity worthy of one of those showoff Japanese restaurants. But there is no applause or apparent salivating on the customer's side of the Treat counter—just a close, truth-in-bologna eyeballing as the sandwiches are flicked into being.

A few doors down, the same thing is happening at Deli City. Sandwich shops are neighbors on a Manhattan street the same way supergalaxies are in space—vastly separate and similar, producing countless tidbits of matter that daub the void briefly.

•

The people who do the feeding are on different cycles from the fed. A young man from Chock Full O'Nuts times his coffee break just before the luncheon crowds spill from the office buildings. He sips, unrushed, seated in a wheelchair parked outside the corner newsstand, chatting with his friend, the newsie, across the papers.

Down beyond the delis, a place called Valentino's Italian Kitchen is true enough to its motif, offering imported macaroni on its fast-food menu. ("Fast food" is a redundancy for most people on a Manhattan lunch hour.) Valentino's is adapting to the block with a fresh window sign: "Notice!! We will also serve onion rings, knishes and hamburgers."

Down from this is a tiny hole-in-the-wall fruit stand crammed with cherries, nectarines and Packham pears that beam with color. Then comes the gaslight look of Suerkens Restaurant, where the shadows on the old tile floor look as inviting as the day's specialty hand-lettered in the window: "Steamers."

And so on around this single block and its trough of street stores. Precious time can be measured in chews if you study the Kwik Times deli, where customers sit and present their jawlines profiled and ruminating in the windows. With adjectives like "overstuffed," the menu is reminiscent of the acidic promise of City Hall press releases ground out down the block.

Across from City Hall Park, a man who seems trapped in a perpetual clinch and gasp is hurriedly wheeled out on a stretcher from 250 Broadway to an ambulance. A pedestrian eating a salt pretzel watches the gray-haired man who seems so far from this lunch hour and its splendid sunshine glistening brightly on the man's brown buckled shoes poking out from the ambulance blanket. Fast as a Sabrett sale, the ambulance leaves, worming past crowds sucking on ices and sodas, and its siren sound evaporates into the lunch hour.

•

City Hall Park is a small place crowded with lunchers staking out choice patches of grass, sunshine and bench space. A young man has come from somewhere on a racing bike, settling down a blanket for a young woman in a breezy-looking dress who takes her shoes off and leans against him. They barely talk.

In this dappled commons, books are being read, hands are being held, thick shakes and diet sodas are drained side by side. The northeast quadrant is suffused with the smell of marijuana smoke, and young office workers are having some for dessert, toking away at the wrapped weed, sharing it like a password to a special state. Some hear the music from one of those thumping tape decks at their feet and sway and pop a bit in the sunshine.

Sunbathing is in all attitudes, shirtless, sockless, shamelessly pleasant with lovers posturing to mix sunlight into their cozying. On the steps of City Hall there is a woman staring so still and straight up at the sun that you half-wonder whether there is yet another charismatic politician approaching.

Out on the Brooklyn Bridge, which ascends in a proud web east from City Hall, a young man is eating cheese and crackers. The wind, strong and flat and straight, polices lunch wrappings from the crest of the pedestrian crossing, dashing them out and away into blue above, green below. Gulls hang on the wind at eye level, and, back down at City Hall Park, the trash barrels are filling up with the crumpled leavings of another lunch hour.

[7/15/78]

3
You Have to Be Special

Move It!

There is an eighty-seven-year-old nag in the Bronx named William Hirscher who seems to scream to life every morning, first with a cold shower, then with a brisk round of dispensing his own hand printed traffic citations to offending motorists who block the curbside path of the city's mechanical brooms on 161st Street.

"You are *illegally* parked. Police Dept.," the flimsy citation says in the Xeroxed scrawl of Mr. Hirscher, who has no authority but his own sense of cleanliness and outrage.

"My brooms are due here in five minutes; move it!" he said the other morning to a flabbergasted motorist. The driver, startled and frowning, obviously did not know how to cope with this new form of civilian impudence, a vigilante in his ninth decade barking orders out of the side of his mouth and then, for good measure, producing a police whistle from under his scarf and blowing it loudly.

Mr. Hirscher was an unexpected peril for the man; a gaping, rough-edged tin can in the path of your average morning New Yorker trying to crawl back quietly to life.

•

"Hey, Pillar!" Mr. Hirscher shouted to a policeman writing tickets a half block away. The motorist immediately scrambled to life and drove off, his face askew with a question that was the Wild East's equivalent of Who Was That Masked Man???

"My cops are out," Mr. Hirscher said as Officer John Pillar came up and said, "Good morning, Mr. Hirscher."

"God bless you, Pillar," said Mr. Hirscher. "This marvelous cop writes up a hundred a day." The policeman beamed at the compliment and told how he had to follow Mr. Hirscher around to protect him on his morning rounds.

"One day a merchant—right there," Mr. Hirscher said, pointing to a store, "comes out after I had cited him dozens of times and he jabs his finger in my chest and says, 'I'll see you buried in your grave.'"

Mr. Hirscher was delighted, not so much at the comedic notion of someone making such a threat to a man forty years his senior, but at the graphic evidence of success in his one-man campaign to keep his self-proclaimed ten-block piece of the Grand Concourse neighborhood cleaned up.

•

A first impression of Mr. Hirscher is that he is a sharp-tongued anachronism worth visiting, a creature of dated true grit on the brink of returning to dust. At 7:55 on a cold morning, with the Yankee Stadium in the background and his breath coming forth in steamy dashes, the reality of Mr. Hirscher begins to set in. He crosses 161st diagonally, stopping to pick up some litter, and immediately this old man begins to marshal people.

In a fifteen-minute stretch no fewer than six uniformed officers from three different city agencies arrive to pay their respects to him and wait while "his" mechanical brooms and "his" patrolmen and street cleaners do their work. (One officer with bars on his olive uniform, resembling a generalissimo of sanitation, grumbled privately: "It's good he keeps after us, but you know what this means—other neighborhoods have to be neglected for this one.")

Mr. Hirscher scoffed at the complaint, saying the more likely alternative was that these civil servants would not be working much at all at that hour but for his grating cleanup campaign, which he sustains by organizing civic groups, flooding commissioners with letters and getting signed compliments in return, including a picture of himself and the Mayor, all of which he flashed about like an ambassadorial sash. In a government run in good part on public relations, these letters, even if part of the defensive routine, can be powerful stuff in the spotted hands of a crafty old man.

"I'll tell you," he said in his own whispered aside. "They're not doing half as well as I want, and I am going to *keep after them*. You know what they say: The creaky axle gets the grease."

The only accurate way to describe Mr. Hirscher's method is in terms of the Yiddish verb "to hock." He doesn't simply complain about things, he hocks people, pestering them incessantly for clean streets so that his talks seem to fall only a fraction short of biting them.

But then he praises people, too, composing and distributing imaginative handbills of photographs he takes of merchants sweeping their sidewalks and of sanitation men and policemen doing their job. "John Lutzyg, Sanitation Man Nonpareil" one recent issue was headlined with a photograph of Mr. Lutzyg, smiling in his sanitation uniform as he wielded broom and shovel.

•

Mr. Hirscher has had all kinds of paying jobs, including teacher at Stuyvesant High and longtime worker in the garment industry. "Do I need a vacation?" he asks rhetorically over his morning Sanka-break. "Am I some nut? No, I get businessmen of property into the gutter to clean."

His brothers have died and most retirees in his early civic groups have died, but Mr. Hirscher keeps hocking. "We should refuse to give New York up to the punks," he says.

His motivation, he said, comes from the Ephebic Oath, a pledge rooted in the Greek city-state that he took as a 1909 graduate of City College. "I said I would leave the city a better place than I found it."

The Ephebic Oath? Anyone who smiles at the gaslight chimera of such a notion had better not litter 161st Street within hocking distance of Mr. Hirscher.

[12/9/76]

On Her Honor
She Did Her Duty

When she was good, the little girl in the brown beanie was very, very good— good enough to sell 1,148 boxes of Girl Scout cookies and, now, to be proclaimed the best cookie seller in Manhattan for 1979. And when she was bad, the worst she did was interrupt an interview to try and sell more Girl Scout cookies.

"Sir, would you like to buy some Girl Scout cookies?" the seven-year-old West Side cookie maven piped up.

By the end of the interview, she had sold five more boxes, impinging on journalistic standards that frown on the purchase of information, but yielding a reckless news beat on how to sell Girl Scout cookies. (The sale is confessed here to head off another tacky First Amendment confrontation with Government.)

The name of the champion seller is Markita Andrews. Remember the name. She could be the next Annie, or Gloria Steinem. She is small and cunning as a Communist-bloc gymnast.

She is perpetually polite, and just as watchful, and she keeps things at the basic cookie-question level even as a visitor is seeking Bruno Bettelheim nuances—how, for example, her superior motivation might be affected by electronic fairy tales, seeing as how the TV "cookie monster" has been. . . .

"Sir, would you like to buy some Girl Scout cookies?"

Yes, yes. We'll try the Thin Mints, Markita, your very own favorite flavor.

88

All about her are cartons of cookies, piled in tiers twice as high (Granola was a new kind this year). The cache is worth a cool, crisp $1,500 at street prices, and Markita and her aunt, Meredith R. McSherry, must now break it down according to the precise mix of customers' orders. The biggest delivery, for example, is going to Mrs. Goldstein at 180 West End Avenue, who ordered seventeen boxes—heavy on the Thin Mints, light on the Tagalongs, medium on the Do-Si-Does and Van-Chos.

Last year, when Markita was six, she was the prodigy in the cookie competition, selling 658 boxes when other Brownies were selling the typical dozen or so to their family and immediate neighbors. This year, she became the virtuoso.

Chance was a factor in the high sales, according to her aunt, Mrs. McSherry, who played the chaperon that all cookie-selling Brownies are required to have. She played shrewd business manager, too, in deciding that the best selling territory was their home ground, Lincoln Towers, the extensive apartment development at West End Avenue and West 69th Street.

"I've lived here since the 1960's and noticed there never were any Girl Scout cookies sold, so I thought this was promising territory," says Mrs. McSherry in a Carolina accent sweet as the scout's Trefoil shortbread cookies.

The territory is ambitious—nine buildings of twenty-nine floors each, more than 4,000 apartments. They set out to cover all of it in the three-week period of competition that began on George Washington's birthday. It snowed heavily that day, and Markita and her aunt went door to door in their own building, 180 West End Avenue, from 10 A.M. to 8:30 P.M. They finished tired but jubilant, with ninety boxes sold.

•

Markita's pitch is simple, standing in the doorway in her uniform with the Wise Old Owl patch, her big dark eyes angled up in supplication, smiling so innocently, always beginning with a polite "Ma'am" or "Sir."

"She's cute," says her aunt. "They couldn't turn her down. Would you?" Mrs. McSherry says Markita's only noticeable flaw—two missing teeth—occurred during the sales period, enhancing the child's technique.

The big breakthrough, though, occurred at the apartment tower across the way, No. 185, where the doorman was strict and stopped them from going door to door after they were three floors into the building.

"We went down to the lobby, not sure what to do," Mrs. McSherry recalls. "It was about 5:30 in the evening and people were coming home from work. I saw a man opening his mail and told Markita to go over."

"Sir . . ." she began, and the rest is cookie history. She signed up forty customers in one evening in that lobby.

•

Thereafter, the Brownie, with her aunt watching like Fagin, deliberately worked the lobbies of the nine buildings on evenings and weekends, selling box after box at $1.25 apiece, and earning 17 cents per box for her Brownie unit, Troop 311, headed by Ruby Rubin, plus a personal reward of a two-week vacation in scout camp.

The official total of 1,148 boxes was sold to 730 customers. She roamed a bit beyond the apartment towers, selling twenty boxes at Beacon Lanes, where Mrs. McSherry bowls, around the corner on Amsterdam Avenue. They also sold more than fifty boxes at the West Side Republican Club where Markita's uncle, Walter McSherry, is active, and a few dozen at the Fifth Avenue Presbyterian Church and the Lincoln Square Academy where Markita is in Mrs. Grabino's second-grade class.

The huge order of cookies was trucked to the McSherry's apartment last week and neighbors stopped to watch the sweets being wheeled in, handcart after handcart. The order included ten extra boxes, a shrewd allowance by Mr. McSherry for breakage. This is a supply that he actually covets for his own sweet tooth, but, of course, Markita began selling them during the interview.

"Sir . . ." she began.

Yes, yes, Markita. A box of the coconut Samoas, too, as you say, Markita.

[5/8/79]

Smoking Guns
in the Big Town

It was a marvelous piece of shooting in a delicatessen on Farragut Avenue in Brooklyn, the gun club president said, an adrenalized blur in which the deli owner said he had snatched a revolver from one of three bandits and had wheeled and shot down the first of them, then the second, then the third. He squeezed off five rounds in a thorough arc of fury, moving so fast it would have taken the cameraman from "The Wild Bunch" to record it all.

"He didn't even break a jar of cranberries," said the gun club president, Gerald Preiser, after giving the deli owner $200 and a "Courageous Citizen" plaque for shooting down the three intruders.

A few weeks earlier Mr. Preiser sent another plaque and $200 to a Texan—a department-store security chief—who was here as a tourist and told the police that he had to draw on two holdup men and smoke one into eternity over at the New York Hilton.

Like they say, you have to be special to make it in the Big Apple.

•

Mr. Preiser seems ordinary enough until he unbuttons his double-breasted blue blazer, swings his right hand to his belt and draws out a .45-caliber Army pistol, already cocked with a round in the chamber and the safety on, the way he always strolls about the city.

It is a startling sight—a brutish shark-gray killing tool with the hammer back, hefted by the smiling garment district executive. Mr. Preiser has never had to use it against urban predators he terms "the Barbarians," but he says he is ever ready to shoot to kill anyone who tries to get the drop on him in "the valley of the Barbarians," which is anywhere in the city.

"Once a gun is trained on you, it's open season, the game is on, and it's not like tag when you were a kid," he says. The game means your money *and* your life these days, he feels.

"I was born and raised here [Manhattan], a classic liberal Jewish Democrat—ask me my positions on housing, education," he says, sliding the automatic back against his belly. He pats the walnut pistol grip. "But when you consider this, I guess you say I'm a conservative—yet I'll vote for Koch."

With his cocked .45, he can vote for whomever he pleases, is a visitor's immediate reaction. Mr. Preiser's view of the extreme delicacy of life is uttered quite casually over the midday pop-pop-pop sound of gunfire on West 20th Street, in the West Side Rifle and Pistol Range that he opened as a second business and heartfelt avocation fourteen years ago. It is a commercial range, one of the few successful ones in the city, he feels, because of its location, service and the limitation on the legitimate shooter's market in the city.

•

There are "only" 30,000 licensed pistol shooters among the city's eight million residents—an alarming fact to Mr. Preiser for which he roundly denounces the Police Department. And only about half the permits authorize self-defense in home or office. The rest are limited to recreational target shooting, and Mr. Preiser contends that the law is so biased that if a target shooter, in his own bedroom, were to shoot a criminal intruder, the person with the gun permit is liable to criminal charges.

He says customers who use the midtown range—lawyers, business executives, a few secretaries at lunch time, plus guards from Lincoln Center to Con Ed to all the major banks—suffer a law stacked in favor of the Barbarians who, by Mr. Preiser's estimate, have up to two million pistols and revolvers at their disposal.

There was considerable controversy when the $200 reward and plaque were first given two years ago to a sixty-seven-year-old building superintendent. (He had talked yieldingly to two thugs, had reached in to hand over his wallet and had come out with "a blazing .38," Mr. Preiser happily recalls.) The rewards, instituted by the Federation of Greater New York Rifle and Pistol Clubs, headed by Mr. Preiser, were denounced as bounties smacking of Frontier mayhem.

But these last few times, Mr. Preiser contends, there has been less controversy and more endorsement from the public, with some enthusiasts sending contributions to the reward fund. At the same time he says it is getting harder to talk "courageous citizens" into accepting the $200 because attendant publicity might prompt some armed pervert in the city into seeking revenge on Everyman, the smiling deli owner.

Also, many people pack pistols illegally, and Mr. Preiser asserts there are numerous nonshooting incidents where, for example, a friend backed out of a subway men's room Wild West-style, with his pistol held on a nefarious looking pair, then merely holstered the weapon without a report to the police.

•

With his thick brush mustache and horn-rimmed glasses, Mr. Preiser stands out in all the wall photographs in his office, posing next to dead boars and swordfish from his hunting trips and live Republicans from his Albany lobbying. The memorabilia are an interesting mix of Hemingway macho and Sinclair Lewis Babbittry.

Out on the basement range of sixteen target bays, 50 feet deep, the sense of the vicarious seems as pungent as the smell of burnt gunpowder.

"I'm going in," Mr. Preiser tells a range assistant. "Run up a silhouette and give us some earphones."

On the line, Mr. Preiser faces a crouching, mean-faced,

point-blank paper gunman 20 feet away. He draws his .45 and in ten seconds of acrid, startling thunder drills the target with eight rounds in a fist-sized circle in the middle of the chest.

"I got his pump and other vital organs," he says, turning away from the shredded paper enemy.

[1/31/78]

Chuck the Knife

Talk about a captive audience: Charles D. Kelman, M.D., goes on at Laff's nightclub on East 54th Street the other night, and not only is ringside packed with patients who see him well because of the cataract surgery he did for them, but one of those so sighted is Lee Salomon, a big agent for the William Morris Agency.

"You're a beautiful audience, ladies and gentlemen," says the doctor at the top of his song-comedy-and-saxophone routine, looking Vegas-chic, his surgeon's hands casually whipping the microphone cord into place with the show biz élan that he's craved all his life.

Indeed, the audience's indulgence of its own beauty in full line and color and shadow is a fact well born out in the preceding cocktail hour, paid for by Dr. Kelman for 150 patients plus physicians in town to study his special ultrasonic surgery technique for cataract removal. Banging down a bounty of glinting summer cocktails, people are staring into each other's eyes with a passion unusual for any East Side boîte.

Dorothy Tasman, glaring happily through her one repaired eye, is a good measure of how ready the audience is for this unusual ophthalmologist's monthly Walter Mitty go at show business.

"I'm shouting it to the world," Mrs. Tasman says over the noise at the bar. "This man is the greatest."

•

Dr. Kelman beams and says it is smart, with 9,000 ex-patients to choose among each month, to stack his audience with some like Mrs. Tasman who are awaiting their second cataract operation. Somehow, they're more willing to laugh and applaud.

But seriously, in moving right along into the red and green and blue and orange pinpoint spots of the stage, Dr. Kelman says he sheds in his nightclub act much of the tension and doctor-patient impersonalization involved in his weekly run of two dozen cataract operations.

He kids his clientele as its members grin at the tiny tables in the dim, smoky club. "Would the patients in the audience please wave their canes?" he jokes, as if he had failed in surgery.

In a parody of "My Way," he informs the doctors he's been teaching all week that if they goof, don't call on him in a malpractice suit: "I couldn't lie," he sings, backed by his four-piece band, "I'd testify/It wasn't my way."

The forty-nine-year-old physician's act is authentic down to the chesty opening of his striped shirt. He gets what he hungers for—applause, quick laughs across the icy hollow of a highball glass, timely barump-barips from the drummer for punctuation.

•

Mr. Salomon, the wheel from William Morris, looks like one tall, tough audience in dark suit and gold ring, but he melts a bit at the sight of an ordinary nonstar, Frank Albino. "Frank had the operation same day as me," he explains, patting the man on the back. The agent's eye is not only clear, but shrewd, making quick calculations on a bonanza in his field—a luncheon booking of three casino acts for Atlantic City—versus the ten patients he saw Dr. Kelman line up one day.

"You want the Concord?" Mr. Salomon says to the doctor. "I'll get you the Concord. No big money, and you'll have to be the opening act, but I'll get you the Concord."

But Dr. Kelman already has played the Concord Hotel, along with the Fontainebleau in Miami and a summer cruise ship and a benefit at Carnegie Hall he organized and filled with 2,000 patients and friends. Some of the frustrated and affluent among the public have the vanity press to turn to;

Dr. Kelman has vanity show business, costing, he says, about $1,000 for the monthly nightclub rental, the band, drinks and hors d'oeuvres.

It is not a complete shock for his patients the night the doctor finally sheds the surgical gloves and comes on finger snapping with his opening, "This could be the start of something good." For his bedside manner includes a glass of champagne the evening before the operation, and a limousine pickup, too.

•

Some of the patients are heady enough to venture their own material. "Try the Skylab cocktail," Mrs. Tasman advises at the bar, timing her pause for the punch line: "two of those and you're not sure where you're landing." Barump-barip.

"Obviously I need this," Dr. Kelman says, surveying the room and his ego. He wanted to be a jazz musician and his father said he could be anything he wanted—after he first became a doctor.

He mocks himself with jokes about price-gouging physicians (but seriously, he loves the A.M.A.). And in an iatrogenic confession of his past try at other specialties, he sings, to the tune of "Mack the Knife," that while earlier patients succumbed, "they don't die now/'Cause I do eye now/I'm your good friend, Chuck the Knife."

The best thing about Dr. Kelman is not his material, but his lack of inhibition. "I sometimes wonder which is more important: this," he says, gesturing to the waiting, watching audience right before he goes on, "or making them see." He smiles at such a remark, heading onstage. It feels good to shout, "Kill them Doc," after the physician. Barump-barip.

[7/17/79]

Sanctuary

St. James, L.I.

It began with the gift of a small monkey from husband to wife thirteen years ago, and now the wife finds herself every lunch hour making cream-cheese and jelly sandwiches for thirty-one monkeys who live in her house. The monkeys have the sandwiches on toast, if you don't mind, cut into cage-convenient morsels adapted from the cocktail parties of human evolution.

Please try and understand about the monkeys, the husband and wife explain at their breakfast nook, where they are casually joined by Suzy, one of their spider monkeys, who pops into a chair, watches a visitor, nibbles a doughnut and seems to be planning some sort of light day for herself.

A woolly monkey extends a long furry arm from his cage opposite the breakfast nook, his palm offered with the watery gaze of a professional beggar. He seems understandably offended by the sight of the privileged Suzy. She ignores him and pays more attention to Casey and Ursula Kwarta, the hosts of this menagerie household in a modest white-shingled house at 50 Sunny Road.

•

There are four other woollies caged nearby. One of them is bent arthritically, pathetically, the Kwartas explain, from his years of being "loved" in a cramped bird cage of one of the many witless romantic humans who buy a baby monkey to relieve their own affection mechanisms. The animal grows, and the human becomes bored, particularly with the onset of naturally aggressive tendencies. When the cuddling

99

wanes, such creatures can be tolerated by only a few knowledgeable, patient humans such as the Kwartas, who run the only private simian sanctuary in the New York City area.

The Kwartas feel good about the sanctuary, but desperate, too, at times—they once had sixty monkeys, which is a lot of cream cheese, but had to scale back. There is no overwhelming monkey odor in the Kwartas' cheerful, paneled home. While a half dozen monkeys live in the house with the Kwartas, most of the others live in a monkey house in a converted garage that has an adjacent outdoor cage, a zoo-like structure built by Mr. Kwarta on his single-acre homesite.

Life with the monkeys is such that Mrs. Kwarta, a sinewy woman with the scars of monkey bites on her hands and arms, goes virtually around the clock, hosing down and repapering the cages and dishing up vast amounts of fruit and monkey chow spiced, as the monkeys prefer, with Captain Crunch cereal.

She arises at 7:30 in the morning and goes to bed at 1:30 A.M., exhausted from serving the monkeys, who invariably are glistening and chattering the next morning for more of the same treatment. In the last twelve years, the Kwartas say, they have been able to get away from their house for relief for only a single day. "We went to Great Adventure," Mr. Kwarta says, "to see the baboons."

The Kwartas may seem difficult to understand, but they are very fine company, kind and decent, and far less strange than some of the people who try to drop off their pets as word of the sanctuary spreads.

•

"They'll be crying, some of them, as they leave," Mr. Kwarta says drily, "crying so hard they forget to get a name and a mailing address so they could send a few bucks to help feed their little pets." Mr. Kwarta, a sales representative with an electronics company, supports the licensed, nonprofit sanctuary out of his own pocket and his wife's labor and figures he's barely breaking even.

100

The budget isn't spared by Suzy the spider monkey, who gets up from the breakfast nook and heads into the living room, suddenly reaching back to snatch a quarter pound of butter from the table. She sits down inside and savors it like a cigar. There is no way not to laugh, and it is difficult to tell who is aping whom as Mr. Kwarta scolds, "Bad girl," and Suzy smacks down the last of the butter and sits back.

Outside, two tiny squirrel monkeys are running free in the fall foliage up in the backyard trees, scrambling, searching, as if for the springtime inchworms they relish. A capuchin monkey with an impish, fringe-bordered face is roaming on a tether, sneering like a gargoyle at the Kwartas's German shepherd but then grooming the dog as it stands there. Pebbles, the household's most-favored woolly, who sleeps with the Kwartas, is languishing in the sunshine on the redwood deck by the swimming pool, a pool the monkeys use for gazing but not plunging into.

"Hi, boys," Mrs. Kwarta says in greeting to what seems a rugby team of monkeys romping in the main cage. Hands are extended, faces presented, lips pursed by the boys. Mr. Kwarta starts singling out the monkeys that have been stranded by human divorce proceedings, at least a dozen by his count.

"What we get, really, are the children of broken marriages," Mr. Kwarta says.

Mary Bloom, a volunteer with the Manhattan A.S.P.C.A. who tries to place abandoned exotic animals, says there is no one else like the Kwartas for the right blend of affection and practicality needed for monkey care. (Mr. Kwarta knows when to half-bite monkeys' arms and shoulders in affection and when to brandish a billy for protection.) Mrs. Bloom says the market is glutted with urbanized, often abused monkeys that have such talents as recognizing a Zabar's shopping bag as a treat cache but no ability to fit in with zoo colonies.

Lately when Mrs. Bloom calls, the zoos have no help to offer but rather ask her to find homes for their excess. She has witnessed weird urban love scenes such as the parting of a heartbroken apartment dweller and her macaque monkey, who was surrendered wearing a pink-lace dress and a snowsuit. The apartment dweller had taken a human roommate and the macaque had eaten the roommate's kitten, and so goodbye to that.

The Kwartas dream of opening a sanctuary out West with hundreds of acres, but they say the stress may get to them first, particularly the strain when one of their favorites dies. This year, Priscilla died. She was their prize woolly who had the run of the house and particularly enjoyed watching the fireplace on winter days. Mr. Kwarta, grief-stricken, built a small coffin.

"Yeah, we had kind of a funeral," he says, gesturing with a hand bearing a long monkey-bite scar. "I had some of the monkeys gather around for the burial, and they kind of watched."

[11/13/78]

A Voice Terrible
Yet Mouthwatering

YONKERS, N.Y.

We're here at Carvel College with John and Barbara O'Malley, who are graduating in uniforms white as the vanilla. We are toasting them with pink champagne and listening to Tom Carvel's terrible voice.

He agrees it is terrible—awfully memorable, he hopes, on his terrible-voiced Carvel ice-cream commercials that rise up on the air waves regular as Grendel at the castle door.

That voice is so identifiable, sounding like muffled laundry in a footlocker, raspy and suggestive as an anonymous, but benign, phone caller ("Have you tried our Thinny-Thin products?"). Never mind that it sells ice cream; Mr. Carvel's voice performs the greater public service of parodying all the hot-combed voices of the broadcasting marketplace.

•

It was tracked to its source here because people listening to the radio all day long have to stop and say things like, "Oh, not that guy again," when Tom Carvel comes on with his adenoidal huckstering. He'll introduce the O'Malleys or some other freshly trained Carvel couple who sound so nervous, as if the world of soft ice cream they are entering were frozen wedlock.

"I believe in the product," John O'Malley says as solemnly as a bridegroom into the commercial tape recorder while Tom Carvel officiates.

Tom Carvel is smart enough to know that, as people

look up and half groan at the sound of his voice, they remember well the name of his ice cream. "We'll play this back," he tells the nervous O'Malleys after a thirty-second interview that presents no threat to Barbara Walters and Anwar el-Sadat, "and if it's not good, we're going to use it."

He leads the laughter among a group of ten men and women seated at the graduation luncheon in vanilla-white. They are the latest batch from his intensive two-week training course that turns out fresh mom-and-pop entrepreneurs as steadily as the machines that Mr. Carvel designed flute out the ribbons of vanilla and chocolate in 750 stores in sixteen states.

Tom Carvel goes into his semiweekly gaudeamus, speaking around spoonfuls of the graduation dessert—a sweet, cold sundae, topped with his latest experimental topping of crunchy, flavored wheat germ. "How do you like the new crunch?" he asks merrily, a seventy-one-year-old little boy with ice cream on his gray mustache that has an Arthur Fiedler curl. He resembles the old Esquire magazine logo roué, but with a more innocent lech, ice-cream innocent.

"Girls, don't let your husbands get into the register," Tom Carvel tells half of his graduates and the women smile appropriately at the headmaster. "I'll tell you—when he gets going and breaks out a big roll of singles, he'll seem very attractive to the girls down in the saloon."

Commencement wisdom is dispensed in that voice, with Tom Carvel speaking at the head of the table. He presents himself as a friendly, proud ethnic-become-millionaire, and he has an antic, earthy quality. He complains that there are all of these "anti-anti-anti leagues" to stamp out the ethnic jokes and stereotyping that are part of his vocabulary and faith in humanity.

He relaxes the graduates with a Polish joke. Then, speaking in fond memory of some past graduates, Mr. Carvel recalls standout commercials where he found the accents as decorous as his new crunch. He never heard a better description of the Carvel product line and willingness to please, he says, than that which came from the lips of a man named Bruno: "We gonna make waddayouwant." Fresh-frozen waddayouwant, and more laughter from the graduates as Mr. Carvel grins and scrapes the dregs of the sundae from his dish and licks his spoon.

"I love dialects," he says. "This country is made from accents."

He is Greek-born of the family Carvelas, the son of an agriculturist who knew wine and yogurt making. "I have been called 'greaseball,'" he says, obviously proud that making an ice-cream fortune was his sticks-and-stones reply.

•

Once, he thought that he would be a mechanical engineer, then a jazz drummer on the borscht belt, then an outdoor dealer of old-fashioned ice cream from a trailer that he built himself after he got tuberculosis. The trailer broke down on a profitable curve in Hartsdale, N.Y., and he stayed there for business, with the first real Carvel born after several years of mechanical engineering by Mr. Carvel. He holds fourteen patents now, and the big one is on his machine built around the notion of using a small barrel and high refrigeration for instant freezing and freshness—6 ounces of soft ice cream every ten seconds instead of 6 gallons of hard ice cream in a half hour.

All of this is prologue as the latest Carvel College graduates go forth to open stores on life's highways.

"As a registered nurse, I appreciate Carvel as a food," Barbara O'Malley says in her graduation vow.

"A nurse, huh?" Tom Carvel says. "Is that why you're rubbing my knee?" His joke gets a big laugh from the class and he smiles as if life is one big, crunchy sundae.

[7/25/78]

The Overall Drift

DOBBS FERRY, N.Y.

The drizzle is soothing on Main Street and Bill Kalt's small apartment blends with the midday calm of America as he turns on his tape recorder to hear the monthly word about what's been going on.

"Hello, my friends, this is Dr. Beter in Washington," says an authoritative voice. "Today is March 29, 1979, and this is Audio Letter No. 44. It has now been fifteen months since I revealed in Audio Letter No. 29 that a new Bolshevik revolution was getting under way here in the United States . . ."

For $6 a month, Bill Kalt keeps in touch with the conspiracy he thinks is going on. He receives Dr. Beter's monthly, hourlong Audio Letters on cassettes from Fort Worth and plays them in his clean, humble apartment here on Main Street.

The words spin out each month in the same strong voice. The notions are startling, of course, to anyone unconvinced of the conspiracy: the murdered Pope, the "ad hoc gang of four," Cabinet officers ruling Washington, Henry Kissinger's double cleverly passing himself off in gossip columns of the controlled press.

"I can now reveal that the Kissingers' jet suffered a midair explosion," says Dr. Beter, who gives precise coordinates ("54 degrees, 40 minutes, 57 seconds") of where he insists the secret assassination took place and where the conspiracy took a doppelgänger twist.

•

The tapes are stored as neatly as the set of Beethoven symphonies across the small room, lined up in Mr. Kalt's sizable library of classical albums and books on the conspiracy. In addition to the tapes, he gets various newsletters for a few dollars each month, regularly as some people get cookbooks or tennis magazines.

These come from a few psychics (like Paul Shockley, trance interpreter) and other sources Mr. Kalt has come to trust. He copies and mails on, from his own busy Post Office Box 299 here, what he finds believable to the others he knows who track the conspiracy.

"I throw out two-thirds of what I run into," says Mr. Kalt, a polite, gentle and well-spoken man of forty years, the sort who waits in the drizzle on Main Street with an umbrella to greet a guest. "I run into some weird paranoids, a lot of weirdos in this field."

But he knows what he believes, and he finds the twists and turns of the news so relentless and the Government's reassurances so incredible on so many things, from inflation to Three Mile Island to the oil crunch to the arms-limitation talks to the Guyana suicides to the Mafia, and so much more, that Dr. Beter seems to have some relevant things to say to him each month.

"I'd rather believe that than the news," Mr. Kalt says, and a visitor has a pang of sympathy.

•

We all get tired from being hounded through the days by the separate crises and confusions and surprises and personalities and shocks and botched explanations. They seem an endless spiral; but Mr. Kalt sees an inexorable circle, and his keener sense of geometry can seem enviable.

Not too long ago we all reeled back from the news of Jim Jones's morbid Utopia. The tear-sheet explanation Bill Kalt has been circulating lately carries the tale farther round the bend, but the bend seems almost familiar. The tear sheet is entitled: "Guyana massacre was set up by F.B.I. & C.I.A.

to smuggle heroin into U.S. to destroy the churches and to enslave Americans.''

Well, yes, maybe. We'll see. But let's wait for the final official explanation, and then the inside books denying that, and then whatever fresh shocks indubitably will come forth.

Outside Dobbs Ferry exists so simply, up from the Hudson, reassuring as the midday drizzle. When Mr. Kalt goes across Main Street to see Murray in the village copying shop, it's like "Our Town" updated. Friendly hellos. Murray puffs his pipe and casually makes copies of sheets that put the conspiracy up to date by wrapping in all sorts of details, even Presidential hemorrhoids and electronic banking, "the mark of the beast" (as in the Book of Revelations' foretelling of the loss of personal identity).

In friendly farewell, Murray uses the universal motto of America's commercial conspiring: "Have a nice day."

•

Mr. Kalt admits he can't vouch for everything. But he says he does believe, after disallowing certain racist and paranoid excesses, the basic outline of a world plot by families of international finance to dominate governments through political, economic and spiritual means. These range from "self-tapping telephones" triggered by certain words of official suspicion, to the C.I.A., the K.G.B. and the Vatican.

"The evidence is massively coherent," Mr. Kalt says. "I do not believe every word, but I believe the overall drift."

The overall drift. For $89.50 you can catch up with it through twenty-four Audio Letters, gleaning from a list with such interesting titles as "Decline of the House of Rockefeller," "Plans for Interplanetary Russian Empire," "U.S. 'Gestapo' and Dormant Postal Service Powers," "Water, the Ultimate Weapon."

Mr. Kalt says he never would have listened to these things nine years ago when he left the religious life as an economics teacher and moved on to civil-rights and settlement-house work, to human-potential studies, to Arica, to the Seagull Mind Institute, the Fiske-Hoffman Process of Holistic Therapy. But eventually, he says, he thought and read, doubted and watched, and now he awaits the monthly tape on the conspiracy.

A siren goes off on Main Street as Dr. Beter is intoning: "They'll stop at nothing . . ."

Mr. Kalt checks his watch and offers a firm explanation. "It's not noon, so that must be an actual fire alarm," he says.

[5/17/79]

About Nayaug

The spirit of New England eccentricity flared up reassuringly here last week when E. P. Mangan, a local historian who likes to lie and fabricate history, announced he was running for President. He promises no taxes, no progress, and seems to be running on the general theme "Why not the worst?"

He could be dismissed as simply another quadrennial political loon except for the fact that he has the backing of his fellow residents here of a place called Nayaug, the self-proclaimed fifty-first state marked by a roadside sign announcing: "On this spot 357 years ago, nothing happened."

Residents of this mythical section of Glastonbury declared their "state of mind" seventeen years ago, spurred by the pomposity of the suburban status quo and the threat to Yankee independence perceived in the League of Women Voters and other mirthless co-conspirators.

"That's right, the League of Women Voters," says Ruth Witherspoon, Nayaug's social director. "Haven't you noticed how the league was formed and right after there were two world wars, a flood . . ."

•

The "flood" refers to the lovely Connecticut River, which runs by this 300-year-old town south of Hartford. The more she spells out the league's coincidence with modern plague, the more believable it sounds to devoted Nayaugians gathered in the living room of Jack Finney, Nayaug's Venerable Scholar of Latin, the ossified state language.

"And don't forget, the homogenized cigar was invented right when the league came along," Mr. Finney adds, clinching the case because, as everyone knows, the Connecticut Valley's fine-leafed tobacco was no longer valued after the introduction of the amorphous-leafed homogenized cigar.

If you examine the roots of Glastonbury, first settled in 1635 by colonialists who found Massachusetts too crowded, you can see why there is a Nayaug and why one of Nayaug's first official acts was to send notice to Queen Elizabeth that Cornwallis was forgiven.

For, in a few minutes' drive down Main Street, a visitor can cover first the cemetery where Glastonbury's pioneers rest in a winter-weary field studded with marble gray and centuries of names and eroded sentiments still stonily poignant. The ages hold Gideon Hale, a warrior in the French and Indian War, and Jemima Hubbard, who left only four months into life and rests near a sober caution: "The wise in God will put their trust; the young may die, the aged must."

•

And so, quickly past the clean clapboard houses, the trim Town Hall, the monotonous commerce, down to the other terminus of Main Street, which includes a McDonald's with its golden symbol arching quite like the Turner Memorial Gateway back at the cemetery. Between these two sets of arches a body needs a few laughs, and thus Nayaug arose, named after an old Indian tribe, inevitable as Utopia.

According to the Mayor of Nayaug, Jim Kinne, the fifty-first state is totalitarian to the extent of trying to skewer all those people who go around in life with clipboards and gavels and throat-clearing harrumphs before they speak their orders to the rest of us. "Nayaug's only law is you can't take yourself seriously," Mr. Kinne says.

Thus, when Nayaugians finally convinced Ella T. Grasso, Governor of a neighboring state, to pay a state visit, they watched her closely as she stood on the tiny reviewing balcony above the Olympic Pizzeria, side by side with Elmer Gardiner, Nayaug's Governor. Jack Finney solemnized the occasion with his usual outburst of maniacal Latin, then the Governor was invited to say a few words.

She stepped forward, but was stopped sharply by Ruth Witherspoon: "No, no, not you, Ella. The *Governor,* Elmer Gardiner." Elmer said something deliberately fatuous and soon Ella began smiling, and Nayaug's purpose was justified. By the end of the visit she was relaxed and her husband was an avid supporter of Nayaug's contribution to international diplomacy, an eight-minute period of open kissing in a crowd to solve problems. Crucial to the latter is the presence of Ruth Dufford, a cute and kindly widow who used to run a chicken farm and now mostly kisses people.

•

More than Adams or Emerson, Nayaug's spirit seems rooted in Bruegel and his addiction to celebrating the tiny, leering deviations from the norm that relieve life's relentlessness. When Chet Hodge retired as the butcher at Gardiner's Market, Nayaug held a three-day festival. It included the slow flagstaff-lowering of a loaf of cold cuts, with incomprehensible prating from Jack Finney and the usual bass-drum solo by Canada Wille, plus a historic tour of Mr. Hodge's house. His aged, scowling father wanted no part of spoofing, so visitors had to parade around in the dark while Ruth Witherspoon pointed up to such famous rooms as the one where Mr. Hodge was potty-trained. Chet Hodge is considered famous in Nayaug for once saying, "Give me love . . . or a good baloney sandwich."

The interesting thing about Nayaug lately is that it is getting more and more attention, and not just from jaded media workers craving relief in the surreal. (E. P. Mangan's Presidential press conference was so hectic that Nayaug's poet laureate and only militant feminist, Hilda S. Moe, walked out, quite understandably, in protest.)

But politicians come around, too, some fairly begging to be put down. Alas, not all those who might benefit from such a visit have been to Nayaug—California's Governor and New York City's Mayor come to mind as regrettable absentees.

There is enough growing attention and infiltration that Nayaug had better beware of America's dangerous habit of devouring its own eccentrics. As Jack Finney puts it in a warning about non-Nayaugians bearing gifts: "Timeo danaos dona ferrentis."

[3/29/79]

Big Deal

From across the way in Manhattan, the ballpark beckons in cream and blue, like a saucer of light next to dark ribbons of water. The confidence of outsiders is such on a World Series night that they are willing to park their cars across the river on the streets of Harlem—down West 164th Street toward the Caroline Club on Eighth Avenue—and walk over the Mc-Combs Dam Bridge to the Bronx and Yankee Stadium.

These streams of baseball fans are predominantly white. They sport suburban coats as the weather chills, and they feel secure enough in numbers to be willing to walk as aliens along someone else's sidewalks for the chance to avoid the expense and tangle of stadium parking.

The streets fill early with the outsiders, and by the second game last night, a steady trickle of fortunate and affluent with tickets are discovering a short cut to the stadium—right through a hole in the wire fence of the neighborhood handball courts erected as a local friendly gesture by the Yankees.

The trespassers are diffident as they go through the fence with picnic bags and children. The black and Puerto Rican youths ignore them and keep at their paddleball games in their preserve. The ticket holders go on by within conversation distance, moving ahead silently to claim their places at the big event.

North of the stadium, as the ball park lights send a white blush up into the darkening blue city night, the outsiders park in the streets of a housing project that is home to

Andre Atkins, a tall, thin, black sixteen-year-old who is a part of a youth culture that can make stadium visitors nervous.

"It's like the night of the Ali fight," Andre says, describing the mass of interlopers on his project streets at 170th and Washington Avenue.

•

The youth culture of the stadium's surrounding poverty neighborhood was dubbed "feral" a year ago when locust-like jostling and foraging by youngsters frightened the outside crowds of ticket holders as the police only looked on, intent on getting their own in a labor dispute by job inaction.

This series, the police are out in active numbers to rival the groups of youngsters scurrying outside the stadium walls. The situation hardly seems feral. In fact, it can get down-right overpoliced from Andre Atkins's viewpoint.

He comes out practically every ball game all season long, if only to stand in the street, and the police arrested him one recent game. "They said I took some woman's wallet," Andre relates. "And if they didn't catch the real dude later, I would be doing that dude's time right now. The woman gave me an apology."

The feral danger of the stadium, then, is in the eye of the beholder. And for most of the youngsters watching the ticket holders arrive intent and delighted, the operative word is not very heavy sociologically; it is "fun." The fun of staying out and feeling free, of meeting friends on the fringe of a great event, of planning no greater mischief than the time-honored search for a way to sneak into the ball park.

"Hey, George," Alan Mingo drops a triumphant sneak's shout down from the right field ramp onto his friends clustered outside on River Avenue.

"Allie got in!" one boy says, looking up. "Hey, man, how'd ya do it?" Alan is not saying, but the rest of his friends from Walton Avenue make some guesses, "Starsky, on our gate," one says. They translate, naming a particular gate and policeman friendly enough to turn his back at key moments.

The Walton Avenue gang has the advantage of being in the eleven-to-thirteen-year-old range and they are smaller than Andre Atkins and his friends. They are cute enough to sneak in more easily.

In this group, too, "feral" is a matter of perspective. One busy youth named Tito comes over and offers work to Anthony Lopez, a ten-year-old. "I need you," Tito says. Anthony is to assist in manning one of the movable souvenir vending racks outside the stadium, and he squints and figures he might make $5 for the night.

This is good. ("Work incentive," visitors might enthuse in their box seats.) But Neil Senior explains that sometimes after particularly emotional games, "the older guys [ticket holders] come out of the stadium drunk and push you and rip you off."

Every problem has its adaptation, even reverse vandalism, and the thing to do is to get associated with "the group"—a federation of vendors that includes the larger and wiser local teen-agers.

Andre Atkins is outside the stadium trying to hustle a vending spot with "the group." "I was down at the Garden for the Commodores concert, helping the scalpers." This concert had its feral quality earlier this week when scores of youths raced through mid-Manhattan robbing and knocking down pedestrians. "I didn't see that," Andre says. "I walk away from that stuff 'cause the cops come and break heads."

•

Andre finds no opening with "the group," so he and his friend, Greg Germany, another sixteen-year-old, simply hang around the crowd, watching the smaller Walton Avenue kids try to dart in toward the first-inning sounds brimming over the stadium. They assay distinctive limousines.

A very long, deep-blue Continental pulls right up to the River Avenue entrance like Cinderella's coach, and four middle-aged men dressed in the dull quality of executives emerge, obviously smiling with a sense of looking special there under the rattling subway el. Greg puts his hand to the window and peers into their limousine.

"What you see?" Andre asks.

"They got to sit like this," Greg responds, demonstrating the face-to-face configuration of the limo's jump seats. "That ain't so great."

Andre nods and keeps watching the crowd and having fun standing around.

[10/13/77]

4

Ceremonies

In a Flash

In royal blue caps and gowns, the graduating class of Public School 109 sang to their parents and teachers. "I am music," they sang. "I write the songs that make the whole world sing."

From the auditorium stage, you could see full face how touched the parents were, how they beamed. A breeze came through the open grill-covered windows, and the sun shone hot on the housing project across East 99th Street.

On the stage where the honored guests sat, one of them, Arnold D. Kates, was so enjoying his connection to these children—he was graduated from P.S. 109, in this same building, sixty-four years earlier in the class of '13—that he began humming and snatching at lyrics. "I am music," he, too, could be heard singing not quite to himself.

All this week there has been a binge of memory-making in schools across the city as youth squinted past mortarboard tassels at life so far. And there has been a complementary binge of memory-unraveling on the sidelines.

At P.S. 109, there was a kind of staring by some young and some old people as if through each end of the spectrum toward the other. "Pomp and Circumstance" was sounded at 10 A.M. Thursday, and the color blue came down the aisle and was watched by the color gray. "Oh, they're wonderful," Mr. Kates said as he sat on the stage.

•

There was something for Beverly Washington to remember. The slender girl, beautiful with dark skin and scholarship, was about to begin her valedictory address with breath-catching nervousness when a seat seventeen rows back collapsed with a crash and then an instantaneous giggle from the graduates. This thunderclap and laughter seemed to ease her way and clear the air for the optimism of Beverly's speech. Something for the class of '77 to remember.

Three score years before, in the class of '17, there was Abe Gewertz, who was on the stage last Thursday watching the special entertainment offered by Danny Mercado, strumming a guitar in cap and gown and singing, "Oh Freedom."

Mr. Gewertz remembers that the special entertainment offered at his commencement exercise was a Shakespeare recitation: "Miss Molt picked Mark Roebuck to do it. It was from Julius Caesar. You know, 'This was the noblest Roman of them all. . . .'"

Ah, Miss Molt, says Mr. Gewertz, "Mary A. Molt, a great teacher." He describes a very strong woman, dressed from neck to ankle in heavy dress with celluloid collar and cuffs and sweptback hair. "A disciplinarian. She stressed learning the language and literature. There were a lot of first generation immigrants among us, she knew what we needed."

•

The commencement program notes back then showed names like Nat, Ben, Moe, Abe, Julie, Samuel, Harry. P.S. 109 was a male cloister then. "A lot of us married girls from P.S. 150. We'd meet at the 92d Street Y." On Thursday, boys and girls were together and the names were often lyrically Spanish: Carmelito, Angel, Maritza, Felicia, Carlos, Wilfredo.

"Many, many years ago, we were students in this school," said Mr. Gewertz up at the podium, speaking to the graduates. "We lived in this crowded neighborhood, in tenements that were cold in the winter and hot in the summer. You can understand that we were poor."

Mr. Kates is watching the parents. "Look at that," he says quietly. "Some of the fathers took time off to come watch the graduation. Good people."

Brenda Adefioye, the mistress of ceremonies for her

fellow graduates, nervously is checking ahead to the next item on her schedule. In the front row, a boy bats the tassel on his mortarboard.

Mr. Gewertz tells the children he is not here to brag about the graduates of sixty and seventy years ago. "That would sound like a lecture on ancient history."

What can be new in these messages and memories of commencement, looking back or forward? Arise from the slum, Mr. Gewertz says, with hard work under the teacher's hand. "It won't be easy. It will mean years of hard work and effort, of overcoming the obstacles that the future contains. P.S. 109 is proud of what we became. Make P.S. 109 proud of you."

Mr. Gewertz and Mr. Kates give out $25 bonds to four scholars in behalf of the alumni association. They are genuinely surprised when Mr. Keuletsis, the assistant principal, presents the two alumni with plaques of honor, and everyone—the students, parents, Mrs. McLean of the P.T.A., Mr. Galina, the principal—applauds. New commencement memories have been made for old grads.

•

P.S. 109 seems self-renewing as the fifty-six youngsters and the two old men face each other through their ceremony. Mr. Kates will never forget Miss Schiff in the fifth grade.

"Rose Finn Schiff, a wonderful woman," he said, holding the plaque from the class of '77. "She gave me a book and told me to keep it, that some day I would be ready to read it. I remember it was Ruskin's 'Crown of Wild Olives and Ethics of the Dust.' I never did read it. Now, after today, maybe I'm ready."

On the stage, Antonio Baez came up for his award, and was a royal-blue blur, almost racing off in shyness. "Tony!" his sister shouted, standing in the audience. He stopped, startled, and looked up and out, right into her camera, and he was caught thus in a flash of light for the future.

[6/25/77]

A Perfect Day
to Become an American

Even as America grew yesterday, it was reproducing: Flinching with early labor pains, Margo Dayan, a radiantly pregnant immigrant from Mexico, had to be rushed out of turn from the 329 petitioners for citizenship gathered in Brooklyn, so she could pledge allegiance and renounce all foreign princes and potentates with more than the usual sense of emotion.

Naturalization beat nativity by a safe margin when federal Judge Mark A. Costantino interrupted a court case and swore Mrs. Dayan in as America's newest citizen, without benefit of his usual speech on his own Italian roots and the continuing beauty of the American dream.

He saved that for the jubilant, unlabored throng waiting in the main courtroom for the weekly ceremony of citizenship that has made Brooklyn the busiest and biggest naturalization center in the country. Close to 30,000 immigrants become citizens in this courtroom every year, all sworn in beneath stylized murals, salvaged from the old Ellis Island immigration station, depicting an old America, laboring with pick and shovel.

The crowd yesterday was of the new America, an America more of middle-class immigrants, young and better educated, and far more pluralistic in their gathering than the city's old throngs of Irish, Italian and Middle Europeans.

The new citizens came together from fifty-five countries of the world and offered words of gratitude from a spokesman-member, Nichan Tchorbajian, an Armenian from Syria who already is running his own electronics company in

Manhattan, having found the streets paved with computer chips.

•

The patient, multihued crowd offered a gasp of delight when the largest homeland source, producing forty-nine new citizens, was announced as Jamaica. And the people generously applauded the one Russian in the group, Inna Gorbatov, a doctoral student in French literature at City University, a fresh, bright face in the crowd, eons removed from the world of steerage.

A visitor had little sense of being among neophytes. Constantine Alexiou, a forty-three-year-old immigrant from the village of Alona in Greece, stood tall with his mono-grammed, combination-locked attaché case, an ear cocked for the business-call beeper on his belt. He bragged of his success in music publishing, and proudly claimed author-ship of "The Astronaut Song" ten years ago in a hybrid of patriotism and commercialism that is itself a badge of Americana.

"I did a demo tape and Mutual played it on 940 stations," said the happy immigrant.

Judge Costantino did his first citizenship ceremony over twenty years ago on Staten Island, where the crowds were usually Italian and Irish. "I would have them turn and face the window which overlooked the bay and the Statue of Liberty," the judge said. "The moment was ecstatic."

•

Edward P. Rhatigan, supervisor of the Brooklyn court's naturalization section, ran the three-hour process like the proud father of a massive family. He told them what to expect each step of the way, and relaxed them with the sort of immigrant anecdotes that only offend second-generation Brahmins. (He says there really was an old lady who memorized her civics according to city landmarks and when asked who the first President was, replied: "George Wash-ington Bridge.")

Mr. Rhatigan saw to the final name changes made by 96 of the 329 petitoners. A government lawyer, Kenneth

Hurewitz, made sure no one was fraudulently shucking a debt-ridden past in the last-minute changes which involved, for example, the decision of Harry Gerolymatos to change his name to Harris Gerolymatos.

The crowd seemed to savor the exotic beauty of its own names. "Marin Michael St. George Hanson?" Mr. Rhatigan called, searching for a single absentee. "How do you like that name. His mother was good to him, right?" The crowd replied with friendly laughter.

•

The literacy test is handled very easily by 95 percent of the modern applicants, according to Judge Costantino. Few immigrants come now with the old idea of sacrificing themselves stoically for their children's sake, he said. "Rather, a fellow decides that his type of personality would do best in America for the kinds of success he wants to enjoy."

Salim Nasir, a lawyer from Pakistan who beamed as his four children prepared for citizenship, described his motive: "I decided it is better to be a citizen of the country, the people of which reached the moon. Even if I do not reach the moon, I want to be among the people who reached the moon."

He explained the moon was a metaphor for his true feelings, which are rooted in his early university studies in Pakistan when he majored in the American Constitution. Unlike most Americans, Mr. Nasir has read his new country's Constitution repeatedly and written a treatise on it. The genius of the document is one thing, he observed, but its practice is even more interesting and complicated. "I am free to run for office here—providing I have what? $1 million?" He smiled and clearly had caught on to the new land.

•

Mr. Rhatigan shepherded most of the people over to the League of Women Voters table, where they registered to vote. "Remember, I'm going to run against Jimmy Carter, so vote for me," he told the people who laughed loudly, only a few nervous minutes away from taking the oath.

"Oh, you have my vote, Eddie," came a shout of endorsement, in a beautiful Guyanese lilt, from Katherine Mabel Dundas, a handsome matriarch delighted with this day.

The ceremony was simple and lovely. Hands were held high, promises made. "America is you," Judge Costantino said in his speech. "Nothing, nothing is too farfetched." The 329 new citizens left the court, squinting into bright sunshine, joining the lunchtime crowds, blending in perfectly.

[5/2/79]

Marriage
Municipal-Style

The rotary rubber stamp of Myrtle Bradford puts love on the public record in three-quarter time. Cha-gung, cha-gung, cha-gung she goes across the official document, numbering another license to marry, perchance to love.

Outside her station, the third of four waiting areas in the Municipal Building's marriage bureau—a kind of motor vehicle department of the heart—there is a wind sweeping across City Hall park. The magnolias outside the Tweed courthouse look frail and misplaced.

None of this is romantic, with pedestrians streaming and bumping by like hulking fish. But there are passages of sunshine and the impulse of love driving Geraldine Sposato and Adolph Continanza like spellbound salmon across the Park Row traffic rapids to the marriage bureau.

They just catch John Jaich, a city worker in a neat blue suit, before his lunch hour and they go into the municipal marriage "chapel"—a narrow windowless room with white vinyl wallpaper and a stained-glass scene of a dove holding two gold bands above a vaguely fruitful tree. In less than a minute they are married.

They are seconds into savoring their state with an exchange of smiles and stares as Mr. Jaich already is turning from them, inserting their license into his municipal time-stamping machine so that—thwack—the good news goes forth across the recorded ages without benefit of church bell.

At this moment, they are fine, a man and a woman in their forties delighted to have each other after an earlier divorce for each. It is an occasion to have heard them exchange the plain difficult words of marriage. Their sole official witness, Mrs. Continanza's mother, Irene Sposato, has a silent glistening gaze of bittersweet joy.

•

In the next room, the newlyweds have just been entered as No. 37330 in a Dickensian-looking ledger by Sam Kessler, a clerk, married thirty-seven years himself, who takes a rather unromantic head-counting view of things. He is in charge of the chapel waiting room, a tired place done in the traditional tones of municipal ennui, but a room which usually is mobbed on a Friday afternoon with scores of couples, babbling relatives and grains of rice crunching under foot. His worries include the exit door from the chapel, which opens out but which nervous grooms regularly claw inward at so that the handle has been torn off.

"When I got married it was a much more serious thing," says Mr. Kessler recalling his own municipal marriage in Queens after which came a ferryboat to Weehawken on a honeymoon trip. "I don't think people even know the idea of honeymoon any more—a lot of the women are pregnant. But in the Depression days marriage was much more a thing of, well, not exactly dread, but it was serious. All you had was the money in your pocket. No welfare."

The Continanzas' first marriages were big church affairs back in their Brooklyn neighborhoods, and this new one, in weekday clothes with no music or religious flourish, impresses the bride. "It scares you the second time, too. But you want to do it."

One nice thing about the marriage bureau is that, unlike so much of government, no one makes a big deal about its performance, issuing press releases, demanding inquiries and curative remedies. Marriage licenses have fallen off more than 20 percent in the last five years, to 58,000 in the five boroughs last year. But so far no one is building a mayoral candidacy on this fact or accusing the banks and unions of killing love, or working the porn and fiscal problems into this for a theory of what's wrong with life.

The subject is better left to feeling than analysis. Go into the bureau's record rooms, where lawyers for the dead, criminal investigators, and divorcing couples go in search of past marriage certificates, and get something of an oenologist's perspective. There are shelves of ledgers going back a century, with such labels as "1972, grooms A to Z." (There was a smitten man named Aala and another named Zwipf that year.)

•

No one at the marriage bureau seems greatly involved emotionally with the forms and ledgers and the white vinyl chapel. In fact, there seems far more emotion, if enmity is included, across the street at City Hall.

But the City Clerk, David N. Dinkins, oversees the bureau with a certain humanistic view extending beyond the monthly data that rise like tree sap as winter ends. He is certain as he goes to work in the morning that he can spot a marriage-minded couple in a crowd on Broadway. "They have that look," he says.

Over at station 3, Myrtle Bradford watches, too, as her rubber stamp moves in three-quarter time. "I look at some and think they'll never make it," she says. She wishes more of the couples seemed more serious about the step as they put down the $5 for the license, and she worries about the future of the very young ones.

She does not doubt the motives of the people on line, however. "That mad exciting feeling—love, you know— there is that. But I have found there are more reasons than love for getting married." Sometimes a couple wants to make more of an impression than an inked nuptial number, so they chat. "They'll ask me things like, 'Is everyone as happy as we are?' " Mrs. Bradford says. "I tell them what they want to hear: 'Sure they are.' " Cha-gung, cha-gung, cha-gung.

[4/19/77]

Birth by
Remote Control

In pain and panic, the pregnant woman was on the floor of her apartment in Brooklyn, suddenly into a breech delivery with no one there to help her, and her friend on the other end of the telephone nearly hysterical, hanging up, trying to call the emergency ambulance.

All the bobbling of time and spirit—"Oh God, I don't know," the friend peals to the emergency operator—is frightening to hear at the switchboard of the city ambulance service. But then Beryl Romano, a registered nurse, puts on a headset and cuts in with a voice built of West Indian beauty and emergency-room experience.

"Stop that crying and let me have the woman's phone number," Nurse Romano says. She gets the number and dials it.

It is five minutes after the pregnant woman called her friend, and the telephone rings by the woman's head. She answers it on the first ring, whimpering.

The lilting power of Nurse Romano comes across immediately. "Hello, are you the lady having the baby?"

Is she ever. The woman wails, "Yes" and "It's coming out!"

And Nurse Romano, miles away from the woman in another borough, says, "O.K., listen. I'm a midwife. I'll tell you what you're going to do." There is sheer beauty to her willingness to be assertive. "You're going to cooperate."

For the next sixteen minutes, to listen to Mrs. Romano work the phone from the emergency ambulance service is to be with her in the woman's apartment on East 52d Street.

She even thinks to attend to the pregnant woman's two-year-old daughter. "Is she there with you? All right, turn her face to the wall. Don't let her see all this stuff so it doesn't affect her."

•

And so, by telephone, the nurse takes the woman breath by breath through birth. "You bear down very slowly with the pain. I don't want you to push. . . . Push while the pain is coming, but not at the height of the pain. . . . Bear down, Honey, very gently." Inch by inch, a child is born, feet-first. And inch by inch, Mrs. Romano questions, soothes and advises, getting whimpers and cries, yes or no from the mother.

"No cord on the neck? That is good. . . . When you get a hard pain now, I want you to pant. I don't want you to push. . . . It's out? All right, have a look and see if it's breathing. . . . Is it crying? I want you to make it cry. . . . Make it cry, Honey. Just hit the foot on the bottom. . . . Put the baby on its side. This is important. The baby's lung has got to drain. . . ."

It is exhausting to hear the child born, as other operators stay busy with their headsets, dispatching ambulances throughout the city on less-promising missions. At the end, with the baby breathing and Nurse Romano assured the baby is warm not cold, you can hear the ambulance attendants arrive, and the woman weeping fully.

"Don't cry, don't cry," Mrs. Romano says very gently. "They are going to take care of you now." The authority and lilt are still in her voice as she ends the call.

This is one of the better moments at the city's Emergency Medical Service, the communications room where 125 ambulances are dispatched about the five boroughs. Usually the phone operators never hear how the calls turn out, life or death. And usually the special registered nurses on hand for all the busy shifts earn their money by trying to screen out fakers who call demanding an ambulance and exaggerating their problems.

•

According to Donald Rowan, a former police inspector who directs the service for the city's Health and Hospitals Corporation, there are callers who want to use ambulances as taxis. By keeping records of the repeaters (there are no specific laws to curb the abuse) and by having the nurses, all veterans of hospital emergency rooms, screen calls, the service refuses ambulances on about 150,000 calls each year, but goes out on 500,000 others.

The service is one of those city agencies dogged by its own statistics, in this case response time. Some have been scandalously long, and that is what the public remembers.

In the telephone room with the operators and nurses, the calls arrive incessantly, and you can channel-hop and monitor them like crackling swatches of wartime serial dogfights. One call: "Man down on street." Next channel: "Ah, look out." Fourth call: "I don't know what's wrong with her." Fifth call: "Give us the cross street. We need the cross street."

The problem of response time seems as complicated as all that noise and need and anxiety. Officials accept blame for weak response time in the past, but they say that new management techniques—having the ambulances roam neighborhoods at the ready between calls—and the latest telemetric and radio systems have reduced the time substantially in the last two years. It has been cut by about four minutes to an average of 8.8 minutes a call, and officials insist, despite criticism, that this is as good as any major city.

•

But the problem of heeding distress calls in this glutted city is endless, and in two of every five calls answered no one is found waiting. Further improvements, if they are to come, will have to be obtained, Mr. Rowan says, from the heart of the statistics—the public itself. There are thousands of people in the city every day who call ambulances for such occasions as going for a routine clinic appointment. Operators have notorious anecdotes: The man with a doctor's appointment who called instead of using his own car because he didn't want to lose the parking space on his block.

Even with nurses screening calls, Mr. Rowan feels further protection against fraud is needed, and so he hopes to introduce soon a system whereby ambulance attendants who suspect malingering will be able to call medical authorities to check on their suspicions. At present, the policy is to pick up anyone waiting at the end of a call, no questions asked.

Under this new system, the ambulance might actually roar up, reject a member of the public on the street, and drive off to show faster response time for someone else in greater need.

[4/15/78]

Coming of Age

There are more ways than fire to measure change in the Bronx. Up in the great union housing projects by the Van Cortlandt Reservoir, life seems holding up well, but the bar mitzvahs are down.

"We used to have forty or fifty bar mitzvahs a year," says Rabbi Jacob Sodden, sipping J & B scotch from a party cup. "But now, what? Nine or ten. Young Jews are good at revolution, but they're not reproducing like they used to."

This, however, is not a moment to be regretful, and the rabbi toasts the dark-eyed twelve-year-old Latin girl who is the center of attention at this Sunday party at the Van Cortlandt Jewish Center.

Whatever the state of the generations, the center is redolent with the old ways of youthful celebration. There is music and dancing and the spicy aroma of kosher foods catered fresh and hot for the birthday of Cynthia Carrasquillo, daughter of the center's caretaker, Victor, a lively man San Juan-born and New York-bred. This day Victor has filled the center's party room with a blend of Puerto Rican relatives and Jewish friends and congregants for whom he was cleaning and opening up the center for shul and Shabbos only twenty-four hours earlier.

•

Religiously, the big event lately for the Carrasquillos is the pending acceptance of their son, Victor Jr., as an altar boy at Our Lady of Angels Roman Catholic Church down from the center. But socially, their focal point is the center where Mr. Carrasquillo branches out through the neighborhood on all sorts of home repairs and trouble-shooting errands. When it was time to celebrate his daughter's coming of age with a big party, there was only one place to hold it, at Mr. Carrasquillo's Jewish center. "It was important for my daughter to see me spending on her," the caretaker says, articulating an age-old aspect of the rites of passage.

As the celebration goes forward, the scene is a microcosm of much of the modern Bronx. Older Jewish guests are smiling, watching the children of the Puerto Ricans who not too long ago were the borough's New Wave, but who themselves now must adjust to such newcomers as the Albanians who are buying up apartment buildings in great numbers lately.

Mr. Carrasquillo has cut across all this with the guest list. It includes eleven of his daughter's friends at the head table—an honor guard of dark and light Hispanic beauty—and other children, black and white, including the son of one of the new Albanian landlords and the son of a Jewish father and a Puerto Rican mother who had one of the center's rare bar mitzvahs last year.

•

Through the pluralistic swirl of the party, Victor and his wife, Nilsa, distribute the kosher food they themselves paid for, making sure everyone has a party favor, from the senior citizens to the young teens attempting nonchalant movement to the disco music.

After another sip of the J & B, the rabbi pronounces on the scene at the head table: "God works his miracles in many ways." Then he turns to Leonard Stoller, the center's secretary, and resumes a discussion of the shape of Bronx politics, where the rabbi has been gauging the latest vyings of Jewish and Puerto Rican blocs.

So the Bronx lives. And if you are invited to the house next door that the center provides for the Carrasquillos, you can see details of the intertwining. You can look beyond the rosary-draped statues within, through the window to the caretaker's backyard, where there is a permanent metal frame for the Succoth canopy used by the congregation. In the summer, when it is bare, it stands among the Carrasquillos family cookouts.

The two buildings face the reservoir road, and among the caretaker's first duties two years ago was to talk the teen-agers into ceasing the rock-throwing that was breaking windows in the synagogue and house. "I said, 'Look, I'm a Puerto Rican and went to work for these people. Why destroy what we are doing together?'"

•

Back in the center, the tables are filling. There are the families of Victor's two sisters, Lydia Torres and Evelyn Ayala, gathered about thick sandwiches of lean corned beef. There is five-month-old Jesse Modlinger, wheeled up in a baby carriage by his mother. There is the center president, Irving Balsam, who baked the cake for Cynthia. There is Mildred Epstein, a longtime center congregant, and her daughters, Abby Panken (and her husband, Saul) and Renee Stoller, who works at the center and had despaired of finding a good caretaker until Victor came along. "He is much more than a caretaker," she says.

Her husband agrees. "All the others ever did was clean," he says. "He does favors for the whole neighborhood."

"We love him," Anna Tuvim says. And Victor, dishing out the food, replies: "I'm feeding you, sweetheart, so you're saying that, right?" His mustache bends a bit in a smile.

It is time for photographs, and Victor, who carries a yarmulke for whenever he is near the sanctuary, puts it on for this occasion. It is basic black, and several congregation women complain it is not fancy enough for their beloved caretaker. They promise to crochet him something better.

"Something pretty as me," he tells them, and everyone laughs.

"Make him a white one like the Pope," Rabbi Sodden says, his mind clearly off the lost bar mitzvahs as he poses with Cynthia Carrasquillo on this special day.

[2/1/79]

Commencement

The housewives of Northside graduate today in a triumph of blue-collar feminism
and ethnic enrichment that will go unnoticed because it
seems mundane. It is only a community celebration in a
parish auditorium that is mundane the way evolution and
procreation are mundane.

Tucked into the Williamsburg section of Brooklyn,
Northside is one of the back-muscle neighborhoods of the
city, tough and crucial, and unknown to people in places of
greater power—Manhattan to the west, the suburbs to the
east. It is a place where upward mobility can be an
incredibly drawn-out process and where movements cast
flickering shadows at best on their way through salons and
media centers elsewhere.

But the housewives of Northside, and some of their
daughters and mothers and sisters, are graduating after
years of having implicit, unacknowledged power in all the
block associations, P.T.A.'s, church socials and well-run
walkup homes that have kept the neighborhood strong
through decades of immigration and uncertainty.

•

No one is moving on to another place with today's
commencement. They are all staying, working out of a four-
year-old powerhouse of social forces, the National Congress of Neighborhood Women, situated poetically in a
second-floor factory room on 145 Skillman Avenue over a
quilt-making company that the women have nothing to do
with.

The graduates are receiving two-year certificates after
having lived through the adventure of the first half of a

special sort of college education. The curriculum is administered through La Guardia Community College of City University but tailored by the National Congress members to make a virtue of Northside roots and the hidden power strains of housewifery.

Thus, the history and writing courses at the experimental college, conducted within the neighborhood at convenient off-hours, have produced such essays of personal research and honest beauty as "My Italian Grandmother, Theresa" by Elaine Carpinelli. She is third-generation in the neighborhood, and graduates today—a wife, mother, and National Congress staff worker offering financial-aid counselling to the next class in the neighborhood college.

There are thirty-eight pioneer graduates today. The new class has one hundred. For Mrs. Carpinelli, this occasion can only be part of a history once hidden, the story of Grandmother Theresa, who raised six children on Devoe Street in Brooklyn after surviving, as worker and mother, the great 1912 mill strike in Lawrence, Mass.—the "bread and roses" strike over the exploitation of women and children.

"My mother and I remember hearing many mill stories from Grandma and each time she told her stories with the same enthusiasm as the time before," Mrs. Carpinelli wrote. Fifty-six-hour work weeks at the looms were larded with housework at night while the man of the house rested in his traditional role. Mrs. Carpinelli has put each memory to work for her new self in Northside. "Now after reaching into her past, she is even more special to me," she said, "because now I discovered the woman Theresa who lived inside my Grandma."

•

Part of the National Congress success is simply in bringing the neighborhood women together to find strength in their similarities.

Thus Jean Kowalsky was one of those touched the night Mrs. Carpinelli read out loud all about Theresa. Mrs. Kowalsky earlier had read her essay, "My Russian Mother-in-Law" about the life of Julia Butko Kowalsky, a handsome ninety-one-year-old neighborhood resident who went through Ellis Island in 1913 and two days later got a $4-a-week job in a jute mill on Box Street, Brooklyn, starting a long life of work and reproduction, and, Mrs. Kowalsky stressed, of the best lessons of humanity.

Similarly, the courses in government for the graduates stress their neighborhood, exploring ways to use such traditional strengths as block and church organizations to intrude into the politician's realm. The Northside women became known for blocking the plan to close their local firehouse. Just as important, the National Congress cornered twenty of the federally funded Comprehensive Employment Training Act jobs that politicians have tried to monopolize.

There is no elitism evident. Laura Polla Scanlon, the forty-year-old president of the board, comes into Northside with a doctorate in literature and a strong grounding in 1960's politics and feminism. But she feels her real strength is her own working-class roots in Auburn, N.Y., in an ethnic hamlet like Northside where her parents worked in a delicatessen and macaroni factory and where she broke out in the same way as the women of Northside, through education.

The women of Northside sound remarkably free of recriminations about men and the past. They identify more than ever with their neighborhood, and their particular self-discovery seems less selfish than that of other revolutionaries.

Florence Montijo, a graduate and new paralegal worker, holds dear her years of motherhood. But the great thing about the National Congress discovery, she said, is that her daughter, Brenda, has decided to push out from her own working-class woman stereotype in an office and has enrolled in the new class of the neighborhood college of Northside.

[1/21/78]

A Fitting Tribute

Forty years ago, Wilford English and Dorothy Cook were married at night in a Georgia cotton field, exchanging vows very quietly as the sharecropping land of Sandersville cycled through another spring.

They were keeping their vows a secret from high-school authorities to assure the graduation of Dorothy, who had high hopes because her family ran the one black-owned general store in nearby Soperton. Only two others in the cotton field witnessed the couple's marital beginning, Wilford's brother, Wilbur, and Uncle Clifford Jordan, a Baptist minister.

"We went down the road after to a little restaurant, had a Coke, and Wilford and I went to our separate homes, that's all," Mrs. English recalls. Not quite.

Four decades, nine children and twenty-seven grand-children further into life, Mr. and Mrs. English celebrated their fortune by gathering with everyone last Sunday on the land they love and call their own—Bedford-Stuyvesant, the great Brooklyn ghetto that has ties as close to the cotton fields of Georgia as it does to Manhattan across the river.

A magnolia tree was in chalk-and-pink blossom outside a brownstone on Willoughby Street as scores of kinfolk arrived at the corner of Nostrand Avenue, turning heads as they paraded into the Masonic hall in tuxes and gowns. There were hugs and exclamations, and the Southernisms seemed easy on the streets of the Brooklyn area to which the Englishes had moved after four years and four babies in Georgia.

The return to these streets found Wilford and Dorothy's clan piecing itself together from such places as Brunswick, Ga.; Montgomery, Ala.; Chicago, Detroit, Hawaii and the suburbs of Long Island, too.

•

"Bessie! Why it's Bessie," an older woman walking through the doorway babbled as she looked kindly into another woman's face. Across the foyer, a younger man was being introduced with pride of reproduction: "And this is Tyrone." And down the hall, one-year-old Ronjari Buie was trying out the dance floor. He was wobbly but handsome in a tiny Afro and a tiny dude's outfit, looking up at all the other people who had happened since that night in the cotton field.

As much as marking the most personal sort of family history, the anniversary also seemed to close out for the English family an era for their beloved Bed-Sty, an era where the streets seemed merely tough and not so mean and unyielding to good people as they do now.

The Englishes had it as hard as any other pre-civil-rights black family, driven North by farm poverty to the ghetto. They had to take welfare now and then as Wilford English took the jobs he could find in a sugar factory or as a house painter. But Mrs. English recalls her children, packed but happy in four rooms on Sutter Avenue.

"You could let your children play in the streets then," she said. "And I remember the school [Public School 133 on Tompkins Avenue] had whites, blacks and Puerto Ricans, nicely mixed, in the '50's. No one was bringing up this race thing."

So, in a relative way, the Englishes were saying they had, if not the best, at least the better part of the ghetto. They were saying they had got out in time, when church and school and self-paid college degrees and Civil Service meant a good deal. And there were educators, policemen, hospital workers and a stockbroker at the family gathering to make the point.

•

"One key thing was momma and the church," said Rhena Vaughns, a daughter. "She pushed us in the old way, and that really helped."

Mrs. English had her daughters gospel singing when they were five or six years old, and the Rev. Charles Walker thought they were so good that he featured the English Sisters as a group at his Morning Dew Baptist Church on Nostrand Avenue.

As the English family returned yesterday on that same avenue, their gratitude was as much a matter of place as people. "We all came the same route, through the ghetto," said Michael Gourdine, a broker with Merrill Lynch who married Joyce English. "This is where we began."

Mrs. English, having known more of life, knows there is something loving and deep to be sensed as well back in Georgia, so she returns there every year for renewal. But her husband stays in Brooklyn.

"No reason to ever go back there," he says, not expanding but just saying that, for him, the South was done long ago. Some of his kin say his attitude is quite understandable—his skin is darker than Dorothy's, so he suffered a shade or two deeper. Prejudice is so ridiculously chromatic.

•

For all the past, Mr. and Mrs. English seemed the two least suffering people, North and South, on Sunday evening as they sat together receiving tributes, renewing their vows and even kissing in public, an event of great delight for the young and old in the hall.

Mr. Walker, who now has a church out in Jamaica, Queens, read Scripture on the miracle by Jesus at the wedding, when ordinary water became rich wine. The preacher looked at the Englishes and their children and said, "There's no such thing as an end to a divine work."

There was plenty of music, and as beautiful as the disco-bobbing silhouettes of the younger Englishes were, there was nothing to match the tribute paid by the English Sisters.

Five of the daughters stood together to sing again their gospel music.

Arm in arm in blue gowns, they sang their mother's favorite, "Born Again," with a shifting tempo that got everyone involved, foot-tapping, hand-clapping. "You must be," they sang, "don't you see—you've got to be—born again."

[4/18/78]

A Small Ceremony of Life

J ust in time for his fiftieth wedding anniversary, a father came home from the hospital with terrible but funny tales of the man in the next bed in the middle of the night.

"Can you help me?" the man in the next bed asks abruptly in the darkness, in one tale.

The nurse's call button apparently is a mere placebo at night, for no one appears when the father presses it. From his years of illness, the father has no real voice left, so how can he reply to the man without slowly getting out of bed, finding his cane, groping over to the beseeching neighbor to mouth words hoarsely?

"I want a cup," the neighbor dictates, maintaining an edge of imperiousness—the kind W. C. Fields could joke about so well in the afflicted, the kind that saw this old man seize control of the TV set even though his neighbor, the father, was paying for it.

The father fumbles among the limbo accumulations of the sick room, finds the hospital-issue stack of plastic cups and slowly carries one over, his hand shaking a bit as it has been lately.

"Not that kind!" the man in bed hisses.

•

It's a beautiful Beckett scene as the father describes it in his lip-readable rasp when he finally gets home to a two-family house in Queens. Listeners laugh at a good narrative that measures what is involved in life.

The father is down to 104 pounds, but his silent laugh is the same, and the story goes over so well that he asks for a beer to celebrate his freedom from the hospital routine—

baby food and tests, baby food and tests, plus the nasty neighbor in the darkness for redeeming social value.

On his way home, going down in the hospital elevator, the father is glad to be back in street clothes even if he is in a wheelchair. At the nursery floor, a newborn is carried aboard by a maternity attendant who seems bigger than life and who smiles like no one else in the hospital as she takes the infant forth, trailed by a depleted mother, a beaming grandmother and a new father all too willing to bare his foolishness.

The old father sits and listens as the new father tries some small talk in the elevator.

•

"Do they like to go outside?" he asks the attendant loudly, treating his daughter—the swaddling is pink—as some generic exotic fauna.

The attendant is very kind. She resists the temptation to clear her throat didactically like Dr. Joyce Brothers and reply: "No, studies show they should be kept in root cellars with plenty of compost." Instead she smiles and says, "Well, yes—you know, a new experience."

Everyone but the infant smiles kindly as the elevator descends toward all the new experiences awaiting everyone.

Outside, the sun is finally warm. "I never felt anything so good in all my life as the sun outside the hospital," the father rasps later, declaring his own end to a rough winter that included a broken rib from some mysterious tripping and a harrowing January of thirty straight days of cobalt therapy. "I've been cold all winter."

The man slowly walks into his house. The view from here is less dramatic than the hospital view, which was tantalizing with a fold of golf fairway bearing carts of players mindless of the hospital. But home has an honest Queens view of alleyway and rose bushes, orderly life.

•

His wife kisses him grandly and notes he is back fifty years to the day they got married. "The bad penny returns," one of his children announces. The father had lost track of the days in the hospital and stops in delight at realizing the coincidence.

He sits at the kitchen table, which is the only authentic way to touch down at home in Queens. As the others lip read his rasp, he talks of rediscovering the flavor of things since the cobalt faded—notably ice cream and beer. Everyone vows a good vacation this summer up by the beloved Saratoga race track, with full supplies of ice cream and beer.

His wife brings out something special just received in the mail from an old, old friend—four photographs of the man taken five decades back, before she was a mother and he was a father. They show him in the winter snow of long ago with a group of friends, a weekend outing of young men staring confidently at the camera, all lean and unknowing. People at the kitchen table recognize traces of future grandchildren in the early image of the man. He sips his beer and looks at himself.

Life is best if manipulated a bit with a photograph or some words. A photograph really is not about the past. It is a premeditated continuation of the present. After the photographs are passed around the kitchen table, it is time to honor the continuing present of the mother and the father.

There actually is nothing left to give after fifty years, but a wrapped package is presented. This package contains another bit of manipulation, a scroll obtained from the office of the local Bishop, who is as honorable as the best politician in seeing to the small ceremony of ordinary life.

The mother and father are shocked to see their names printed fancy above a simple prayer marked by golden church symbols and dates sharply inscribing the years that define the occasion.

They are pleased to accept the scroll. It is another instant in the fifty years, handed across the kitchen table of the mother and the father.

[6/16/79]

147

On Alice's Birthday

Tomorrow is Alice Matthews's birthday, and if you ask politely she will tell you about her ninety-three years, from the time she saw the dappled firehorse that led to her elopement from Indiana seventy-four years ago, to the night here in her welfare room where she saw the spirit of Louis XIV and he had his beautiful white horse lay his head on the counterpane of the bedridden woman to comfort her.

None of these stories is sad. Mrs. Matthews sees to that. She represents a small drain on the city's Human Resources Administration budget. But she herself is a major human resource of memory and good company who belongs as logically in the slick Big Apple ads about the city's strengths as she does in the roach-ridden room that she graces at the Hotel Earle off Washington Square.

Only a lucky few New Yorkers benefit from this resource, and get to hear the stories and see how classy a human can be at ninety-three.

There is the cleaning woman, Jessie, who comes around once a week; the visiting nurse who sponges the blind, arthritic woman and does her nails; a volunteer friend, Jean Serrie, who stops twice a week to talk and listen, and a former volunteer who is now just a friend, Debbie Carter, who still comes by.

•

The rest of the city misses out on Mrs. Matthews's stories as she sits in a pink bed jacket and uses her hands like two blue-streaked birds to punctuate her life anthology. It encompasses a fabric of hard detail (the name of the barber tending the chair where a long-ago fiancé, Jack

O'Malley, dropped dead) mixed with emotional milestones ("I was only three but I remember crying when they packed me for the orphanage and, oh so clearly, I remember the stranger asking, 'Are you taking her to a home?' "), and a counterpoint of spiritualism ("My father was a faith healer, but he couldn't heal himself and I never got to know him.").

Does anyone recall Mrs. Matthews serving as a chambermaid at the Taft Hotel forty years ago? No problem, because Mrs. Matthews would rather tell about her earlier career as a showgirl billed in 1908 as "Alice Veniere, the Laughing Soubrette, Choral and Refined Singing." The picture of her young beauty then is topped off by a parasol.

Show business arrived soon after the dappled firehorse. She had been a waitress in Locksport, Ind., and always chased off to the fires because she liked to watch the horses. "There was one beauty and just as I reached out my hand to pet him, I see between us the face of a man who would turn out to be my husband two weeks later."

The man is Carl Philomon, a traveling magician, who, it turns out, is accomplished at billing and cooing, but more importantly levitates and decapitates his bride on numerous stages across the nation for years to come.

Her first joys in New York City include a $28-a-month apartment on East 17th Street seventy years ago. "Five flights up, nicely furnished. We had a Newfoundland dog— 'Here, Prince Rupert,' we'd say—and a nice deli downstairs where we'd buy a roasted chicken on Sundays for 50 cents and have a feast." One of her last joys before she became confined to her current, ascetically furnished room, was the day at a local center for the elderly when she heard an old man at the piano attempting "My Hero" from "The Chocolate Soldier."

"I couldn't keep quiet and just boomed it out," she said, beaming. "That always was my surefire encore number. And people said, 'Oh my, oh my.' "

•

As an elder in this city, Mrs. Matthews cloaks her stories in no mantle of wisdom. She tells of her spiritualism

("I always had the spirit eye . . .") in terms of experience, not wonder. And she still has not been able to decide about the existence of a God. "Well, I don't know. You hate to say no, but you hate to say yes."

Louis XIV, she adds, was no random bit of madness, but a useful apparition who warned of a fire that was actually happening at the hotel. The smoke, she says, ruined her singing voice.

None of Mrs. Matthews's stories end sadly. The one that begins with her crying on her way to the orphanage ends several years later, with a beautiful woman coming up the sidewalk as Alice and her friends exclaim at the windows of the orphanage. "It was my dear mother come to take me with her. See what life does to you?"

And she says her present chapter is not sad, either. "Oh, I have a little cry sometimes when I think of my two sisters—I lost them two days apart. But I get over it."

Her sweet tooth helps. She likes the dried apricots that Jean brings as a gift, and last birthday there was a chocolate cake that she still talks about in another neat little story.

Mrs. Matthews sits in the Earle Hotel, like a bright resource work of human witness and imagination left on a dusty shelf. She is exhilarating, and people should wish happy birthday to the Laughing Soubrette.

[10/6/76]

150

Up for Sale

It is the last day of winter, and the widow at 24 Johnstone Street is putting forty years of possessions up for sale in her house—her clothes, her furniture, her books, her silver.

All the hearth-weary, life-worn, straight and bent possessions of a dispersed family—Mason jars, an Exercycle, tablecloths, a faded lace dress, a dark velvet cape, sheet music ("Avalon" and "Any Bonds Today?"), a pile of rugs, a gaggle of shoehorns and ashtrays, buttons, bowls, a 1939 World's Fair shopping bag filled with old Octagon soap bars, the grandchild's crib, the late husband's framed university diploma—all are laid out with tiny price tags through the sunlit rooms of the house.

The widow is leaving in an eruption of personal history, ending a household by transacting separate beginnings for all its stuff, a benign dispossession into the hands of avid strangers. The widow, Ruth Hoffman, is smart, friendly and handsome and is choosing a muted, mercantile way to scale down her life by letting a horde of bargain hunters into it.

"I've had forty years here of pleasure, plenty of sadness and illness, but good times—loads of wonderful memories," Mrs. Hoffman says, standing in the upstairs hallway by a rack of her old dresses, all tagged for sale.

"If you have been part of a house, your lifeblood is in it and it's paid for itself," she says, across from her bedroom, which is taped shut and full of her true goods, the ones she is keeping. "I don't think this house owes me a thing."

•

By contrivance and by default, ours is the age of materialism, and the hundreds of tag sales now beginning to brew in houses mark the beginning of the true suburban spring, the turnover of matter. Mrs. Hoffman is moving and has decided to sell rather than cast away pieces of her life.

Her son, Harlan, has come back from California for this week to help her. When he looks out the window at seven in the morning, he sees shoppers parking their cars on the quiet suburban block three hours early, holding the newspaper ad, forming their own line to his mother's doorstep to wait to get at her things.

Linda Hanson, a local housewife and tag-sale entrepreneur who is managing Mrs. Hoffman's sale, already has spent several days getting to know and tag all the things. She has spotted the Icart lithographs, leaning forgotten in the basement, and knows they're good for $150 at least. She has spotted a long-overlooked Art Deco box and amazes Mrs. Hoffman by tagging it at $15. She has gone through the house with notebook and magnet (to test for brass), scale (to weigh silver) and fine-tuned eye from eleven years of tag sales.

And out on Johnstone Street, as the people line up (a few jostle and argue oafishly), Mrs. Hanson spots the familiar collectors and retail dealers of all the antique and nonantique oddments that Americans hold dear. She also is pleased by the long babbling line's collection of tag-sale addicts, who cannot resist the chance to poke and possess another human's things.

•

The wandering through four decades of possessions has put Linda and Ruth on a first-name basis. With everything unsecreted and arrayed, Linda knows the sale day can be hard on the owner, particularly a widow witnessing more ending, piece by piece. She often will have the family take an older person out for breakfast to miss the traumatic intrusion. But in this case, she thinks Mrs. Hoffman can take it.

In fact, Mrs. Hoffman shows her stuff spiritually as well as materially as soon as the first wave of shoppers is let in to rush, to peer, to handle, to prowl, to try to bargain down from the tag prices. She can't resist offering little tales that go with various possessions, enriching them. The sadly beautiful marble-topped bureau came from three maiden ladies in Baltimore years ago. The ermine stole came from Russian emigrés her uncle, a professor of Egyptology, had met in his wanderings.

She wonders about two men—"Persians," she says—who bargain compulsively about everything, from toaster to furniture. One kisses her as he would his mother, and she says, "If you think that's going to make a difference. . . ." And it doesn't; the tagged prices hold.

•

If you simply watch, the shoppers seem almost insectivorous, bumping past one another in the tunnels of Mrs. Hoffman's stuff, reaching and touching, even sniffing at times, driven by some special code. If you listen, you find some are merely crass, impersonally stocking their stores with another's personal things.

But others are plainly human. A gray-haired woman, after slowly climbing up to the front bedroom, duels a bit over price, but comes away with a $15 crib and announces proudly: "This is for a great-grandchild." Mrs. Hoffman, who seems to have held to that price lest a certain memory of another child be demeaned, says: "I'm happy you got it, dear."

It is hard to see the unburdening for all the change in Mrs. Hoffman's life, for on Friday she will move to a small apartment several blocks away from the stucco house where she lived so long with a husband and two sons. The emotion of all this may be mitigated by the fifty boxes of possessions she already has set aside for her new life.

But there are feelings to this day, as surely as there are goods, and midway through the sale, she suddenly notices that two Borsalino hats that had lent her husband a favorably rakish air, are missing, gone, sold.

"We got them on our first trip to Europe," Mrs. Hoffman says. "I'm glad I didn't see them go. Everything about that trip was important."

She pauses at this, but only for a moment, and is soon distracted by a young woman asking about an old mirror.

[3/22/79]

John Conniff's Wake

Determined to be positive about life's passage, Jim Hyland celebrated his fortieth birthday by bringing a big bottle of champagne to the dining-room table as his wife and seven children watched. He popped the cork and quickly caught the bubbling geyser with his mouth. But the gush knocked his one false tooth into his windpipe and left everyone gasping along with Jim as he was rushed off to Long Island Jewish Hospital.

This was a perfect story to hear Jim, grinning and back in full voice, tell in the hallway of Stutzman's Funeral Home in Queens Village last week when John Conniff was being waked. John's son-in-law needed a laugh and this man Hyland, who specializes in ludicrous self-humor, was never one to let a friend stay down. There was laughter, good laughter to go with the intense conversation and tears and silence and prayers at John Conniff's wake.

In sum, it was as good a tribute as could be paid to any man, a haphazard brocade of life's signs and sounds offered beyond his open coffin.

His grandchildren cried, but they went for ice cream, too. And some old friends grew dry and slipped out to Jamaica Avenue to a place that has McSorley's ale on tap.

The nuns kept coming like the snow. John Conniff's sister, Rose, has been a nun for fifty years, and she brought them out from all over—the young nuns from a Newark ghetto school who were graceful and hopeful about life and death, and the old nuns, some gnarled by long years but still able to get to their knees for a prayer for John.

•

In the three days at Stutzman's there was a warm-toned attendant who regularly asked the universal question of mercantile America: "Is everything all right?" But otherwise, everything was all right as far as things can go with death.

Gray-haired women with the deeper Irish roots did not hesitate to look down at John and say openly that he looked good—"grand" used to be the word for this. Some of the youngest visitors with mere Irish-American tendrils were exasperated at such talk.

But the old ones had the great advantage of speaking from the bias of decades of memories of John Conniff, a man of quiet affection who never stopped doing small and large favors in private ways for everyone he knew. And even those he didn't know, for when it snowed on his day off from the subways he used to go to work free of charge, just to clear the ice from the stairways of the stations he supervised.

His neighbor, Mr. LaRocca, wondered who would be able to fix all the faucets and doors for the widows in the 93rd Avenue neighborhood, now that John had died. John's widow, the former Mary Murray from Belfast, already was figuring out the noisy steam-heating system that had been one of the manual mysteries of John's success as a good provider in the family's secure, bright row house in Queens.

By the time he died, the house was all paid for and had new siding and storm windows and clusters of houseplants thriving beyond John's careful hand. He had long since finished building a basement room and thrown plenty of parties there, himself having danced at all of them with Mary in a fleet, gliding Peabody version of "Hold That Tiger."

•

The people who came to Stutzman's said that John was thoughtful from one end of his life to the other, showing love in brushing his two daughters' blond hair when they were small and safe, and lathering and shaving the whiskers from his friend Dave a few years ago when that man was having his own life's final trouble.

John was remembered for lending everyone something and preferring not to get it back. His deviltry went no further than slyly escalating family water fights in the summer by suddenly appearing behind someone with a bucket of water when the others were only wielding water pistols, and by encouraging Uncle Jerry actually to take a hose indoors to finish things off when the rest of the drenched, laughing clan moved on to buckets. Outsiders could only marvel damply at the fun in the Conniff family.

When his birthday would come (his seventieth was due in May) and his daughters would ask what he wanted, John would say, "Peace and quiet." And he'd get socks and shirts instead.

When retirees from his generation on the subway came to Stutzman's, they told Mary wonderful stories of how John had helped them and encouraged them to follow his path up from the token booth to supervisor jobs. There were tired brogues in the group, recalling Mike Quill's impish palaver from long-gone transit crises, and there was a black man in the group, too, and a man named Gonzalez, and they all offered respect and prayer for John.

•

What was surprising, some said, was that while John was a taciturn man, he spoke up well at his retirement dinner. He declared that transit had not paid much, but that he was happy because it was enough for his life goal of providing a home for his family.

At his funeral mass at St. Gregory's Church by Cross Island Parkway, a relative read from the Old Testament Book of Wisdom about how the souls of quiet, just men like John were in the hands of God and "in the time of their visitation they shall shine, and shall dart about as sparks through stubble."

Before Mary Conniff was left to herself, she had a close group at her house for drinks and coffee and cake. There was more talk of John, and there were some silences and quiet stares, too. Jim Hyland's champagne story was added to life's continuing retelling and drew big laughs. The laughter, as always, was welcome at John Conniff's house.

[2/10/77]

First Flight

Kennedy International Airport was a mess of impedimenta Thursday night, with anxious travelers trapped in hot metal clots of auto traffic. They were jammed and crawling so near yet so far from the jetliners that came and went endlessly and grizzled the sky with plumes of jet exhaust.

The idea of vacation seemed an act of nihilism as the police struggled futilely to handle the car traffic and drivers delivering frustrated and frantic travelers began flailing at their auto horns. The angry bleatings were shredded and snatched up by the larger jet sound, the way the carillon from the airport chapel spoke back to the din with a this-too-shall-pass-away tinkle.

Recreation is no simple word and these days it borders on the religious for its power to stir souls and move mountains closer. So the airport presented a final test of faith before believers were taken up into the sky.

•

A glance at returning travelers dragging their possessions through the International Arrivals Building showed a considerably exhausted, sour-faced lot. The sight raised serious questions about the folly of fulfilling dreams to go elsewhere, but the people just beginning their travels were too self-absorbed to notice. Everyone seemed bumping about like ants dragging their crumbs and twigs clear of a giant colony exit.

A bystander spiraling his spirits downward in such anxious generalizing finally was rescued by the sight of a sixteen-year-old blond girl who walked up, prevailing over the auto traffic, to secure a single seat for her first trip abroad alone.

Such an event, if noticed and savored, can cancel any amount of mass holiday depression.

Against the crowd of darkly handsome travelers massing at the Chilean Airline counter, this girl, named Laura, stood out. Teen-agers work hard at not seeming exotic, but there she was alone as a blonde at the airline counter. The clinching bit of exotica was her chewing bubblegum while wearing earrings.

Her younger brothers carried her luggage and were very quiet at this event of the first solo flight from the nest, however round-trip. They would not see her again until September, when they would all be much older as time is measured in summers. By then she may no longer call her three brothers "you guys," the way she did at Kennedy.

"You guys," Laura said firmly to her brothers, "don't say any tear-jerking lines to me, O.K.?" She had already had a round of goodbye tears with her friends, so no more, please.

Other passengers were in similar glum-happy cycles. Some had the richest-looking luggage, others lugged rope-lashed boxes. There were infants in arms, crying, sleeping, looking about, hungry for the world.

The mood of airport chaos had dissipated even though the crowds and traffic jams had not. A young policeman who had seemed so ineffectual at traffic control earlier was much more interesting now as he flirted with a beautiful Iberian ticket agent outside the windows in the hot evening breeze.

•

Laura took out her passport and was checked in as her brothers watched as if memorizing this for future reference. Upstairs in the waiting lounge, she made a final check of her flight bag, proudly showing a new, small recorder for the marathon of taped music she was taking with her. Her basic summer goal is to see a new place, make friends and learn Spanish as an exchange student, but things had already become more interesting with talk of riding horses and having a maid with her host family.

At a quiet moment in the wait, her mother offered her a collection of photographs to glean for mementoes, and suddenly the girl was sitting there with a lap full of pictures of the family, the family house, the clumsy family cat, the family cat in snow, and so on back into time. She chose some, didn't say much, and smiled no thanks when it was suggested she might want to take a picture of herself playing soccer to impress young men in Ecuador.

•

Her maternal grandmother, true to her reputation as a connection for sugar addicts, arrived with two boxes of freshly baked cookies, one for the plane, one for the airport. There were final thoughts on what might make things easier for the host family, but when the attempt was made to purchase a bottle of twelve-year-old Scotch to ease the visit, the duty-free shop said this was not possible because the plane was making a domestic stop at Miami.

Laura was doing all right—no tears, and when the summons to board came she gave a final caution to her brothers against tear-jerking lines. "Just be like 'See ya,'" she instructed, acting out a mood of casual passing for their benefit, a beautiful actress going into summer stock.

At the boarding gate, things were not so easy. A mass of families were hugging in parting, but the crowd itself was a distraction until one woman was seen walking away crying openly. Some tears from Laura followed, then quick hugs all around. Her brothers looked stricken for an instant.

She moved away through the gate into the summer, and someone said, "See ya."

[7/1/78]

5

Like Magic

A Ride Like No Other

It is not that you can't go home again to Brooklyn. It's that, once you're there, you can't seem to get back on the Cyclone roller coaster.

The Cyclone is not an ordinary roller coaster. It is one that was worth a small boy's stealing $10 and $20 bills thirty years ago and going off to Coney Island as a third grader in company with a fifth grader (known generically back then as "a near occasion of sin") and riding up into the night with such whipping force that a hamburger was flung out of hand down toward the scary pool of dark inner space through which the tracks dipped and rose and curved on their creaking latticework of bone-white pilings.

Standing in that very inner space at sunset three decades later, the boy is as long lost as the burger. The sound of the clacking ascension of a train of fresh young silent passengers up the first and highest hill of the Cyclone is trepidation itself slowed to onomatopoeic syllables.

Clacking up through the sea breeze with the rest of Coney gaudy and tired below, clacking way up to the top of what now must inexorably become a 90-foot drop, the nose of the train rises into view like Finnegan at his wake. The red train plunges as wine spilled from a table edge, right past the witness in the inner space standing next to the parabolic bottom.

•

And, oh, look at the sweet fool in the front car smiling preenishly and disdaining the usual white knuckle handhold and clasping his hands atop his head. This passing Mona Lisa blur is Michael Edwards.

He can't stay away from his childhood, either, and so drugged is he by the geometry of falling through the air in a leatherbound car and rising and circling back down on scraps of screaming that he is making the Cyclone his master's thesis at City University's film department.

Mike was nine or ten years old when he snuck away from a school outing to Steeplechase Park, a sweet departed part of Coney's ornate past, and came down Surf Avenue and approached the Cyclone as if it were a sporting house. Fifteen years later he still screams on the thing, but oh, so voluntarily, he says. "I want to get that aspect into my film, the helpful screaming."

Mike can get into variations of the Rosebud theme as he hand-frames his creative energy along these dips. With his mustache that bends with gravity's sudden applications, and with other footloose biographical notes (bulldozer operator in Europe, leather-sandal maker in Rockaway) he makes the Cyclone sound like organic psychedelia.

•

Much more blasé, as he gnaws clean the steak bone from his take-out dinner and mans the simple master controls of the Cyclone, is Gerry Menditto, the operations manager, who was born in Coney Island thirty years ago and grew up, way up, on the Cyclone.

He, too, hasn't really gotten that far from the Cyclone, and he walks the tracks of the ride, all nine hills of it, every morning to make sure every bolt and scare is in place. He spends so much of his life clambering about its skeleton and arranging each clacking 100-second excursion (at least fifteen hours a day, six days a week) that he has built a barn, a green barn, in the diagonally dappled shade of the Cyclone's big beach curve. His horse lives there without a whinny most days as all about him humans shout. The horse is named Cyclone.

To Gerry, Mike's ride this evening sounds well. No, he

doesn't analyze the passing screams forced through leers of fright. He hears the rattle and shush of the cars a special way. "I picked up a lot of my problems by sound," he says. "I can hear a small crack in the track, a wheel that's beginning to wear."

He makes most repairs himself with fresh strips of three-eighth-inch track steel or thick lumber underpinning. The cars can be detoured out into a repair shop, stocked with countless compartments of spare parts and a few photos of naked women, right next to the main hill.

•

For major structural repairs—fresh steel support or renewal of the "bull wheel," the giant belt-driven motor that looks like a mammoth watch cog—we must go farther back in Cyclone's time to Ralph Juliano, born sixty-three years ago in what used to be called Stein's Flats near the old Coney Island trolley depot. Ralph worked on the ride back in its first year, 1927, preceding Gerry along the tracks, and then his uncle made him a principal in Peluso Machine and Iron Works, an honorable guild of mechanics who serve as a kind of hospital for the shudders and flouncings of Coney rides tired of the daily grind.

"The Cyclone is a nice, simple belt drive, no gears, beautiful," he says, describing the engine that gets people up the first hill, after which gravity completes the trip.

Ralph and Gerry and Mike sit around in the office shack and talk of coasters like Hemingway characters telling of the bulls. Mike regrets that a visitor refuses to ride again, and the visitor contends that the Cyclone is a fright he no longer needs.

Ralph can take you way back through the crowds and fires of Coney past, years that consumed a dozen forgotten coasters—the Rough Rider, the Scenic Railway, Dragon's Gorge, Ben Hur, Drop the Dip. "The Cyclone was always the best," he judges.

Mike says his film will zoom in on fright, particularly that of Emilio Franko, a man afflicted with a speech problem that kept him silent, who got on the ride twenty-nine summers ago and astounded his companion by speaking at the end. Mike checks the newspaper accounts; Emilio's first reported comment was, "I feel sick."

[6/7/77]

An Epic Reading

He has warmed up the snug tavern on West 72d Street with a tale of death in the Great Hall, and now the gentleman with the magnificent speaking voice leans across the wine and begins the grand words that summarize two odysseys, his own and Homer's:

Sing in me, Muse, and through me tell the story
Of that man skilled in all ways of contending . . .

Richard Dyer-Bennet, a well respected balladeer in the city's finest concert halls and a professor of theater, is off again on the crackling, lilting lines of Homer's ancient "Odyssey" in Robert Fitzgerald's modern translation.

The spoken words come forth in graphic strokes and are welcomed as a private sampling of Mr. Dyer-Bennet's ingenious challenge to himself: to set the "Odyssey" down in all its epic length and beauty on twenty-four hours of recordings in the spoken form in which the world first heard it nearly three millenniums ago.

This exhausting task of love is to take the next five years of his life, by the reckoning of Mr. Dyer-Bennet, who, at age sixty-five, seems exactly the polished and self-willed instrument required for such unusual art. In the tavern, he is not merely reciting, he is weaving voice and glance, tone and meter, shifting himself for each new character in the tale of human wrongs and wanderings and revenge. He pauses. "It's dynamite, absolutely dynamite," says the man who has entertained and studied audiences for the last twenty-five years.

The National Endowment for the Humanities has

awarded a $100,000 grant for the first two years of his project. Such a simple idea, it seems, to bring lyric imagination back from the book pages and let it flow full strength in the original path, ear to soul.

But the idea, he feels, could only have eddied up from his life thus far. From far back in his British childhood, when his grandmother read the "Odyssey" and the "Iliad" to him as entertainment for a six-year-old, this task was coming. The first line he ever memorized as a child, a line which gave him his first startling sense of death, was a Homeric climax:

And in the ears of Patroclus the din of battle
rang no more.

"Unbeknownst to myself, everything I've done so far, every bloody thing, has been in preparation for this," he says. He relishes the retreat he begins this winter, in a specially equipped recording room in his country home in Great Barrington, Mass. The equipment is designed so he can operate it alone, working in the middle of the night if he pleases. He has a fireplace, a "good bottle or two," an intelligent wife, and a tennis court. What more, beyond Homer, is there in civilization? he asks.

The clinching moment financially came when, after submitting all the National Endowment paperwork, he journeyed to one of the government-gray warrens in Washington and recited some of Fitzgerald's Homer, drawing a crowd of Ph.D.'s and bureaucrats from their work to hear.

Better still was an earlier, less certain moment when he tracked down Robert Fitzgerald at Harvard and was received by the poet-scholar to explain his lovely scheme. Again, he recited a sample.

"I asked Fitzgerald, 'Do I have the right feeling for this?' " Mr. Dyer-Bennet recalls. "He immediately replied, 'Oh yes.' "

He proceeded with the professor's blessing, and part of the recording regimen will include cassette mailings and trips down to Cambridge to consult the translator and a second classics scholar, Cedric Whitman. He also will stay in touch with Alice Wilson, a Stony Brook professor who was one of the first to encourage him after he got the idea six years ago when he first read the Fitzgerald translation.

"Every now and then I'll nip out and try my latest bit for them," Mr. Dyer-Bennet says.

In preparation, he has read all of Fitzgerald's own poetry, a necessary spiritual link, he feels, in the word chain going back to Homer. The first year of the project will be spent in a read-through recording of all twenty-four books of the "Odyssey"—a careful initiation, he says, for a sense of how themes and meters and emotions crosshatch through the narrative. The following year, the final recording will be started, piece by piece, until there, together, will be twenty-four hours of Homer, Fitzgerald and Dyer-Bennet—an electronic monument for which the artist already has received distribution inquiries.

Mr. Dyer-Bennet has a voice to match his face, strong and lean, but shadowed by all sorts of characters, real or concocted, that emerge for the right story. His own ear never quits. The other night he sensed a Homeric echo in a scrap of TV testimony from a veteran of the battle of Leyte who recalled the burial of the Japanese suicide warriors: "We weighted them with five-pound shells, and slid them into the sea." He quotes the sailor in a gentle cadence and says of course he had to send the scrap on to Fitzgerald.

He does not talk melodramatically of art defying death. He is more in keeping with the Harvard poet's own discreet sense of tradition across time: "Let us hold fast to what is good, hoping that if we do any good those who come after us will pay us the same compliment."

So, in toast to Richard Dyer-Bennet's next five years, lean across the wine with him and hear an old story in his ready voice:

Of these adventures, Muse, daughter of Zeus
Tell us in our time, Lift the great song again.

[12/5/78]

The Torres Can Take It

The score is 1 to 1 when Sister Marguerite turns on her car radio after finishing her classes at St. Francis Prep.

Sister Marguerite's brother, Joe Torre, is manager of the New York Mets, and she follows each opening-day pitch out in Chicago as she goes through traffic back to the Torre home in Marine Park, a strong Brooklyn neighborhood that is as rich in baseball these days as it was in the time of Joe Torre's prodigious sandlot play.

Baseball is rooted like earthly produce there, and each spring finds the Torre family still in their old neighborhood, rooting and competing on any number of levels of hardball.

In this fresh new season, it is very important to the family that Joe Torre manage a good year from his Mets, mastering its youth and inexperience so that major-league hope might return to Shea Stadium. But it also is important that the other Mets, Michael Torre's Mets, the team for which he is catcher in the Little League, have a happy year.

Michael is Joe Torre's fourteen-year-old son, a polite and quiet lad at an ambivalent age where, Sister Marguerite notes, he toys with a guitar as easily as a baseball bat. If there's any player in Brooklyn who competes under pressure, it's got to be Michael. Not only is he a Torre—of the fabled baseball line that gave Marine Park and the major leagues two smart hitters, Joe and Frank—but the name of the league he plays in, embroidered on everyone's cap, is the "Joe Torre Little League." That's pressure.

This year, inevitably as grass grows and the big league Mets have to forget last year, the Joe Torre Little League foresees its greatest season of growth, with 500 boys and girls on twenty-six teams. The big excitement is that the schedule has been tripled, to at least thirty-three games for each team, and it will stretch through the summer to Labor Day. The kids like this big-league, hot-stove touch. In the past they were done by July because local fields were limited.

The extra games result from an interesting deal with City Hall. After negotiating with three administrations, the league has taken over a piece of city parkland at Avenue U and East 38th Street, a swatch of creek land that was ignored and filled with reeds until this spring. With City Hall too broke to stake a new ballfield, the Little League parents are somewhat nervously financing a $60,000 baseball park. It will have two fields, simple dugouts and grandstands and, on the smaller diamond, a beautiful infield of sod—lush and green as the Yankees' payroll.

Last week, the word went through Marine Park: Intruders cut the fence in three places and got onto the new field, before the first fungo fly had been chased and the grass fully rooted. Tire marks messed the outfield seedbeds. Strips of the thick infield sod were rolled up like carpet and stolen. Dugout panels, installed by parents, and fence braces were busted loose.

"No matter what, we'll make opening day," says Harry Stein, the league's treasurer, staring at the damage from behind the mud pile that will be home plate. He's not sure how to raise $5,000 for the repairs, but he says there's no way to hold back baseball in Marine Park, particularly with Joe Torre himself due to inaugurate the field on April 29.

In the sunlight and in the oceanfront breeze crossing the scarred, untried field, Marine Park seems entitled to its share of the special optimism of baseball that sprouts in the earth and blossoms in human playfulness.

·

A few blocks away, this same force pins Sister Marguerite and Michael Torre before the TV set, watching the family's fortunes with the high winds and green grass in the Chicago park where Joe Torre signals his team from the dugout.

"Kingman hit a homer, God love him," Sister Marguerite says in mock generosity of a Chicago slugger traded away by the Mets. She and Michael stare at each pitch on the TV set, which has a happy-looking family picture and a china Madonna on top.

"One man away, top of the seventh, Mazzilli on third," Bob Murphy, a Mets announcer, summarizes. "Hebner lays off, one strike."

Hebner is this year's big, new hope for the Mets and Sister Marguerite tells him through the TV to come on, do it. He swings and hits a weak fly to left that tails off as the fielder lunges.

"Oh, oh! Yes! He dropped it!" Sister Marguerite shouts. She jumps up and just plain screams at her brother's baseball team. She smiles at the hit a second time as the Cub outfielder, her old friend Kingman, scrambles on the TV replay. "He's not much of an outfielder anyway," she says, smiling in sweet contrast to the Billy Martin-sting of her judgment.

Then, Stearns and Montanez get on and the Mets have the bases loaded with Henderson up. Sister Marguerite says that Steve Henderson is the nicest young man, that she said rosaries for him as a rookie.

He hits a ground ball up the middle and Sister Marguerite jumps and screams again as it goes through the infield. "Yes! Yes! Stevie baby!"

Michael sits absolutely still watching the game, accustomed to his aunt's wild reactions. The screen shows his father for an instant, and he is just as still in the dugout, but he, too, may know his sister the nun is screaming back in Brooklyn.

The rally—a genuine Met rally fresh as Chaucer's

spring—continues, and Sister Marguerite dashes to the phone to call another Torre, her sister, Rae.

"Rae? I had to call to tell you: It's 8 to 3! . . . What do you mean 'losing'? They're *winning* 8 to 3!"

She swoops back to the set, and Sister Marguerite's opening day joy expiates all the sins of M. Donald Grant. It becomes clear there is no way that the Torres, family and league, will be denied additional hardball on opening day at Marine Park.

[4/10/79]

A Death-Defying
New Day

There is this clown living in the West Side railroad yards who gets up every morning, walks his dog, buys the paper, has breakfast at the diner near 34th Street and 12th Avenue and then goes over to work bossing other clowns.

Upstairs, in the backstage area of Madison Square Garden, they are oiling the elephants' feet and smearing vaseline in the wrinkled whorls near the beasts' small, startled eyes to prevent the heartbreak of psoriasis or something when the Boss Clown, Frosty Little, arrives to start the makeup chores and other preparations of the day at Clown Alley.

Out in the arena, everything is dim and still, all the tethered shiny trapezes and their frail ladders on high, the glinting Babel of guy wires, the large cage of wire mesh for the opening big cat act—all is ready, like a long day's fretwork of ideas assembled for dreaming.

•

In a chain of small, wheeled cages backstage, tigers, leopards and panthers pace separately, waiting for the bit of whip and meat and fiery hoops and music and applause that is their special daily jungle.

A young woman in a zippered jump suit comes riding through the cavernous backstage on a bicycle and sets Stephenson's Dogs, a friendly, busy pack of troupers, to yapping. The dogs are behind a liberal-sized playpen fencing stretched outside the motorized trailer home of their owner.

The Stephensons have clothes lines up, filled with fresh

morning wash drying in this large air-conditioned room that resembles a kind of survival ark of the energy crisis, with animals and Winnebago campers parked together. These circus people have specialties with animal acts that keep them living and sleeping in Madison Square Garden—through the nocturnal snorts of the animals—rather than back at the circus train on the West Side.

A child from one of the trailers comes gliding by on a skate board, ignoring the white beauty of the Liberty horses tethered side by side for their morning grooming. Across the way, Rudi Lenz is in his undershirt, cleaning up his circus equipment and his trailer home, and he stops for mail from the woman on the bike and he says good morning and thank you.

It is the most natural of moments—a new day—and even within the giant corridors of an entertainment hall in the middle of Manhattan, this nomadic hamlet of humans and lower-ranked creatures makes the new day fresh and honest.

"I been out already, down to the grocery [a co-op on West 26th Street] and got the boys their salad for the day," says Mr. Lenz. He opens a bag of appetizing lettuce, pineapples, carrots. "Such good cucumbers for the boys." A bag of chocolate bars is tucked away, too.

The boys—four chimpanzees—are peering over his shoulder out of their glass-walled cage, delighted at the salad makings.

"They are eating well. They are playing well. This is a good city." Mr. Lenz doesn't see, but three of the four chimps go into a funny chain-stepping strut behind him like human vaudevillians—part of the chimps' act, or something original for the morning?

•

Obviously Ringling Bros. and Barnum & Bailey Circus performers are entitled to their superlatives later, out in the arena. But right here and now, things are as low-keyed as the hot coffee being sold over at the backstage pie wagon, where some of the roustabouts in blue coveralls lounge and chat, then pause to watch a darkly beautiful woman in a velvet bathrobe walk by, ignoring them regally.

One of Frosty Little's clowns is reading the paper, half made-up in white face framed by his own modishly long hair so he looks more rock star than clown. He actually laughs out loud at a newspaper comic strip, and so seems extra innocent as a clown.

"It's not that hard to get going in the morning," says Frosty Little, a fifty-one-year-old former land surveyor who says he quit that job at great risk to go off finally with his heart's desire, the circus. "If you come to work depressed, it's hard to stay down—you know, when you sit at a mirror and start putting on a clown face."

For all their death-defying, once-in-a-lifetime, never-before-attempted business routine, the circus people are quite relaxed as they get ready for work. They don't seem much like the railroad commuters passing six stories below, who are more comparable to the gray and linked and swaying elephants being led back from their oiling now, with barely a thumping direction or two.

•

The perfect master of the big cats, Gunther Gebel-Williams—tall, decisive, Nordically handsome—appears like a sun priest. He goes into the empty arena with one leopard.

Watched by Piccolo, a dwarf animal handler, Gunther gently strokes and almost converses with the cat, and he coaxes it into hiding in a secret compartment so it will be ready to pop out like magic in the opening extravaganza. The transaction seems pleasantly unnatural, a conspiracy of two species.

"Between shows I like to take the makeup and costume off and go outside and watch the people pass by," says Frosty the Clown Boss. "That's a circus, you know."

Soon some of the people start to come in and take seats in the arena, which remains in a kind of suede gray mood until the opening color spotlights sweep the ring and the aerial apparatus folded overhead like surreal dental machinery.

Frosty has his early wave of clowns ready to warm the customers up. He has sixty-three gags ready for the laughs. The elephants backstage are stoically receiving their first gaudy mantles of the day, and Gunther's leopard is staying nice and quiet in hiding in the arena, ready for the opening scare.

[5/3/77]

Touring the Tombstones

Why not go giddy into that good night?

When their fifteen-year-old son died in an incredible birthday accident in 1909, Cornelius and Carrie Millet decided to tell of his demise plain as night on the headstone: "Lost life by stab in falling on ink eraser, evading six young women trying to give him birthday kisses in offices of Metropolitan Life Building."

Down the hill and around the bend in the older part of Woodlawn Cemetery, near the east bank whose original vista of elysian Bronx fields has since turned to apartment houses, Herman Melville lies under an even more startling headstone. The stolidness of death and Melville's thrust at immortality through the power of words are summarized by his simple white-granite stone on which is carved a large unrolled scroll that is absolutely blank. There, in the space for his final words, Melville left nothing and for eighty-seven years this page has stood as tantalizing as some in "Moby Dick."

•

"It's still controversial," Jeanne Capodilupo says staring at the scroll, which is encircled by a graven vine.

With thin sunlight falling on all the acres of stonework and old trees, the scene she surveys has the eerie beauty of her own name—Capodilupo means head of the wolf. But Mrs. Capodilupo is a chatty, nonmorbid, charming member of the living who flits gracefully about the graves of Woodlawn, resurrecting all the names and tales of the strange and famous dead there.

She is regathering lore that was itself taken to the grave

when Charlie Augustoni, a cemetery worker and master of local anecdote, died and took his own place in Woodlawn.

"I love Woodlawn," Mrs. Capodilupo says, sounding like that voice in the lush TV commercial invitations to rush off to the good life in the Caribbean. She has a Dickensian wisp, strolling up to the stones like Christmas Future. But she lives up to her oddly spunky job title at Woodlawn, "community affairs coordinator."

Such a kinetic-sounding calling seems contradictory. She is the designated live wire in a universe devoid of electricity. But Mrs. Capodilupo is making the most of it, reaching outside to the living (setting a musicale for vaudeville buffs at George M. Cohan's mausoleum), putting out a newsletter (no cost-of-living stories, of course, but headlines like "New Mausoleum Proves Popular"), inviting tours by headstone rubbers, bicycle clubs, and students from an undertaker school.

The latter were enthusiastic enough as they paraded across and among the 230,000 at Woodlawn. Anyone is interested to hear that Duke Ellington was the only one cemetery officials ever permitted to have two markers, because of the tree-split layout of his plot. He lies beneath a pair of tall plain stone crosses engraved: "The Lord is my Shepherd."

But the one hundred undertaker students grew particularly reverent at the bust-headstone of Stephen Merritt, a celebrated turn-of-the-century undertaker who had much to do with peopling Woodlawn and who managed to reach ninety-two years of age before having to submit to the trade himself.

•

Founded as a rural resting place on a rye farm in 1863, before the South Bronx was ever built or burned, Woodlawn attracted a large, fashionable crowd of the city's merchant princes early in this century. The rural lanes of mausoleums echo the city's era of great retail families: Woolworth, W. R. Sloane, Macy, Hearne, Kress and, of course, Penney, just around the corner as in life. Commerce seems as much the common denominator as death, and the Berkey photo people even have images of cameras and films in the stained glass above their crypts.

Mrs. Capodilupo is trying a new emphasis for the cemetery, insisting that there is something for everyone there, even some life. Bird-watchers come to spy on an occasional eagle. Architecture buffs inspect mausoleums constructed as miniatures of classic buildings. Historians can stroll among five Mayors, Confederate and Union generals, and stop and wonder at the unmarked mausoleum, grand and time-darkened on a hilltop, of Jay Gould, the robber baron who took his jewelry with him to his sarcophagus, but lost it when the expense of armed guards became too much. Feminists can stand on the grave of Elizabeth Cady Stanton and note the seven children she bore and regathered to her beyond time.

Some of the most interesting markers are for the missing dead. The Strauses, Isidor and Ida, who went down with the Titanic in 1912, are commemorated by a handsome stone funeral barge in miniature that is inscribed: "Many waters cannot quench love—neither can the floods drown it."

•

The age of such family opulence has receded with time, tide and the graduated income tax. Lately, people have been buying smaller spots, niches, in the "community mausoleums," large ground-level buildings shared in common like an apartment house. Studying the tiers, you can see that some living buyers even engrave the marble cap of their empty wall crypt with their names and birth dates and leave a dash with a temporary blank space for what must follow.

Down below the handsome Woolworth Memorial chapel, Mrs. Capodilupo wants you to meet Rudy Fighera, a busy man in blue work clothes. He runs the crematorium, a silent, gleaming, ship-shape place with four ovens and a wall panel of buttons controlling fuels and dampers, retorts and afterburners. A visitor, while impressed with Mrs.

Capodilupo's openness, wants to get back topside to a slower dust-to-dust motif.

"I understand," she says. "It's a matter of preference. Personally I lean more toward the ground." She is outside again, casting a lively smile across her Woodlawn community.

[4/11/78]

Keeping Up with
the Phippses

In his chauffeured Cadillac on Rockaway Boulevard, Sigmund Sommer has a brief, merry look on his face as he makes his daily escape from the multimillion-dollar pangs of the real-estate business and passes through the iron-gated entrance of his other world, Aqueduct Race Track.

He owns horses the way he owns buildings—richly, seeking profit from carefully calculated risk. He has horses in four of this day's races and he will watch all four of them lose from an exquisite vantage point in the track's trustees' dining room, possibly the only Big A locale where humans are pampered as royally as the thoroughbreds are down in the barns.

Mr. Sommer shows class in losing, something to be expected in such a hushed, élite setting. Looking down on the finish line like a choir of seraphim, the select diners include Lucien Laurin, the celebrated trainer of the great Secretariat, at the head of one table, and, table-hopping genially, Ogden Mills Phipps, chairman of the New York Racing Association, whose name is borne like the finest social silks among the brahmins of the turf.

No one appreciates all these distinctions more than Mr. Sommer who in little more than a decade as a thoroughbred owner has scored well at the finish line, very well, often leading in victories. But he knows his front lawn is in Great Neck, not Lexington, and his talent is more in the short-run turnover of horseflesh rather than in the blending of generations of bloodlines. He deals in margin, not tradition.

"The Phippses, Bradys, Mellons—they really make all

this possible," says Mr. Sommer. "There'd be no racing if it weren't for the big old families. They keep the bloodlines going with glamour horses so that every once in a while a fellow like me can come in with a fluke."

•

Such humility can blur in the homestretch, however, for Mr. Sommer celebrates the fact that the finish line is "the great equalizer" not only of horses but also of the diners in the trustees' room. He works hard to find his flukes. He spends heavily when he wants to, bidding sizable amounts at yearling auctions. Used to the executive's role after sixty years of life, he declines to discuss one celebrated, costly purchase at Saratoga a few years back, more a creature of beauty, it turns out, than competition.

"You can have perfect bloodlines on both sides, but if it's not a champion, it's nothing," he says, offering the equine variation on the three principles of real estate: location, location, location.

Through the day's card, Mr. Sommer nibbles lightly at the buffet in the trustees' dining room, puts away several straight Scotches, and makes some bets with hundred-dollar bills by way of a discreet track aide who hovers about. "Put six pieces [$600] on my horse in this race," he instructs quietly as the man bends to hear.

Very little crowd noise reaches into the room. The planes going into Kennedy seem operating in pantomime, and far around on the northern horizon is the nearest reminder of Mr. Sommer's other world—his three luxury apartment towers newly built on the Queens-Nassau border that have not exactly gone wire-to-wire in filling up in the city's depressed market.

Mr. Sommer says very little about the real-estate business except that lately it is "awful." "If I didn't steal three or four hours every day at the track I'd probably hate my business," he says.

•

In the quietude of the trustees' dining room, life, even luxurious life among the thoroughbreds, can seem as cyclical as the race course. As one diner says, the dessert choice always seems to be between apple pie and cheesecake.

Mr. Sommer peels back the crust on some pie, pokes briefly at the apples, and seems saved from La Dolce Vita by a redeeming kind of gruffness. "C'mon," he says after watching his third horse of the day finish far back.

Then it's out of the trustees' room, down an elevator, and out through two V.I.P. doors. There, finally, is the missing noise, the sort of grandly anxious hubbub that can only be heard on the main betting floor of a race track. The sudden scene is of a sneering, quacking throng, poring over race forms, reaching into pockets, queuing up for nowhere, trying to boil life down to its post-mortems.

Mr. Sommer has the brief, merry smile back again. "This I love," he says. "The bums that are here. The wise guys. The shysters."

He gets a respectful hello from a sort of race-track official, but he shoulders his way apart from the V.I.P. doorway and goes over to a bar where he nods to a man dressed in black like a dude-ranch hand who says, "Hey, you drinking?"

"You buying?" Mr. Sommer responds. The man in black is, and after downing a gift Scotch, Mr. Sommer scoffs at the man's choice in the next race, the feature. "You're such a drunk, you're hallucinating," Mr. Sommer says, and he moves on, encountering and needling more of the Aqueduct hangers-on, agents of agents and glorified hot walkers he cherishes. "They're beautiful. See that guy? Never works a day but he always manages to have $50 in his pocket."

•

The millionaire builder-horse owner smiles as if the real knack at Aqueduct is to be a connoisseur of souls, not horseflesh, and he moves on down to the paddock to watch the saddling of his last chance for the day, a splendid dark horse of shining strength and gentle gaze, Great Above.

The horse is beaten out in the stretch and Mr. Sommer allows himself one small muttered obscenity, another

186

Scotch, and a glance at tomorrow's program. There are more Sigmund Sommer entries listed, of course, and he will be coming back in his Cadillac from his buildings to watch his horses.

[4/28/77]

Killers

Every week Bernard Brown goes back in
time to crash his cares against a flat gray
wall. He leaves his good address on the East Side and
drives his Cadillac Fleetwood up to a small city park in a
humble part of the Bronx where there remains a gift from
his boyhood—a passion for handball that he describes as
narcotic and beatific in his fifty-fourth year as it was in his
fifteenth.

The six Bailey Avenue Park handball courts, across
from one of those transmission shops that spill auto innards
into the neighborhood, are intact and have no graffiti on
them. In the city's sadly battered park inventory they seem
unique as Stonehenge. These courts are defended and kept
immaculate by Bernie and fifty or so other men who return
each week from all sorts of life styles to cling in sweating
joy of their common denominator of handball.

Bernie Brown glides to a stop at the Bailey Avenue curb
and gets his equipment bag and plastic webbed lawn chair
from the trunk of the car. "It costs about $30 a year for
handball," he says, laughing as a man who also spends a
small fortune on tennis clubs in better parts of town.
"Tennis is social. Handball is serious, vicious, wonderful."

Abe Greenberg, a lawyer with a mat of gray hair on his
chest, is warming up, tightening his leather gloves and
driving the hard black handball back and forth to the wall,
slap-pop, slap-pop. Abe says handball may be a dying
sport, succumbing to the hammer blows of the paddleball
craze, but it is matchless for no-nonsense competitors.

"There are neighborhood guys who make it as millionaires and have to come back to get a good game of handball," Abe says. "The only important thing about a handball player is whether you can hit a killer."

A killer is a winning shot that cannot be returned, finessed with a lovely sting of the palm that sends the ball into the tightest possible angle between wall and ground.

•

Out on the court, Manny Storch, who has good killers and alters his Wall Street hours to fit in weekly Bailey action, is ready for the first game, lean, bearded and quiet as a saxophone player. The fourth player is Phil Furlong. "I am with the transit," he says, his brogue, despite decades of the Bronx, still green as County Wexford.

He is warming up with what is called the "Irish swing"—a slashing underhanded scoop shot, like a bolo punch, that Bronx Irish players have had for years, a throwback to the four-wall handball of the old country.

"When I grew up in the Bronx, everyone called handball 'Irish handball,'" says Bernie, wearing plain gym shorts and high-topped sneakers that would never do in East Side jogging circles. This is news to a visitor from Brooklyn, who grew up thinking of handball as more of a Jewish game.

"Some of the great ones were Jewish guys from Brighton in Brooklyn," Bernie says. "But you had the Bronx Irish champions, too, and for years the big tournaments have involved the best of the city's Irish and Jewish players. Kirby one year, Jacobs another. Puerto Rican and black players are starting to come on now."

Al McDonald, a sixty-three-year-old retired policeman, arrives, puffing on a cigar that is his trademark, around which he grunts and grimaces as he smacks the ball on the Bailey courts. He has a problem. "I'm going out to the Hamptons, but I'd rather stay here for the handball," Al says. "But there are a lot of Jewish guys in the Hamptons, so I figure there must be handball. I'll find it."

A younger policeman, Jesse Jackson, arrives. "Hey, Al," he says. "How are you doing?" He is as black as Al is Irish and Bernie is Jewish. The Bailey courts are in danger of becoming an ethnic Utopia, except that the hard competitiveness of handball intrudes, and in a minute the men are glistening with sweat, darting about, swiping and grunting.

The physiques are as varied as the accents and skin tones, with middles ranging from the drum-tight to the paunchy. But everyone's legs are log-tight from the sport, even the quick, sure legs of Jack Deutsch, a player who announces his age like a killer shot: "I'm seventy."

"He's seventy?" Bernie says, surprised. The Bailey players, even after years together, seem to know little about one another except each man's shot inventory.

•

Two games are under way and the slap-popping is double time. The men are darting and calculating and slapping, winning and losing points, barely monosyllabic. Bernie is transported where he says he always craves to go, sweating and leaning toward the wall where the only care involves a concrete perpendicular, a slash of muscle, a bit of guile.

In the winter Bernie carries a snow shovel in the Caddie's trunk, and Al and the others come with ice choppers and salt so they can keep playing every week. A few years back, before the neighborhood started getting a little rough, the Bailey Avenue players even held a family picnic into the night, aided by two players from Con Edison who set up utility tents and tapped the street lines for power to refrigerate the beer and keep music and lights going.

"My wife thinks we're absolutely nuts," Jesse Jackson says, delighted with this fact and smiling at the gray wall as if it had psychedelic powers.

"Listen," says Bernie Brown, back at the wheel of his Cadillac after two hours on the courts, heading for the textile factory he runs in Brooklyn. "All I want from life is another forty years of handball."

[6/27/79]

190

The Devil in
New Brunswick

NEW BRUNSWICK, N.J.

The carillon plays gently at noon over by City Hall and out across the old streets of this quiet town, touching the soul of a movie buff to call forth wholesome old dream-factory characters like Mrs. Wiggs and Scattergood Baines.

A man in a yellow sweater stands under the classic small-town movie theater marquee on Livingston Street, squinting a bit, almost as still as a photograph. The passing traffic has a tolerant hum, midway between country and city metabolism. Luncheon strollers are out from offices and stores, and from their passing stream the first few men divert themselves, direct as hunger pangs, under the marquee and into the darkened theater to catch the twelve-sharp showing of the day's porn film.

It is called "Please Please Me"—it's kind of a play on words, don't you see—and you must pay $4.75 to a man in a chilly looking box office to see it.

There are bits of Broadway scattered in the hinterlands in the form of porn movie houses. And if you add them all up—taking nice old elephant of a movie house right here plus the flaking New Liberty up at Plainfield, the old Regent in Bay Shore, L.I., and a dozen other X-specialty houses profiting around the suburbs—what you have is a kind of takeout Times Square.

•

The difference is in the setting. Here the man in the yellow sweater, observed from a bench across the way in a pleasant Civil War memorial green, is standing in a 1930's tableau, opposite a worn, dark, brick hotel of nine stories which has a reedy sign on the roof announcing, "Hotel." The hotel looks barely adaptive, with a Chinese restaurant on the parlor-like ground floor where there obviously once was a more original elegance. A neon sign in the window proclaims, "Open," and lunch strollers are going inside.

Right above the man in the yellow sweater, the marquee's red neon also is lit and the letter "E" in the name of the theater—"State"—quavers weakly. The man in the yellow sweater finally moves—not into the theater to manage the noon showing of "Please Please Me," but down the block 50 feet and through a doorway proclaiming "Character, Health, Knowledge," the entrance to the Y.M.C.A. You never know in a small town; the guy was just passing the time.

Crossing the street down by the United Methodist Church, and swinging back past a diner called Ritz Restaurant and past Dr. Glickman's optometry office, a visitor feels casual enough in the noontime stream, and a quick half-step, half-breath diversion has him in under the quivering "E" in an instant with his money out so he doesn't have to be inspected by passers-by as he buys his ticket.

The man in the box office has cigarette smoke around his hands. He gives 25 cents change for a $5 bill and tears a ticket off a roll, then rips it in two, serving as a silent ticket seller and taker.

•

Porn's magic spell is everywhere, especially in the lobby of old fake-glitter walls that are plastered with coming attraction posters of X-rated films due to follow "Please Please Me" into the State. There is a wide, mirrored candy counter where once the kiddies must have yelped and salivated, but it is closed and there is nothing behind its windows except a quarter-full bin of popcorn looking sour as old sighs.

As the customer reaches for the entrance door, it pops open and another customer is leaving, with the film only ten minutes along. Why? Is the plot chimerical? The denoue-

192

ment telegraphed? There is no answer to be had; there is, most especially, no eye contact as the two pass in the false night.

As the new customer walks slowly down the aisle, blinded by darkness, afraid to feel his way toward a seat, forms on the screen jut and angle like mesa-toned abstractions and the dialogue wobbles out across the rows. It takes a while for the eyes to adjust and for the libido to disengage, but once accomplished you can see the audience—perhaps fifteen to twenty men—scattered about, their silhouettes still and staring, palely roasted by the light patterns bouncing off the screen.

·

The plot involves outlandish variations on a hydraulic theme and, in truth, the audience is more worth the price of admission. It is poignant when an old-timer comes fumbling down the aisle, his gray hair clear in the film light. It is dramatic when the first woman takes her seat with her escort. They seem in their twenties and treat the scene like a lark, whereas everyone else is serious and older.

When the film ends with a groan, it reels again. This way, there is no common crowd of exiting viewers, buzzing in critique. This way, each customer can let a little of it go by and leave separately, anonymously, blinded by the light outside as he rejoins the stream under the quivering "E," as if it never happened.

[5/30/78]

Air Time

Luciano Pavarotti's public is waiting all over the nation as he warms up in a robe and long muffler at the Metropolitan Opera House, working his voice with gradual might like a weight lifter cramming oxygen away. With his right arm on the piano and his left hand in the pocket of the robe, Pavarotti makes his sound lift and pause and fall, natural as gravity.

He soon is ready to go up alone and alive before a public that is vast by classical music standards, a public that could make of this day a heroic event in Pavarotti's grand career. The other half of the risk is that it all might turn out a weirdly American statistical event, a one-man record for super-bowl culture.

Pavarotti has his doubts, which his friends backstage say is good for his voice. He tells Annemarie Verde, his secretary, that he thinks he will die. Make sure he is buried in the ground, he tells her.

Pavarotti is talked of the way Caruso was. Caruso was one of the first musicians to realize the power of recordings to reach an audience and hold it even beyond his death. He made some of the early phonograph records and so his voice remains as an objective standard to peal down through all the subjective debating of tenor lovers.

•

Just so, Pavarotti carries the venture a step further, reaching for electronic immortality with an unusual public recital at the Met broadcast live nationally on the Public Broadcasting Service. His voice is to carry beyond the

3,800 ticket holders to millions more in a public that is written off by the commercial television networks.

"He is so nervous, so exposed," his manager, Herbert Breslin, says. "He knows there are more people who will hear him now than will hear him for the rest of his life."

When Mr. Breslin picks up Pavarotti at his suite at the Navarro Hotel on Central Park South for the trip to Lincoln Center, he finds the master watching a war movie on television. He is affable but tells his manager, "Don't make me nervous."

At the Met Pavarotti first checks the angles of the six TV cameras to make sure there is no offense. He senses something in the air—the stage floor was chemically treated a week or so earlier—and instantly a man is spraying air refresher about, as four other workers polish the Steinway.

•

Even as he warms up, an hour before air time, drinks are flowing up in back at the Opera Club, eye openers for the cultural reporters. John Mazzola, the president of Lincoln Center, checks this room gently, much the way Pavarotti stands and touches the piano veneer out in the main hall as he sings his final warmup. In apparent satisfaction, he touches the shoulder of his pianist, John Wustman, as he puts away the final warmup notes.

The red and cream toned lobby of the Met fills with ticket holders who know they are blessed and will see the tenor in the flesh while television has him only live. Backstage, near the side curtain entry, Pavarotti's little black table has been set up with a white and blue towel, a pot of hot water and a bottle of club soda—the singer might want either—and some tea for the pianist.

The technical people seem taut as their cables, and at four minutes before air time, Pavarotti, dressed splendidly in tails, walks forth from his dressing room through the cavernous backstage, past the towering Eugene Onegin props.

The waiting is mostly quiet and the ice in Pavarotti's glass of club soda tinkles when he sips it and waits for his cue. Bearded and robust, Pavarotti seems to have his nervousness perfectly tucked away under his diaphragm.

•

It will be a minute and a half, he is told, until he takes the stage.

Pavarotti looks at Annemarie Verde. "Just remember," he tells her.

"What?" she says.

"The ground," Pavarotti says, bolstering himself by reiterating his burial instruction. "Remember the ground."

But with all the power of Lincoln Center, the Exxon Corporation, the National Endowment for the Humanities and the Corporation for Public Broadcasting standing there ready to push him on, if necessary, Pavarotti seems to need no urging when the moment comes. He struts forth strongly and in an instant the applause and bravos begin.

He has his handkerchief out, as much his trademark as Satchmo's, and he begins, sweeping through love, death and love again in his first three offerings, and his audience, millions of them, knows the live Pavarotti.

The audience stares and listens, the six cameras are working, Pavarotti is singing, moving through notes he held back on in warming up. He is going all out, singing, sweating, leaning, reaching, and through a sidestage cubbyhole, Edward Diaz, the night stage carpenter who had to give up two house seats to serve this show, is singing along quietly.

As Pavarotti sings, Mr. Diaz, after a decade of backstage work and humming, whispers: "I think this guy is the most fantastic voice I have ever heard."

Pavarotti takes his first brief break, striding to the wings like an athlete with plenty left. He is mopped, made up. He gulps the iced club soda. He is ready to go back but is told to wait twenty seconds. "They have a commercial?" he asks in wonderment at public television.

He gets his cue, goes back out. Pavarotti sings and sings. Forget the ground; Pavarotti is not dying.

[2/13/78]

Music from the Box

Gnawing through the cross-grain of all the city's decibels comes Mike Perez and his "box" of Donna Summer disco music ("BAD girl, BAD girl, talkin' 'bout a BAD girl"), sloshing loudly onto passers-by from his four-speaker, black-and-silver Sony CFM-1 portable AM-FM cassette stereo system.

There is a wisp of Gunga Din about him as he lugs his stereo box and leers, spilling the sound all over the streets, more or less deliberately spattering lyric fragments and piston squirts of melody on crowds who squint on by in the sun, walking unwillingly through the thumping.

"This is my *box*, man," says Mr. Perez, the gleaming boisterous look of the suitcase-sized sound system counterpoised by the small silver ring set in his left ear lobe. "My box is my Roman weapon, my juice box. Listen!"

With too little advance warning he twists one of the controls on the face of the box, which seems modeled after the Concorde cockpit, and full volume is attained on the subway stairs at Times Square. A scarf of torn and bloody sound leaps out and a listener almost ducks reflexively.

"Hey!" Mr. Perez says. "Good, huh?"

•

The box's sound is of a grieving herd, all that has been missing for the final abbatoir touch in the subways. He snuffs it out with the punch of a panel button. Momentarily merciful, the box-meister then begins panhandling, holding his palm up to strangers even as he is strapped to his $90 box.

Mr. Perez needs fresh money for life's sundries, he

explains, chief among which is the better box he covets—the $200 Sanyo box, Model M9994, which has two microphones and four bigger speakers with chrome hubs that pop and throb with the music quite like burlesque pasties.

In the streets, the sound from the legions of walking boxes seem all peanut-butter music: It sticks to the roof of your brain, and you can wriggle your ears raw trying to pry it loose. One entire lyric, delivered wee-breathless-mousey style, goes: "You can ring my bell-ell-ell, ring my BELL!"

•

Up at Crazy Eddie's off Fordham Road, where some of the Bronx box people shop, they already have begun their Christmas sale complete with a baggy-pants, pasty-faced Santa. They have forty different kinds of boxes on display—cacophony to go, at prices better than $300 a box. Even children buy.

Jon Wettingfeld, one of Crazy Eddie's salesmen, explains the selling technique, zooming up both antennas on a Sanyo box, boosting the bass and treble to maximum, getting the stereo dial needles bouncing like Groucho's eyebrows, and zit-zutting across the FM dial to 92, WKTU, where the disco throbs all day, loud as Grendel's pulse-beat.

The following is snatched from thin air: "Some HOT STUFF, baby, tonight. Gonna get some HOT STUFF, baby, tonight." Clearly the message is the same as from pre-box days of yore. It is the sentiment of a once-controversial song that went, "I'd like to get you on a slow boat to China."

"It's a form of escapism," says another salesman, Ray DiPrinzio, venturing into some David Susskind explication on the Meaning of the Boxes.

"Sisyphus would have enjoyed carrying this," Mr. Wettingfeld says, trying to batten down a throbbing box that seems to need a silver bullet in lieu of an OFF button.

The best box sociology is offered by Joe Kelly, a thirty-three-year-old family man who nevertheless is a street person who owns three boxes and always has one with him, even when he is at work transporting prisoners from upstate jails back for trials in the city. He is, mercifully, fed up to his woofers with Donna Summer disco, and he keeps a slice of Herbie Hancock flute jazz ready in his cassette chamber.

"I know with my friends—some Spanish dudes and some Brothers, too—seven out of ten have boxes," Mr. Kelly says. "It's a great street thing. Everybody loves their music. You walk with your box, you meet people."

He emphasizes that no aggression is intended by the box people, however shardlike their music seems. Mr. Kelly is believable, but of course he only speaks in behalf of one of the thousands of boxes whose thwacking sounds ricochet about the city.

•

The boxes are liquid wealth in the street market. Mr. Kelly routinely tells of putting up his fists to two subway marauders who tried to steal his box, and he is not surprised that the alleged motive in a recent Bronx murder trial of a fourteen-year-old boy was greed for another boy's fine, loud stereo box.

Mr. Kelly suspects that most boxes he hears around town "one way or another are ripped off." But he is philosophical and he says general street tolerance is, for him, worth the pastoral experience of a Central Park box evening. He tells of box people gathering a dozen or more strong by the park fountain and tuning into the same disco station to shower music on the roadway disco skaters who lately are updating the park's Currier & Ives tableaux.

Mike Perez even enjoys his box's occasional rest periods. "I can think something in my mind and it comes out of my box in stereo," he says. "Listen."

There is nothing there. But he is so unblinking and serious on this point that it is a relief when he finally flicks a control and lets some Donna Summer slosh back onto the street.

[8/14/79]

Eggbag

Eggbag the cat is asleep in the back of the magic shop, and Eighth Avenue looks almost greasy with the afternoon rain. There isn't much magic on the avenue and the hookers stand out under their golf umbrellas.

In the magic store where Eggbag the cat sleeps, with a pawnshop on one side and a naked-lady emporium on the other, a few locals wait for the cat to wake up and do his card trick. They kill time talking of human magicians.

"Have you seen the new guy, Presto?" Johnny Burns asks, leaning on the counter that has all the magic magazines and the false fruit and fish to squeeze into tiny balls for hiding. "Presto is great. A black guy, fantastic magician, can blind you up close or way back."

Two officers from the beat come in to buy some magic stuff, and the owner of the store, Russ Delmar, an old vaudevillian, goes into some lovely sleight-of-hand with them, doing the shifting silver dollars, the moving pen and an eight-card cover ending with all the cards the same.

The shorter officer of the two loves it when Russ makes him blow extra hard for the abracadabra moment. Russ has strong, clean hands, and the tricks go perfectly and he kids his audience. "You're not too smart—How'd you ever get to be a cop?"

"Nice, Russ," the officer says, still watching his hands. The police enjoy themselves. It's better than standing outside with the hookers and golf umbrellas.

They buy a dirty illusion to put on the lieutenant's chair back in the precinct, an old New York favorite—imitation dog-dropping. It's not first-line magic, but Russ sells some of the usual novelties, too, along with professional grade tricks and illusions. His biggest illusion now is the shoot-the-woman, which goes for $150. (You want to know what it is, buy it. Or, as Russ says: "How do I do it? I do it very well.")

•

Russ's store, the Magic Center, has been scaled down in its thirty years on the west side of Eighth Avenue north of 46th Street. Once he had ten salesmen demonstrating tricks costing up to $600. He still has good stuff, says his friend, Ken Martin, a local actor, magician and Chinese food chef. But Russ has scaled down, mainly enjoying showing magic to the kids who come by and taking care of Eggbag the cat, who was named after the trick in which an egg is palmed out of a felt purse. Russ is near seventy years old, but he looks fifteen younger from all the adagio dancing and unicycle juggling he did fifty years ago in vaudeville.

Where is Eggbag the cat? We want to see him do his card trick. "Eggbag will be along," Russ says. Well either that or we'll go for this guy Presto. "Presto is like wine," Johnny Burns says. "He is good."

Strange-looking people come in out of the rain, a few looking desperate, and stunned, as if they had come from an accident. But it is only the neighborhood they're coming from. Russ is friendly to all and does sleight-of-hand, even when he gives a quarter to a panhandler, and the panhandler appreciates the magic.

"Wait till you see the cat," Ken Martin says. "I saw that trick first time, I almost fell on the floor."

Russ goes back where Eggbag the cat sleeps. Once three hookers came in and offered to rent the backroom for $100 a day if Russ would put a cot in. He said no for morality reasons as well as the fact that Eggbag slept there.

•

After a while, Eggbag the cat comes out. He is an even gray-white color, like a shirt that's been washed without bleach. He ignores everyone and yawns elaborately, stretching his front paws out and curving his back up the sudden way humans pop their knuckles.

What Eggbag really wants is to steal one of the magicians' dummy mice from the glass showcase, as he does every day, and knock it around the floor for his daily macho hunter fix. (He has never gone back out on Eighth Avenue since he sneaked into the store two years ago.) But Russ keeps hauling the cat to the counter. It's show time.

"Pick a card," Russ says to a visitor, holding a deck out. (It is the three of hearts, but don't tell the cat.)

Russ puts the card back in the pack, has the visitor straighten the deck. Russ fans the cards in front to Eggbag the cat. "C'mon, Eggbag."

Eggbag the cat sprawls on the counter as if he is trying out for a Mae West movie. Even his whiskers are blasé.

"C'mon, Eggbag," Russ says, kind of pushing the fan of cards toward the cat, and the cat suddenly bites one, as if it were the hand of human kindness, and he pulls it out in his teeth and lets it flutter down. It is the same three of hearts.

He does it two more times. Not bad for a cat. One of the visitors confides that it clearly was a trick.

Granted. But what can you expect on a rainy day on Eighth Avenue in a place called the Magic Center— divinity?

[12/20/77]

6

The Work of
Many Hands

Witness for
the Prosecution

When the Canal Street trade fell off at Magoo's Cafe about thirteen years ago, Tom Chaipis, the owner, let a limited number of high-price prostitutes into the place to attract a John trade of executive types who started taking quick cab rides over from the financial canyons for special refreshment.

The shift in clientele worked too well. The Johns were willing to pay the $18 "dining minimum" for meeting a woman to rent. And the prostitutes, while heading out from the humble bistro to motels to consummate their deals, would pay Tom Chaipis $5 or $10 additional from their $50 fees to help keep Magoo's open. But the police came around, too, and Magoo's was put on their pad of regular payoffs.

The economics of Magoo's soon became a treadmill, the way Mr. Chaipis recalls those ten years, with the pad growing tenfold to $1,000 a month for the separate payments to members of the precinct, division, borough and even headquarters offices. At what to that point was the most ragged time of Tom Chaipis's life, Magoo's had become basically a bent marketplace in which one man's lust was financing another man's law and order.

"I am not naïve," Mr. Chaipis says, sipping coffee in the back of Magoo's at Walker Street and Avenue of the Americas. "I knew what I started. Before you know it, though, you're in up to here—." He put his hand across his open mouth like a knifeblade. "And the question becomes how do you get out."

●

After forty-eight years of life, Mr. Chaipis is a moon-faced man with a glance that arcs warily between the pragmatic and the sad. He seems willing to answer any question you put to him. He is not Candide, but the description of "hapless" applied to him recently by the state's highest court seems appropriate. His only moral strength, he says, may be painful honesty once he gets caught, not courage before the fact.

Thus the question of how to extricate himself from the tacky symbiosis of pad and mattress was answered for him late in 1973, when he was indicted on felony charges of promoting prostitution. The police arrested him at his home in Fort Lee, N.J., while some of his six children and neighbors looked on.

As he pondered the worthlessness of the pad, Mr. Chaipis was approached by the special state prosecutor's office on criminal justice corruption and offered a choice. He could suffer felony penalties on prostitution charges and lose his business, or he could testify against bigger fish on the police pad and receive a promise of copping a misdemeanor plea and keeping his liquor license.

●

The way he figures the cards of life are shuffled and dealt, his decision was inevitable as the initial turn to prostitution. He testified, and to such an extent that the State Court of Appeals praised him for "substantial . . . considerable . . . significant contributions" that were "extremely valuable to the public but not without grave danger to the witness."

He testified before two special grand juries and before several Police Department hearings, forcing the retirement of high-ranking police officers and ending the pad. Through the year of testifying, "it was like being squeezed through a pipe," Mr. Chaipis says. By day he would testify. By night he would get dozens of death threats, some of them night-long, ten minutes apart.

"They got to me when they used the name of one of my

kids," he says. "They called and said, 'Zoey has ten days to live.' That tore me up."

He went ahead with the testimony, offering names and incidents in his high-rasp narrative. "I was miserable, but I knew I had their promise I would come out of this with my business."

Right then, a growth in his mouth was diagnosed as cancer. As Tom Chaipis sat in a frenzy in a hospital, waiting for an operation that would likely remove his right eye, a letter came from the State Liquor Authority announcing he would lose his liquor license at Magoo's because of his misdemeanor record in prostitution.

"My God, I couldn't believe it," Mr. Chaipis says, sounding like Job on a self-generated dung heap. "What was the point of all that I had done? Of anything? The prosecutor's word to me? What was I doing?"

The doctors saved his eye, but removed his right upper jaw, leaving Mr. Chaipis with a somewhat sunken aspect that seems an almost biblical mark in his tale of flesh and the spirit.

His lawyer sued to get the state to live up to its promise, and last week, after a three-year court fight, the Court of Appeals overruled the Liquor Authority and lower courts. The court said that Mr. Chaipis had been done wrong and deserved special consideration because his detailed testimony on corruption far outweighed "his own execrable conduct."

•

So Magoo's stays open down on Walker Street, minus the pad and minus the girls. Mr. Chaipis says some of the girls married customers they met through Magoo's. He liked the girls, and he gets patriarchal in retrospect about his role: "I was never a pimp; if anything I freed them from pimps." He says he had nothing against the police, either. "It was just everything went like this," he says, jamming his fingers together in a fleshy gesture of hopelessness.

Mr. Chaipis laughs at some questions. "You think if I was organized crime I'd testify and dig myself deeper into this mess?" And he says there is no moral comfort in testifying about corruption. "I wanted to run away, but I have six kids to raise."

Magoo's had a good crowd the other night, drinking and dining on things like omelets and burgers, none of the patrons looking crassly on the make. They are from SoHo, from the post-pad neighborhood renaissance that has saved Magoo's, Mr. Chaipis says. At least seventy of them have festooned the walls with paintings to pay for meal tabs he lets them run up. "It's all all right," he says. "The majority of people are people."

[4/4/78]

The Seventh Cycle

Mr. Laws tells spellbinding stories about the night the rats danced in the street outside the old Ruppert brewery. And a nimble man named Lucky lobs rat-poison briquets into the gutted tenements like a grenadier in wartime Berlin. And Mr. Davis has to use a pickax to crack into backyard piles of "airmailed" garbage 4 and 5 feet deep where the rats despoil—great blankets of organic matter, a slum of manna for the rats.

The problem multiplies at the rate of a plague—more than 100 million new rats born each year in the city—so it is not surprising that the city's extermination program is measured in what sounds like biblical terms: We are in the seventh cycle (and eighth year) of poisoning, uprooting, harassing and maybe even strengthening some of the rats in the city's 2,119 most infested blocks. And without question all those involved—Mr. Laws, Lucky, Mr. Davis and most of the rats—will be back again on the same blocks when the eighth cycle begins.

Life is as much a race for the rat controller as it is for the rat. Life is a holding action, a containment, according to the best plan and hope of Elwood F. Dupree, the director of the city's pest-control bureau who roams the 2,119 infested blocks in handsome checked suits and a leather overcoat, and who waxes scholarly and respectfully on the subject of the rat.

Mr. Dupree pauses outside the hovel that once was 117 East 115th Street as Lucky lobs in the briquets that offer fish-and meat-flavored versions of a poison that ruins the blood-clotting mechanism, and so makes the rats die by internal hemorrhage.

"You know the rat cannot regurgitate like we can," Mr. Dupree says, explaining how this special strength in eating is the rat's Achilles' gullet with the toothsome poison. Lucky smiles in the broken basement corridor of the building and holds up a dead rat, not a fresh kill—because the poison is cumulative rather than fast-acting—but evidence that the enemy is mortal.

"What we have in this city is the Norway rat," Mr. Dupree says. "An Olympian who is an excellent swimmer and climber, travels on telephone wires if he has to. A stocky 1-pound creature, up to 9 inches long from head to tail."

•

The anticoagulant poison, Fumarin, works well and is safest in terms of humans. But the problem is endless because female rats have as many as forty babies a year.

Those are lively odds for the rat. Moreover, there once was and it is likely that there still is a hearty strain dubbed Super Rat discovered like an invincible turtle in the city's archipelago, the South Bronx, two years ago. It looked the same—coarse reddish brown, greasy fur, two protruding incisors—but it was able to consume ten times the fatal dose of Fumarin and survive quite well. It turned up among the fifty or so live rats the city traps each month and has analyzed.

A drastic countermeasure was taken. Doses of zinc phosphide were distributed through a thirty-block area. This is an acute poison that paralyzes the heart, but it is so strong that it must be retrieved within two days along with rat carcasses, or else cats, humans and others might be poisoned. Mr. Dupree said Super Rat had extra vitamin reserves for some reason to fight the anticoagulant. But the heart poison stilled great numbers and Super Rat has not shown up in the monthly cross section for over a year, except for one isolated case in the Lower East Side. Most likely, Super Rat lives, he said, but hasn't been caught.

Mr. Dupree's corps of 525 workers roams the worst of the city's slums, neighborhoods containing 1.5 million people and a majority of the city's rat population, which he estimates includes at least a constant stock of 8 million. They are night creatures, not particularly aggressive toward humans (particularly since humans seem to provide for them so well, Mr. Dupree notes).

Rat bites—more than 200 cases were reported last year—result from a clash of reflexes, Mr. Dupree explains. The child is put to bed with a bottle or other food and jerks about or cries at the arrival of the hungry rat, which defensively nips out.

The memorable moments in the rat program, which in the "concerned" '60's was called a "war," occur at building demolitions. A city exterminator, George Laws, recalls the flight of rats that attended demolition at the former Ruppert brewery, a public hubbub of rats displaced from rich stocks of water and grain. "Man, they were all over the street and people were swatting them with brooms and shovels. Bus drivers were going after them."

•

Ron Bryant has watched South Bronx youngsters play night games, saving bottles to fling at rats in a kind of urban fox hunt. "I've seen six rats climb right up a wall." He is in the education program, following up the pick-and-shovel men who remove more than 40 tons of compacted garbage a year from apartment yards. He knocks on apartment doors and asks people not to airmail their garbage out their windows. "It's a hassle when they have no heat, water or money, and all you want to talk about is rats."

In the midst of this, the seventh cycle, Mr. Dupree gets calls about other pests. "Woman from Queens says, 'Hey there's all these caterpillars eating my beautiful backyard trees.' I said, 'Relax, woman, any day they'll turn into butterflies and flutter away.'" Great whoops of laughter from Mr. Laws, Mr. Bryant and the other rat-killers. "Oh yeah. Butterflies!"

[1/6/77]

Of Bay Rum
and the Unisex

Miss Vicky is snipping away in layers at the next chair but listening closely as George congratulates himself for not behaving like a lot of other old barbers by fighting the unisex. He talks of it that way, "the unisex," sounding like an old blacksmith talking of an early automobile as "the machine."

"When the unisex came along, a lot of guys couldn't do it—all they knew was the regular haircut—and they lost their customers and had to get out of the business," George Dubois says, fingering his white pencil mustache as he sits in the Gotham Hotel barbershop.

"Don't talk about the old barbers, George," Miss Vicky instructs, her cutting hand poised in a hummingbird blur. "Tell him about all the famous people you've cut."

"Well, yeah," George says, thinking back. "Mike Todd. And Erroll Flynn. I gave Erroll Flynn his last haircut over in his room at the Shoreham Hotel."

Dutifully, he name-drops some more about the elegant traffic in hair right here off Fifth Avenue and 55th Street. But George, whose own white hair glistens handsomely from the regular care of Miss Vicky, does not at all resist getting back to the subject of old times, before the unisex. For him, this is the story of Genesis, for he was born to barbering, the son of the Gotham's original barber, Sol Dubois, the nephew of three barbering uncles, with the elders' tonsorial practice rooted in the old country, in Venice. A rich tale of turn-of-the-century migration. . . .

"And Frank Sinatra, don't forget," Miss Vicky prods from somewhere in the present.

Well, yes, George admits to having had Old Blue Eyes in the chair. But closer to his heart is the survival of old Uncle Al, the last of the four original Dubois brother barbers. "Uncle Al quit the shop here when he was eighty-eight," George says. "And he still comes over in a cab—a $28 fare from Jackson Heights—to have me cut his hair."

Having yielded his chair to Miss Vicky and the unisex seven years ago, Uncle Al is running up the years like his cab fares and now is five years short of one hundred. George, who is seventy-five years old, has a selfish grin, accented by his Thin Man mustache, at the long life of Dubois barbers.

•

"After fifty-six years as a barber, I got no varicose veins," George brags, pulling up a trouser leg on a skinny but wholesome shank as Miss Vicky exclaims, "No, no, George!"

George laughs at his joke on the unisex generation. Miss Vicky says to the hair she is cutting, "How sweet it is," apparently meaning life, not the shank.

George compliments Miss Vicky for having a good sense of humor, a key, he says, to making the unisex adapt well to the old bay rum ways in the Gotham shop.

"She's wonderful, and there's more money in her thing," he stresses. "The unisex is more money, and the women come in now and I like the women."

Miss Vicky pays George the light compliment of being a rake. She is easily four decades younger than George, born of a family of Budapest musicians, a woman, dark eyed and smart, willing to invest some graduate tuition for lessons with Vidal Sassoon after she learned the hot-towel basics at the Atlas Barber School. George says she was the perfect answer to his problems with the unisex, the gradual requests for longer-styled barbering that began, he says— "Oh, let's see, fifteen, seventeen years ago."

"It was with the Beatles, George," Miss Vicky says authoritatively, marking the instant clearly as Uncle Al marks the boat trip from Italy.

"Oh yeah, the Beatles," George says. "You're right, the Beatles."

•

Mirrored in his shop as Miss Vicky snips and listens and edits, George testifies that, all in all, there is life after the unisex. "I'm kind of retired now and only come in two days a week, Tuesdays and Fridays, to handle old customers who want a regular haircut."

When George says "regular haircut," it sounds just as special as his phrasing of "the unisex." It summons back so many departed things, white marble decor, the shiny hot towel cauldron, the Police Gazette, the pink nape of the Depression. George says yes, he remembers all that, but he makes no great bathetic demand for the past. One day in the transition to the unisex, Miss Vicky got rid of the old razor strops slung at the side of the shop's new red upholstered chairs. George adapted without complaint, switching to a safety razor for his customers.

As George tells of the shop, having reflected eyeball to eyeball with decades of people, he seems to have experienced all the healthy range and context a person could want for a full life.

"Judy Garland's husband," says Miss Vicky, suddenly remembering another famous head of hair he once cut. "Vincent Minnelli, George."

That's so. But George tells, too, about the death of his own father in the shop.

"He dropped dead when he turned to get a hot towel," George says. "He keeled over and hit my left foot. I was too upset, the guy in my chair got on the phone and called the doctor, but he was dead. He was seventy-one, never sick a day, all his teeth, all his hair. Not a bad way to go."

After that, thirty-two years ago, the shop became known as George's, says George, who interrupts himself as a new notion dawns: "Now I guess you should identify the shop as . . ."

"Miss Vicky's," says Miss Vicky with a snip.

"Yeah, that's right," says George, cooperative as ever with the unisex. "Miss Vicky's."

[9/8/79]

The Nose
That Really Knows

All the sniffing and hoping turned to ambrosia last month when Thomas Weber got the word: He is the new top nose in town. He was chosen by the federal government to replace an olfactory legend, Albert L. Weber, who is no relation except in sheer ability to smell and pronounce judgment on the freshness or decomposition of foods.

Weber the elder, who was seventy-three years old last week, retires from the Food and Drug Administration office in Brooklyn this June as the government's reigning expert in the art of fish-smelling—one of the two remaining specialists rated "expert" nationally in this field of quality control.

He is delighted to be succeeded by Weber the younger, a thirty-year-old chemist from Glendale, Queens, who was trained by the master, in a class of twelve contenders that was winnowed to four before the choice was made of the areas's new chief organoleptic specialist in seafood.

•

Tom Weber has a handsome Barrymore wedge of a nose that Weber the elder says is prodigiously fine tuned from being at the teacher's side as 800 samples were put to the nostrils in an average year. More than his nose is his attitude, according to the teacher, who has trained about 1,000 fish smellers in his thirty-five years with the government.

"Tom has the right disposition," says Albert Weber. "He will do the work well day after day and be willing to fight his own feelings at times. In this line, we can't let emotions get the better of judgment."

216

This crucial distinction, he explains, is a willingness to approve something that is marginally fresh smelling even if, subjectively, the smeller prefers something better.

A good way to understand this, perhaps, is to witness Weber the elder at play—taking a vacation cruise on a Caribbean liner where, he knows, one must never take a holiday from the business of smelling fish.

Fried fish is the main course one evening and Mr. Weber smells some in passing and silently rates it as a Class Two, the subtle gray zone of his expertise, midway between the classes of fresh and decomposed to the point of rejection.

Class Two as a smeller is one thing, but as a diner Mr. Weber keeps his counsel and decides to watch a woman across the table eat some of the fish. When she doesn't frown or collapse from some sort of esthetic assault, he orders the fish. (His art deals mainly in esthetic, not toxic threats; salmonella, indeed, has no odor, and cooking can kill threatening bacteria in stinking food.)

"It was, indeed, a Class Two," Mr. Weber says of the fish.

About 20 percent of the fish lots spot-sampled by the F.D.A. fall into the Class Two category, which means they contain borderline cases but can be approved once the badly odoriferous ones are gleaned out of the shipment. Learning to call this category has been, of course, the heart of the journeyman's job for Tom Weber.

"You have to smell as much as you can—memorizing the odors and retraining as much direct experience as possible," he says, speaking with seven years' experience, including three as a sampler of tea quality.

In the clean, quiet seventh-floor laboratory over on the Brooklyn waterfront, Tom's nose is being put to everything Albert knows, in the remaining months before retirement. They distinguish among anchovies ("all anchovies stink; some stink good and some stink bad," the master notes). They include a bit of exotic fare, letting Tom memorize whale steak. They range out some, making sure they get rabbit and frogs' legs down pat.

The most troublesome item is foul tuna fish that has been steam processed to mask out bad odor, then canned. There usually is nothing left to smell, but the senior Mr. Weber says a good organoleptic specialist, who uses all his senses, can spot a honeycomb texture to the fish, a result of bacteria steamed out of the decomposing fish. One advantage he has is a special sensitivity to histamines produced in this process so that, blindfolded, he can touch the fish and feel an itchy allergic reaction in his hands.

Weber the elder figures his successor will earn the expert rating in another year or two, considering his talent and the volume of fish imports in New York. The other current expert is Harold R. Throm out in the Seattle office. In general, 75 percent of the fish these specialists smell could be rated by the layman since they are clearly fresh or putrid.

Of the rest, 15 percent require training, and the other 10 percent is a matter of special experience, of letting the nose dwell on detail the way the umpire's eyes come to know the outside corners of home plate.

•

The nose of Weber the elder is roundish, with a pink liveliness and a small birthmark on the left nostril. It is an organ with a certain Gallic pleasantness, set above a gentle smile, down from eyes that sparkle securely—a Class One face, ocean-fresh. Subjectively, he likes plain natural odors. "I can't stand most perfumes," he says.

A human masks out his own odors, so a smeller who smokes cigarettes bothers colleagues in the laboratory but not himself, unless he touches the fish he is smelling and puts a tobacco smell on it.

Aside from smoking, the Webers say they can be thrown off their mark by shaving colognes on others, by solvents and detergents sometimes used in cleaning the building and by loud noise, too. The senses are interrelated, they note, and one sense taxed excessively can aggravate nerve endings and impede the others.

Just so, Tom Weber was at a Montauk restaurant and

instantly knew the shrimp brought to his table were far gone from fresh—smelling ammoniacal, as they say in the lab. The experience was offensive enough so he could not bear to eat anything, and one imagines him brooding as should the artist who follows Weber the expert.

[4/7/78]

A Real Pro

Macy's is mostly devoid of music, except for those bingk-bingk-bingk signals of the department store code sounding through the shoppers' babble. So Louis Yelnick, who runs men's sports footwear in the midtown store, has an excellent point when he tells how his daytime salesman's job contributes contrast to his nighttime profession of turning the pages for pianists in concert halls around the city as they nod and throb with both hands on the keyboard.

But he does not savor the music. "That would mean chaos," he says. He stays a measure ahead of the pianist and turns the page at the instant he knows from experience that the bottom measure has been memorized.

"Sometimes the pianist, mutely, will look at me with a smile of gratitude because I have served him well," Mr. Yelnick says.

Turning by night, Mr. Yelnick is not so much escaping from his daytime life as exulting in it, he says. He likes men's sports footwear very much, particularly with its new locker-room decor festooned with Adidas and Converse and the other sneaker names. A customer looks vulnerable sitting there, one shoe off and the other shoe on, as Mr. Yelnick disappears to get a pair of gripping low-cuts. The customer sort of corkscrews his besocked foot behind the other leg for security and is left there in the cryptic bingk-bingk until Mr. Yelnick comes back to shoe him.

In his blue salesman's smock, Mr. Yelnick carries his brown-bag lunch to a seat in the employees' lounge, past the vending machines and the chess and card tables.

"I've turned pages for some of the best," he says. "Beverly Sills, Leontyne Price. Actually, I'm turning pages for their accompanists. But I prefer saying them because they have the names."

Quite proudly, he finds he is the only professional page turner he knows of in the city. "Most pianists get their students or wife or mother-in-law to do it," he says. "Let me say, for $50 [his fee], you're getting a bargain."

When he gets a booking, he prepares, if possible, by obtaining the recital score and reading it through, fingering the pages. He learned piano as a boy in Brooklyn and first turned pages as a help for his older sister at home.

The first time he did a turn in public he was in the audience of a recital at Washington Irving High School in Manhattan when, he recalls quite exactly, a man stepped from behind the curtain and asked "whether there was anyone in the audience willing to turn pages for the pianist, whose regular turner was missing."

"Nervous as I was," says Mr. Yelnick, "I stood up with butterflies. That launched me."

•

On the day of a concert, Mr. Yelnick says he goes to work at Macy's with an extra bit of joie de vivre. "I bring a spare clean white shirt and tie and leave them in my locker, and perhaps some white powder to take care of the 5 o'clock shadow."

He gets to the concert hall a half hour early to prepare. "Give it a dry run," he says. "Certain questions have to be asked: Any cuts? Any repeats? Is the pianist long stick or short stick?" The latter refers to the two-piece strut that holds the piano top open, wide or narrow. "Most are short stick."

The featured artist prefers to be off in a separate room, single-minded. Mr. Yelnick checks to see if they might prefer a bit of small talk for distraction. Most don't; he leaves them alone.

"I am usually the third person to take the stage, carrying the music, with the featured artist first and the accompanist second," he says. "Truthfully, I have a certain stage presence. I wear a dark business suit and stay unnoticed."

The piano is usually back of the featured performer, and Mr. Yelnick sits to the pianist's immediate left. "My technique is to sit catty-corner, not parallel." He moves two chairs together in Macy's lounge to demonstrate.

"This way I can reach up and across with my left hand and grasp the right page corner," he says, reaching into the air as people in the vicinity chew and watch. "If I used my right hand, you see, I would blind the pianist temporarily reaching in front.

"Two pairs of eyes watch as I turn. I give it a fast whoosh, and I smooth it down just once." He prefers old pages to fresh music. They peel easier.

•

Once the pages stuck on him and the pianist had to muddle through. "I could hear a buzz in the audience. It was very unpleasant for me." Other than that scar, the turner's burden mainly involves the occasional temptation to sneeze, which can linger for measure after measure until, Mr. Yelnick demonstrates, he yields shrewdly, implosively, with a delicate clicking shudder.

"Pianists can be eccentric," he says. "Once a pianist asked me during intermission to turn 'noiselessly.' That's impossible. I did my best and it went well."

As he turns and the pianist plays, Mr. Yelnick can hear noise other than music. "Some of the pianists hum along and sometimes they make gurgling noises. That can be annoying, but I'm not the featured star; I know my position."

At the end of a concert, as the applause begins, Mr. Yelnick quickly collects the music, arises and moves to the wings. "I stay in the wings," Mr. Yelnick says. "If the featured artist is a violinist, I offer to hold the violin so he or she can be unencumbered." He waits in the wings listening to the applause and, Mr. Yelnick says, he feels entitled to share in it.

[10/27/77]

Lifting a Curse

On Jan. 17, 1949, Arthur Shapiro was browsing in the Eighth Street Bookstore as a student and heard strange guttural sounds in the next aisle.

"I suddenly became aware of a string of curse words," he says, specifying them like four-letter slaps in the face. "And when I looked around the stacks, I saw a nice young woman, very conventional in a sealskin coat, nothing Bohemian, browsing politely through the collected works of Keats."

He found this woman innocently going about her poetic-minded business except for sudden outbursts of obscene shouts that seemed to visit her demoniacally and depart.

He thought it strange, but like a good New Yorker he forgot about it until sixteen years later when, as a practicing psychiatrist, he faced a patient with the same symptom of coprolalia—an uncontrollable impulse to be foulmouthed.

So it was that Dr. Shapiro came to delve into the diagnostic fringe and become expert in a strange disorder called Tourette Syndrome, which visits its victims with outbursts of cursing as well as barking and snorting, and with garish multiple tics and jerking motions that interrupt ordinary activities with involuntary fits, much the way people are compelled to sneeze.

At first Dr. Shapiro found a few cases, then a dozen, then hundreds, and this year he and three other doctors published the first book devoted to this disorder, which has taken a dark toll in isolated, guilt-ridden and even reclusive wretches.

The experience is mortifying, as Dr. Shapiro's files and tape recordings make clear. In an interview a genteel woman driven to despair about her outbursts of "those words"—she specifies them only in embarrassed whispers—is talking to the doctor when suddenly, the way a news bulletin interrupts regular programming, those words burst forth from her lips in carmine tones, and then, Jekyll-and-Hyde fashion, she resumes her gentle narrative.

•

Dr. Shapiro began searching medical literature in 1965, working back through the most common denominator among the symptoms, the tic motions, and found a physician, Gilles de la Tourette, had first discovered this special confluence of all three symptoms—the sounds, the motions, the coprolalia—and grouped it ninety years ago apart from other tic maladies. Since then, he found it largely forgotten or subjected to shifting fashions of medical treatment. It was a "masturbatory conflict" in one era, a "massive inhibition of hostility" in another, but usually treated as a psychologically rooted problem.

In his research, Dr. Shapiro finds some of its victims were the "possessed" individuals of the prescientific world. In fact some of the modern victims had the same thought after seeing the movie "The Exorcist," and actually went to priests asking to be exorcised.

Dr. Shapiro says he sensed intuitively in that first patient that the illness was organically, not psychologically, rooted because, despite the outlandish interruptions, the patient's "personality was intact." Since then he feels, testing techniques used by himself and a handful of other interested doctors hint at a neurological cause.

Until the existence and prevalence of the disorder became known in the last decade—Dr. Shapiro estimates there are at least 20,000 cases and perhaps 100,000 in this country—its victims lived separate, tortured lives, lacking the soothing information that they were neither unique nor guilty in their illness.

They regularly devastate loved ones (one mother cuddling her four-year-old in her lap witnessed his first fit of coprolalia in shock). They develop habits of having to excuse themselves to find private corners to vent their symptoms.

They endlessly blame themselves and question their own sanity. One man desperately visited the same Central Park thoroughfare for a year in the random search for someone else with the disorder, hoping to prove he was not crazy. Another man, Ralph Passarella, went through years of therapies including electric shock and psychoanalysis, and even was on the verge of a lobotomy before hope was found in accurate diagnosis and the application of a new drug, haloperidol, proved effective. There were suicides, too, one of them who spent years as an affluent recluse in hospitals and took his life just as word of successful chemotherapy began circulating.

•

The key remedy, beyond the drug known as Haldol, is in spreading information to see that the disorder is properly diagnosed. A new group of victims and relatives is trying to do this job as the Tourette Syndrome Association at 42-40 Bell Boulevard, Bayside, Queens, N.Y. 11361. (Telephone: 224-2999.) In three years, this group has grown from 300 patients to 2,000.

The association will unveil a new documentary film on the disorder for the public this Saturday at Lenox Hill Hospital, followed by a discussion of the latest findings about it. Even with the drug treatment producing improvement in a majority of cases, there are all sorts of unanswered questions Dr. Shapiro and others want to pursue. There is, of course, the search for the cause, and just as fascinating is the finding that 43 percent of the victims are Ashkenazi Jews from Eastern Europe. Dr. Shapiro and his wife, Dr. Elaine Shapiro, a psychologist, have been gathering data from their cases at the Tourette and Tic Laboratory and Clinic at Mount Sinai Medical Center.

For a psychiatrist like Dr. Shapiro, there is a sweet moment in a Tourette case when, he recounts, a patient realizes there actually are others like him. "They always say, 'I knew it! I knew I was not crazy!'"

"It's a moment when you feel concretely useful to people," he says. It's also a moment of mercy dawning after all the strange dark years of the Tourette people.

[5/16/78]

Some Ball

Sol Sitzer had fresh trouble yesterday with nude women and robed magistrates. He had thought some order was returning to his business, which, for $3.25, sells a customer the right to watch a woman strip naked, smile, dance and kind of writhe theatrically down on a tabletop only inches from the customers' soft drinks—as close as the ketchup would be in one of the luncheonettes Sol used to run.

Sol says that this is not personally seductive, but that it has been profitable for him. "My neighbors in Westchester say, 'Boy, you must have a ball!' And I say, 'Yeh, some ball.' I'm so nervous I got psoriasis," he said.

What the women do—get dressed and undressed all day long in twenty-minute shifts on three tabletops—has been esoteric, if not exotic, entertainment for enough men over the last eighteen months to keep Mr. Sitzer making money for all his obligations. These include his home in Rye, N.Y.; his family (a three-year-old; his wife, who's expecting shortly); and the $6,000-a-week "nut," or overhead, of paying Lisa Jones, Crystal Brook, Ruth O'Leary and the other nude dancers and leotarded waitresses at Jax 3-Ring Circus, on East 53d Street off Lexington Avenue.

•

Sol thought that, just as he has been paying what is estimated at $650 a week in sales and real-estate taxes, he paid his reverse civic dues last Thursday, when Mayor Beame showed up with the law and with pre-alerted television crews and newspapermen to shut the place down.

Sol was philosophical. "It's an election year and we

know he wants to score points with the voters and Citi-bank," he said, referring to the reported anguish of that bank's hierarchy over Jax's flourishing across from the new corporate headquarters of Citicorp.

Jax was closed down for only three hours, since a judge found that the city's charge of the naked women's posing an "imminent danger" was only a one-sided charge until the owners could present their side at a court hearing. "Fair enough," said Sol.

Yesterday the hearing began and, even though the judge made no final decision, he ordered Jax to shut down again until he settles the issue, whenever that will be. And even before the marshals arrived, the morals squad was at Jax yesterday, making their own obscenity arrests.

But the court order was not served, and the shutdown lasted only two hours.

"Imminent danger?" Sidney Sitzer, Sol's brother and partner, asked furiously after returning to the thumping music, dim lighting and worried workers at Jax. "What imminent danger is there in watching a naked girl unless you have a bad heart? This is Catch-22 by the judge. He'll make us wait until our overhead costs put us out of business."

•

Sol Sitzer was equally furious. "You call this democracy? They're stacking the cards a new way every day."

Lisa Jones could not quite understand it either. Thursday there was panic, with the dancers scampering down to the cellar locker room and hurrying into their clothes. Friday she was a minor celebrity. A well-known television newsman showed up with his camera crew, she said, and had her do a full number down to the buff. "They were directing me—get down lower, brush my hair across my eyes. The news guy said I was a real turn-on."

The film never appeared on television, although undoubtedly it was developed and viewed back at news central. "They said it got pushed off the show because of a kidnapping," said Lisa, who has a youthful face, lissome body and dance movements that seem discordant up close, when you can spot her one bit of attire, a small gold crucifix on a thin chain about her neck.

For all the intimate smiling and positioning that she does for the customers, who sit attentively at the table as if she were some animated entree, Lisa keeps herself apart mentally, she says, and has no harsh view of the men who pay to see her. "Sometimes they even seem scared of me," she said. "You can see it in their eyes."

•

Ruth O'Leary, a waitress in a red leotard, said the funny part of the Thursday raid was that, once news stories appeared about the Mayor's disgust with Jax, a different sort of customer came by.

"We get East Side business types normally," she said, "but Friday these raunchy guys started dropping in, and they had certain things on their mind. It was 'No touchee, no touchee' till they got the point."

Mr. Sitzer said that "if you catch any of the girls hustling here or dealing in anything but entertainment, I'll give you the place."

"I don't know about other places but this one is legit. Here, look—the girls are beautiful. Personally, I don't get any kick," he said of his eleven-hour tour as manager before catching the nightly 7:30 commuter train to Rye.

"What we do is create a fantasyland for the customers— a place that can never be real for them, but that entertains them," said Sol Sitzer, growing somewhat rhapsodic. "Where else can you see a beautiful naked woman for $3.25, plus get free chili, egg rolls, pizza and hot dogs— Hebrew National, nothing but the best."

The customers at Jax yesterday, before the city came to shut it down again, included young and old men. Some, obviously businessmen, sat quietly watching the dancers and did not want to discuss themselves. They dealt with a questioner as shyly as they did with Lisa on the tabletop.

[3/29/77]

Thumbs Down

In a way, Mayor Koch has found a perfect mirror-image audience in Queens—sharp, cocky, self-centered and blunt to the point of insult—and we should be happy for him as he thrusts and parries, one against one thousand, the Douglas Fairbanks of urban dialectic.

Shining on the wall of the crowded auditorium is a slide-picture tally of his responses to the acute questions of the eighteen church parishes newly aligned as the Queens Citizens Organization. As he responds about housing, education and transportation problems, boxes are checked off on the slide, his answers distilled to the simplest levels: Yes/ No/ Other.

Clearly, as the organization proclaims, these people are sick of the system and of politicians who qualify things. They have gathered together to pin down the Mayor, monosyllabically, if possible, and to cut his rhetoric off at the pass back to Manhattan.

•

This sea of faces is heartening. Over 1,000 people gathered like political conventioneers under pikes of identity: "St. Mary Star of the Sea" over there, "Lutheran Atonement" back from the stage. This must be one of the healthiest experiments in city politics at the moment. Even if there is a certain colosseum quality to the proceeding (with, however, the Christians this time wielding thumbs up or down on the Emperor), it is good to see the people out and talking issues.

The Mayor cannot afford to ignore the group, which

claims 47,000 families as members. This is a rematch after an initial bristling confrontation in which he walked out of their rigid, rather Socratic forum—which itself is satisfaction for the group in avoiding the usual pat-on-the-hand speeches politicians like to deliver to the middle class. This second time, everything but the shape of the tables has been warily negotiated in advance.

The Mayor arrives precisely as negotiated—8:23 P.M.—and he looks pleasantly brash in a dark suit, sitting absolutely alone before a plush red curtain on the right side of the stage in the Queens College auditorium. In the next eighty-five minutes, the Mayor gives as good as he gets, and while there is some promise offered on some problems, the main effect seems a catharsis, that of the village standing up to the newest mandarin.

•

One interesting point about government left unstated in the meeting is the contrast between this scrupulous attempt at grass-roots control and the Mayor's proposal, on the previous day in another forum, to cede the ultimate fiscal-review authority of city government to the hands of non-elected monitors for the next twenty years. This accession, to federal authorities' demands, is part of the city's hope for a fresh line of credit to avoid, once more, whatever elements of formal bankruptcy have been lacking thus far in the strictures of the fiscal crisis.

With this in mind, it is possible to sit through the Mayor's visit and pick at issues that were supposed to have been settled far from Queens in The Federalist Papers: What is a proper majority rule and how is it exercised? There are constituents in Queens with votes and needs; there are lenders in the land with money and demands.

At one point, as the group demands the Mayor press for completion of York College as a learning and business anchor for Jamaica, the Mayor says that he won't act until he sees a coming report on whether it is educationally justified. Do they want him to carry on old policies if they are erroneous? he asks. The crowd buzzes with annoyance, but the Mayor continues confidently, bobbing his head like a wagging finger: "Would you have me spend $140 million . . ."

The audience shouts start: "Yes! Yes!" Mr. Koch goes on: ". . . of your hard-earned tax money . . ." The shouts: "Yes! Yes!" Mr. Koch: ". . . without having a master plan?"

And when the group asks for input before, not after the plan is set for building a rapid-transit route through Queens to Kennedy International Airport, the Mayor refers them to the existing community board hearing process. "That is where you'll have your hearing," he says flatly.

•

But where are all these master-plan standards and hearing niceties when Manhattan and other powerful precincts get theirs? the people ask contentiously. It is a good toe-to-toe moment, good graphics for the 11 P.M. TV news. But no one asks how the process must be so constitutionally orderly at this level, yet yield so easily for twenty years at the upper levels.

A woman from Ridgewood, seated at the "Meet the Press" type of panel confronting the Mayor, sums up what is at stake: "We're asking to be part of the meetings where decisions are made."

Through all this the audience is alive and noisy, and everyone has a scorecard to track the Mayor's hits and errors, as if this were Shea Stadium.

"Why isn't that . . . yes, it's Gabe!" a woman says to a companion, distracted by a slash of lamplight. Mr. Pressman is there with his camera crew, the chorus at the catharsis, and he is using the audience as a backdrop as he says something hushed into his mike, his brow knitted conclusively.

•

At the end, the leaders of this aggressive meeting and the Mayor seem to have battled to an honorable draw, by one visitor's scorecard. But the Rev. Eugene Lynch, president of the organization, disappointed because the Mayor will not promise the group a more regular entree to City Hall, pronounces a different judgment on the evening, reading from what appears to be a prepared statement.

"You have refused a working relationship with us," Father Lynch declares. "You have ignored the people of Queens tonight."

There are hoots of demurral at this in some quarters, and Mayor Koch smiles. He beams a kind of Jeanne d'Arc gratification as the flames of the priest's rhetoric lick about him. At the end, he exits to applause and retreats to Manhattan.

[5/18/78]

The Sweet Smell
of Bumbling

A few minutes before going on the air, some of the television crew members were out in the hall, making sweet-smelling clouds of smoke with their suspiciously lumpy cigarettes. This seemed appropriate, the modern equivalent of the old-time passing of the jug for a snort, a social time-out at the electronic cracker barrel known as cable television.

There is no easier way to retreat from the sophistication of the city and sample the doodlings of its component hamlets than to switch to channel C or D on the cable, where television amateurs speak in mumbles and drop things and pause awkwardly in dumpy surroundings.

If you don't have the cable you are suffering an exotic kind of deprivation, comparable to the people who did not have a subway el going by their apartments thirty years ago. Ordinary, unknown faces flash past on the screen, just like on the el, and from your home you can ponder your own status of being ordinary and unknown.

•

Through the sweet smoke of the cable studio, a man with a beard remembered that it helped to wear makeup, so he poked around the dilapidated control room, found a jar and came by with a sponge to quickly smear the show's guests, a postal worker who writes poems and a publisher who collects cartoon originals and erotica.

"I think this is great art," the collector, Jeff Rund, declared on the air, as the camera zoomed in on a Bugs Bunny original. "In fact I own eight paintings of Bugs

Bunny, and I have a Daffy Duck that was done for me." For some viewers, the display was a relief from the opening illustration of a lascivious Santa cavorting with naked female helpers.

The hosts, seated on casually ratty sectionals, were Roger Richards, proprietor of a Greenwich Village bookstore who is on the lookout for unsung poets, and Reynolds Russell, an extroverted man obviously born to the medium, even at this closet-sized scale. He dresses like a character in a Peter Bogdanovich movie, wearing a tight canvas cap and a striped shirt with white collar and cuffs.

At his side, on a soap box draped with a cloth, he carefully placed the makings for hand-rolled cigarettes—a tin of tobacco and mauve-colored papers—and he proceeded to make them and smoke them through the show in a kind of graphic ritual that seemed to bolster his sense of urbanity.

•

The postal worker-poet, Dan Krakauer, sat above them on a stool, a polite man with a German accent who found the lights sweating hot, but who realized that the cable audience—as much as a few thousand New Yorkers—was the largest gathering ever for his musings.

"I was in Bellevue Hospital/Suffering from shark bites," he began in his initial offering. Clearly, he preferred some sort of oblique irony, and the hosts grinned appreciatively through his other poems. "If gravity were suddenly turned off/We'd learn about space the hard way," another poem went. Good, nodding smiles from the hosts. "His mother always said, 'Is it you, dear?'/And he answered, 'No, it's me.' " Oh, yeah, said one of the hosts.

Reynolds Russell had promised "a dynamite show" as he began with a brief monologue on a philosophy termed personalism ("You and I are brother and sister . . .") after the camera panned back from the leering Santa. Mr. Russell told of a new neighborhood organization, Everything for Everybody, designed to help the poor "with no loss of integrity." A caller found a spark there and phoned the show, which flashes a number on the screen inviting public participation.

The resulting bit of dialogue involved a mild difference over property rights, carried on in throwaway lines edged in vanity that were disquietingly similar to those uttered on the better couches of the Johnny Carson show. Was this life imitating Nielsen?

•

Fortunately, Mr. Richards restored perspective, announcing that he had left the doughnut box of the show's one sponsor, Twin Donuts of West 14th Street, back in his bookstore. The sponsor's fee is the $10 in cab fares to get to the studio. He apologized personally to the owner by name over channel D. This spot seemed more spontaneous than Ed McMahon with a dog starved for Alpo.

For Mr. Richards, the weekly one hour on cable is an extension of his store, Greenwich Books on Greenwich Avenue, where he invites unknown poets in on Sundays to read their work to browsers and friends. This is a decent community activity by any standard, and he speaks hopefully of fashioning his cable access into a conduit that gets around the awful problems of unpublished poets.

Any small step in this direction, of course, would be the greatest advance in live television since Ted Mack's gong broke one night on the Original Amateur Hour or since those suspiciously maturational children stopped singing "Less Work for Mother" on the Horn and Hardart Children's Hour in the long-ago.

And for poetry, who knows what an electronic horizon might bring. Mr. Krakauer, the postman-poet, might have said something about this the other day on channel D in one of his works: "After he twisted his ankle sliding down the ravine/ He changed his outlook on life."

[1/4/77]

At Home on the Air

Pegeen Fitzgerald is looking out into the green-black night of Central Park, her pale beauty reflected in the wide window glass sixteen stories above the city.

One of her ten house cats—an upwardly mobile striped creature named Public Relations—is preening itself by the plants, as if mindful that air time is only twenty minutes away.

Pegeen is in a simple loose gown of black, so her face floats in the window reflection as she looks out and chats nonstop, pointing there, where she once saw the police flush a naked man from a tree, and over this way where she saw a man walk several times on water for some movie production, and over by the benches, where her favorite wino sleeps, the one who arises in the morning, stretches and pledges allegiance to the flag.

On a table by the window a stalk of punk smolders slowly, the aromatic smoke etching past four waiting microphones set amid a great clutter of books, a bowl of fresh grapes, a scrap pile of ideas, a cache of cigars and pipe tobacco.

"My husband is a great bourbon drinker," Pegeen says, turning from the window where she has been telling an anecdote about O'Ryan's liquor store around the corner. It could have been a cue—the smallest detail of the Fitzgeralds' life seems part of a continuous broadcast—for Ed Fitzgerald enters the room, looking natty and immortal. "I'm Fitzgerald," he says. "How do you do?"

•

In his eighty-seventh year, down to one good eye and one good kidney, Ed Fitzgerald is wearing a black cap to keep warm and to cover the scars in his skull from one of several cancer operations that have kept him alive this decade. He is wearing a tweed jacket, a knitted tie and a long muffler donned in a theatrical toss. He looks prepared for yachting more than for broadcasting.

Trailed by a tiny frizzy of a lapdog, Ed Fitzgerald goes over to check his microphone and tobacco supply, deciding whether to keep his hearing aid on for this show.

Now it is Ed and Pegeen Fitzgerald in their living room reflected in the window glass, and beyond them the city night ripens as they get ready for the 11:20 show-time.

They do not confer elaborately for their program. Their long and luxurious life style has been spun out of sitting and talking and listening together, and it's far too late now to lose their confidence and their talent. They have an audience whose loyalty has exasperated broadcast executives who tried to shut them off the air six years ago. This loyalty extends beyond life, for expiring members of the audience occasionally will their pets to the Fitzgeralds, who currently have seventy-eight cats up in their weekend home in Connecticut.

•

The Fitzgeralds are near the end of their fourth decade together on the radio. They are night people now, having followed the sun through the spectrum of time from the morning, where they are considered to have invented the wife-and-husband discourse show.

There is no easy way to describe what they do. They wool-gather and play off each other with their talk. They steep themselves daily in remembrances, using the airways as their Proustian bed. They talk of a pet show coming in Brooklyn, of a departed friend gifted with malaprop ("'my teet's hurt,' she would say after a visit to the dentist," Ed says, with a quiet smile), of Sky Lab falling, of Ed's fear of subway gratings (his father died when one collapsed as he walked on it), and of civility, which Ed is always requesting of Pegeen.

She more than meets his request, listening very carefully to him, correcting details, switching topics intuitively, reading the commercials elegantly and accurately as he puffs away at his tobacco.

"We're a true soap opera," Pegeen says in summary as she faces her husband once again across the broadcast table.

•

This night they have a guest novelist, one who has written about power and sex on Wall Street.

The Fitzgeralds casually poke and dig the book out from a tabletop pile as their assistant, a beautiful young woman named Tonia Foster, counts down to airtime. They receive the final signal quite casually. Another of their cats snoozes distractingly near the edge of an adjoining table as the Fitzgeralds greet their listeners.

Within a minute or two the subject moves from a new book on whether husbands can be trusted to the "fair and innocent daughters of Eve," as Ed describes streetwalkers, a considerable number of whom, Pegeen adds, "can be seen regularly on Central Park South."

"The most famous is on roller skates," she says, turning to a commercial.

•

Ed Fitzgerald sits happily in pipe smoke, adjusting his muffler, pausing like a pro while his wife reads the commercial. He is very tough. Seven years ago, when he went off for his fifth cancer operation, he cautioned his wife: "Lugubriousness does not become you." She went on cheerful, day after day, and he came back, courtly and rakish as ever. There is nothing more the Fitzgeralds ask of each other.

They have been known to bicker on the air, though with enough wit to hold their audience. He is an elementary-school dropout from Troy, N.Y., well-read and self-taught, once an actor, a Royal Air Force pilot in World War I, and a theatrical press agent. She is a former advertising copywriter who still styles her own commercials and puts her heart in her causes, especially antivivisection and ethical vegetarianism.

After all these years together the Fitzgeralds are unflappable. As she dishes out the commercials neatly, he quickly takes a one-eyed, skip-read through a big magnifying glass at a few pages of the night's featured books. He is switching from pipe to cigar as Pegeen neatly stirs up the night's novel for a minute and sends a soft lob shot across the mike. "Boudoir athletics," Ed Fitzgerald comments, getting to the heart of the matter.

"I thought I'd blush," Pegeen agrees, helping the novel along as the cats drowse and Ed puffs away, on the air.

[6/5/79]

Advance Man

Joe Canzeri, the best advance man Nelson Rockefeller ever had, darted about on his ultimate mission today, watching the mourners' cars, manning the walkie-talkie, seeing his master's ashes into the winter earth.

The burial ceremony was strikingly plain, with scores of family mourners gathering in a small corner of the riverside estate, dropping handfuls of earth onto the urn containing the last of Nelson Rockefeller. Joe Canzeri stood back and watched both as mourner and family retainer, quietly hovering about a ceremony that had the mark of directness and Rockefeller class that the former Vice President demanded every day of his public life through the efforts of unseen people like Joe Canzeri.

"When you work for Nelson Rockefeller, that's the way you do things," Joe said after the ceremony, very sad, very proud, still talking of his mission in the present tense.

The ceremony took twenty-seven minutes and was a labor of love, all within the cold, hard beauty of the hills that Mr. Rockefeller never ceased to praise and rearrange with an affection that he saw grow five generations deep. Mr. Rockefeller so savored the woodlands here as they angled down from his mansion to an unhindered view of the Hudson that he fine-tuned the vista, regularly ordering that trees be moved about, sometimes having a thick, towering growth of some decades moved only a few feet right or left to improve his impression of a glade. Recently, he had one of his outdoor sculptures, Henry Moore's "Family of Man" moved to be seen in a better winter light on his walks and horseback rides.

•

Visitors who witnessed Mr. Rockefeller rattling off orders for twenty or thirty such pastoral adjustments on a weekend marveled at his detailed love of this land and his treatment of it as an esthetic challenge. These orders, of course, were issued to Joe Canzeri, the advance man. Joe never would discuss them in detail, but he said he found this work with the land a key to understanding the complete Nelson Rockefeller.

"His heart, body and soul, his life was here," Joe said as he directed the movement of the family's sad gathering through the private heart of the estate. "No one on the outside could know. You had to see him here to really know the man."

One mourner who had regularly seen the man on his land recalled, in a sad, affectionate chat in the middle of last night, the extravagantly homey sight of Nelson Rockefeller arriving back from a workday in the city, settling down in his helicopter on the pad down from the statuary and lacy court fountain of the main estate house.

"Happy was always out on the terrace waving, with that look she has," the mourner said, speaking of Mrs. Rockefeller's smoky beauty. "And Nelson would smile and blow her a kiss." He would look about his estate, checking the trees and statuary, this mourner recalled, and relax in his luxury, telling friends, as he stared out at the Hudson, that he would want to stay there forever.

•

Nelson Rockefeller was known to treat this earth in ways both fabulous and casual. There was, for example, a midnight flight back home here from a Western political speech in which he flabbergasted aides by telephoning from his plane to someone in the federal government and having the lights on Mount Rushmore turned on. For a few minutes Mr. Rockefeller circled for a private viewing, then continued homeward. "I always figured the guy was immortal

242

after that," a companion of that night recalled today, a mourner now.

In his final place in the earth, Nelson Rockefeller arrived far less extravagantly, being placed in a cemetery glade carefully arranged down to the four seasons of trees and ground cover that are the responsibility now of the advance man, Joe Canzeri. For Mr. Canzeri, after all his years of gubernatorial and Vice Presidential "advancing" in which he saw to thousands of details in places ranging from the Mediterranean to the Finger Lakes, from the museums of Manhattan to the V.F.W. halls of the upstate stump, now is president of the Greenrock Corporation. This is the family company that operates like a village government and manages the many buildings and 3,400 acres of the fabled private world of Pocantico. He was so suited to the endless, frenetic work of advancing that other aides kidded Joe a few years back for being "put to pasture."

But he never really left advancing. And even today with his master finally at rest, Joe Canzeri was still marshaling people about. He had to marvel at how there lingered about this land the kinetic feel of Nelson Rockefeller, and all his trips through life and his breathless comments in passing.

•

This wisp of the departed seemed close by after the funeral when Mr. Rockefeller's forty-three-year-old son, Steven, was ushered down to news reporters by Joe Canzeri, the advance man. The cameramen shouted, "Rolling!" the way they had all those times for the departed father, and the son fielded questions gracefully, politely and even, at times, with a faint echo of the "Rocky" rasp. A familiar reporter put a final question, and Steven began hauntingly by pausing and saying, "Well, Gabe. . . ." And Pocantico seemed for that instant to defy the events of time.

This day, Joe Canzeri contained his grief by advancing even with his chief gone. He sent out for fried chicken for reporters out on the funeral stakeout. He instantly produced a headstone rubbing when questions arose about the final marker. He hit his walkie-talkie button to check on the widow. And then, when this was done, he began advance work on the public Rockefeller memorial ceremony Friday in Manhattan with a kind thought.

"I'm going to call together the old advance gang from the '68 campaign to work this—Nelson would like that," he said. Then, with the funeral done, Joe Canzeri darted to a waiting car and headed back up to the main house to confer with the surviving Rockefellers.

[1/30/79]

A Banquet of Dreams

The dreams of San Yan Wong are deliberately limited, he says, as he sees to the platter of squab waiting all nut-brown like toasted dwarf turkeys. Six days a week at the woks are acceptable because he is making the money for the larger dreams of his two children, he says, as his senior chef, Mr. Chao, smiles down on the platter of crisply sweet-fried walnuts and moves his cleaver like a knitting needle to make a filigree of meaty ingredients for the Three Pleasure soup.

But you never know about children, San Yan Wong says, checking his palette of cooking sauces, white, red and brown, sweet and fiery. "You want child to be success, go to college." He smiles, an honest and boyish smile for his forty-one years. "Some don't listen, have own idea, own way. Maybe be truck driver."

Well, yes, and maybe San Yan Wong's special batter fried oysters won't be devoured in less than three minutes at the New Year's banquet this night, and maybe the duck shiningly roasted in its special sauce will fly from the platter out onto Mott Street.

It is difficult to accept fatalistic talk from a man who can so control some of life's better subtleties—he knows exactly when to cease the steaming of the lobsters in his special broth of white wine and ginger.

•

Last Tuesday, the first day of the Year of the Horse on the Chinese calendar, San and Rosanna Wong's two children—five-year-old Lily and three-year-old Joseph—were permitted to come to their parents' restaurant, Hunan Garden, and stay by the front window to watch the parade and fireworks. If the Year of the Horse is to have any justice for the hard labor of the Wongs, one of the glaring lion's heads bobbing by or maybe even the parading dragon offered the two children enough of a fateful glance to drive away notions of truck driving.

The truth is, though, Mr. Wong will certainly manage to enjoy them whatever is to come through all the Years of the Horse, the Tiger, the Ram and the Hare remaining to him.

Even after all his labor of twelve-hour days at the woks, he is loving and amused, not regretful, when he discloses the first sign of the undoing of the children's palates by Western monotony: "They want McDonald's always. Big Mac."

Mr. Wong's grinning tolerance sets the New Year's mood as perfectly as does the ten-course banquet he personally prepares for his friends to celebrate the New Year. He stays in the kitchen, acting in whisks and twists and decisive flips and arranging the tones and shapes of his courses like platters of watercolors.

He cooks and appears but once during the meal to smile in his white outfit and ask how things are going, and the long table of guests, glutted and besmeared by his artistry, burst into applause as if Horowitz had just stood up from his Steinway.

•

A man named Lee taught him to cook back in China, and San Yan Wong came here in 1963. He lived alone in a room on Spring Street while he worked as a waiter. then chef, sending some money back home and saving for his own restaurant—the limited dream he is now happy with.

San Yan Wong started slowly, shakily in 1970, taking over a sliver of a restaurant at 1 Mott Street at the corner of Worth on the southern curl of Chinatown. The place was called Shanghai Town and it needed something. He put in a new menu with the Hunan emphasis of spicy garlic and pepper. Just as important, he says, he got an idea visiting a

Woolworth's lunch counter one day, and put photographs of his dishes in the menu and the front window, helping the tourists along.

Now he has bought more room in the place next door, an old Italian bar, and is very busy cooking, resting only on Thursdays. On that day he simply stays home and Rosanna cooks; or sometimes they go out to a Chinese restaurant—a Cantonese place like Hop Kee where they like the crabs and snails.

•

San Yan Wong can account for his success as he pleases. His friends at the banquet know Rosanna, his twenty-nine-year-old wife, is as big a factor as his sauces and flashing hands at the woks. She sits with the celebrants at the feast, beautiful in a European-style peasant dress, forceful as any mother in dolloping extra mushrooms and tiny pork chops and squares of bean-paste cake all around.

She had one big doubt when the whole question of marriage and migration first arose, in the brokering by letter and photograph eight years ago between China, where she was, and Chinatown, where this stranger, San Yan Wong, was working hard on his limited dreams. It concerned food, appropriately—whether she would be able to adapt to whatever America's food was. Rosanna smiles now at the irony of it, surrounded by platters of the best Chinese cooking. She has, she confesses, begun to enjoy an occasional nibble at the hamburgers her children crave.

She agrees with San Yan Wong that, the way life goes, it was easier to celebrate New Year's back in China when they were children and had nothing all year. In that context of poverty, the old New Year's treats—money envelopes from the elders, candy and meats and maybe even some new clothes—are very memorable now in this new life.

But from the opening course of eight hors d'oeuvres to the final grand and crispy yellow fish, the Wongs' banquet is not a bad substitute for poverty. The people at the table eat and drink, and wish well a missing friend in the hospital, Ken Martin, an amiable actor who cherishes San's cooking.

They make new friendships, discuss Koch's City Hall, Mao's China and San's kitchen, going forth warmly into the Year of the Horse.

[2/11/78]

7

City Lights

A Gracious Presence

The lady tourist's white hair was back-
lighted beautifully by the Manhattan sun,
and she was told so and said, "Why, thank you."

Amy Turner was polite, posing in the city for a tourist
photograph where light spilled into a point of darkness and
took the measure of her watchful face.

This was her second visit here, a lifetime enough after
the first, which was in 1911, when she was twenty-eight
years old. When you hear the range of dates she discusses—
1853: her pioneer grandparents from Sweden homestead in
Minnesota territory; 1882: she is born in the thriving
Minnesota farmhouse of the Turner clan—it feels as if
unseen stars wheel above the city's sunlight and make her
tour special and solitary.

For a ninety-six-year-old woman, it's hardly a passive
tour. There was the United Nations last Wednesday, the
Metropolitan Museum of Art on Thursday and the American Museum of Natural History on Friday, Lincoln Center
and the ballet on Saturday and services at the modernistic
chapel of St. Peter's Lutheran Church in the Citicorp
Building on Sunday, followed by a Staten Island ferry ride
in which the captain invited her to the bridge.

Yesterday was an open day, to give Miss Turner time to
hone an edge back onto her cane, and today she flies back to
Minnesota, with the unseen stars still wheeling overhead.

The city is graced by Miss Turner's gaze, and especially
by her open mind, in which she doesn't work up to a lot of
superlatives about all the new things she is seeing, the
artifacts and peacemaking scraps, the perishable buildings

and people. Instead, the city gets treated like the black-loam country back home in St. Peter, Minn., where, before she left, a farmer-cousin informed her that the corn was knee-high and doing well.

"I didn't see any knee-high corn," Miss Turner says objectively, peering across the visitors' lobby of the United Nations. "I suppose it all depends on where your knee is."

•

So, obviously, there will be none of the I-Love-New-York tourist hype from Miss Turner, and the unalloyed truth that some New Yorkers wish they knew may have a chance of getting back out West.

Miss Turner is luckier than most tourists. She is not staying in one of those hotels where visitors venture out in their walking shorts and sandals and have to step around a wino congealing on the sidewalk. Miss Turner is staying in Stuyvesant Town with her relatives, Charles Voss and his wife, Ingrid Pierson Voss. They are quiet book- and museum-loving New Yorkers, shrewd enough to know how to get a window table at the delegates' restaurant at the United Nations and humble enough to be delighted by Miss Turner's blood-kin presence in their town.

Her earlier visit sounds quick as a snapshot. She came east sixty-eight years ago with her cousin Esther Turner to visit some relatives named Steele who were stationed at Fort Totten in Queens.

"I remember I overslept and the porter had to wake me up as we came into the city," Miss Turner says. "We stayed at Fort Totten, but took a trip by subway to the Russian quarter to buy some brass things."

"I remember doing this," Miss Turner says, holding her nose closed defensively, "when we walked by all these pushcarts. The food on the pushcarts couldn't have been very fresh. We saw one play, 'The Pink Lady.'"

Miss Turner stops. That's it, her 1911 visit. None of that business of bumping into Diamond Jim Brady or Lillie Langtry the way authentic characters on public television always do in old New York. No talk about never forgetting whoever was the toast of Broadway that summer, or sensing the clouds of war gathering.

•

Amy Turner yields nothing but her own truth, and what she really knows is the old farm life back home, now subsumed by the combines, and her old insurance-office career back in St. Peter, and fifty years of Sunday Bible class and socials—a pleasing skein of time that ended when others, not Miss Turner, faded. Nowadays on Sundays in her apartment at Fourth and Myrtle in St. Peter, Miss Turner listens to three radio shows: the Bible show, the Scandinavian hour and the United Nations report.

"I wanted to be sure to see the U.N.; it didn't exist when I was here last," Miss Turner says, sitting in the delegates' dining room, a comfortable, aimlessly busy place where swords seem to have been beaten into gravy moats.

"I read the Reader's Digest," Miss Turner says when asked about world affairs. "I don't believe everything. Sometimes I get scared. Sometimes you wonder what's going to happen."

Miss Turner is as succinct a tourist as has ever come to summarize the general routine of the world: Wonder some, get scared occasionally, don't believe everything.

•

Miss Turner has brought ninety-six years and a sense of Minnesota to the city. Had you met her on the 20th Street crosstown bus as she headed out to another sight, she would have chatted politely about her life. She'd have told you how she lived alone, gardening, sewing quilts for welfare families and cooking for guests. On special dinner occasions, she decks out the table with brass finger bowls she bought in 1911 in the shop that was past the smelly pushcarts in New York City.

If you ask, she will offer reassurances about the city. "We can have bad things happen in small towns, too, you know," she said. "Teen-agers in St. Peter have been very naughty. They spray-painted the statue of Gov. John A. Johnston, a very, very fine person."

Miss Turner takes life in undramatic, savory morsels, like the chocolate cake she enjoyed at the Metropolitan Museum of Art. Heading home Tuesday, she may leave a few New Yorkers more reassured about the general routine of the world, which, as we now realize, is to wonder some, be scared sometimes and not believe everything.

[6/26/79]

Expressive Diagonals

Edward Hopper is ten years dead and gone from his skylighted studio at 3 Washington Square North, and professors talk about sociology there now in the great wash of light that flows down through the slope of roof glass. Hopper spent fifty years in that light, silently making paintings about the heart of this city, showing people and places defined in solitude and in great angled planes of color and shade.

"Alienation . . . loneliness . . . diagonals of expression. . . ." A group of attentive women stare at a Hopper painting as their guide at the Kennedy Galleries, on West 57th Street, speaks her ideas on why he is worthy. The painting on the wall, "Hotel Room," has isolated a woman in herself, seated on a bed in her slip, staring down at a letter she has read, her face almost lost in shadow, the room a pattern of yellow window shade, white wall, brown furniture. Hopper has made receptively plain things into an abstraction, like the unfolded yellow message that has transfixed the woman.

The gallery's walls are filled with Hopper oils, watercolors and etchings. A new young generation is coming by in crowds to discover them, even as Europeans are starting to buy them, according to Lawrence A. Fleischman, who arranged the Kennedy show with great affection for the artist he knew and used to visit on Washington Square.

•

"Hopper was as sparse verbally as he was in his painting," Mr. Fleischman says, imitating the tall artist poised slightly over his cane as he sat with a visitor. "Observing the man was akin to observing his paintings."

The paintings seem to use city light to slow time down, getting eternity into a slash of shadow and catching the special sort of urban crankiness and loneliness of a half-turned-away face.

There was a man who might have appealed to Hopper's eye sitting across from the Washington Square studio the other day—an old man on a bench, his face half-averted downward as he plucked at something unseen on his shirtfront.

In the paintings, Hopper put his thoughts in old storefronts, roofs, hotels, a desolate cafeteria, city buildings bare and sun-washed as adobes, and always a few people caught isolated in the city. He painted an office at night with a man and woman dealing with papers and, perhaps, some fathomless intimacy.

The gallery world of 57th Street, where his paintings are being shown, does not seem like a Hopper street. At midday, there are little pools of stark shadow, it's true, but they are cast by the awnings—Jasper, Wally Findlay, Henri Bendel—that march along elegantly, and Hopper liked his store windows treasureless.

The front window of Public School 59, on 57th between Second and Third Avenues, may come closer, with a paste-up student painting of a city street. There are odd flat buildings in it, and the figures, while smiling too much for Hopper, seem worth thinking about.

•

"She was very lonely that last year," says Joseph J. Roberto of Mrs. Hopper, the painter Josephine Verstille Nivison, who died a year after her husband. Mr. Roberto, the staff architect of New York University, admired Hopper and quietly observed the two painters in their late years, when the university acquired the Washington Square property.

"She didn't have many visitors," says Mr. Roberto, who points to traces of yellow paint on the stair-runners leading to the fourth-floor studios. "Hopper painted them bright for her. She had cataracts and didn't see too well late in life."

In the south studio, a gray room about 35 feet square, a sociology professor sits by a window and looks up from conversation. So does her companion, as a visitor sees Hopper's big easel, which he made himself, forgotten in a far corner and decorated with plants.

Through an open doorway is the north studio, the same size, with its own skylight, and here Mrs. Hopper painted. Between the two artists stood a closet-sized kitchen space. Painting was their world here, obviously all there was for years and years. What has happened to this world? Are its remains gathered for sale now up on 57th Street?

"I have his palette," Mr. Roberto says, leading the way up from the studio to the roof of 3 Washington Square North. A dim passage, a door is opened and, like flash powder in an old photograph, the sunlight bursts outside in great angles and planes off a great chunk of the world of Edward Hopper.

A very special part of his city paintings focused on this very rooftop, and here, as he painted them, are the same vent pipes poking upward and the sloped and oblong masses of the stairwell entries and the outer side of the skylight that shed so much force down to Hopper over the years. It is like finding a still-life fruit bowl, brilliant and vital fifty years after an artist painted it.

Hopper once tried to summarize his sparse style: "What I wanted to do was paint sunlight on the side of a house." The light descends to the studio a decade after the eighty-five-year-old Hopper died down there, and it seems *his* light and *his* rooftop still. Mr. Roberto, squinting in the blade-like sunlight that casts shafts of shade about the roof, takes out a sheet of paper listing Hopper's last studio possessions and wonders whether he should try to piece them together as a museum.

The list is as spare and mysterious as a Hopper painting: "Clock. Easel. Upholstered chair. File cabinet with folders of information collected by Hopper. . . ." And not much more.

[5/31/79]

Ladies' Haven

There are all kinds of bromides printed on the walls of the tenement building: "Love and never count the cost." And: "Go without fear into the depth of men's hearts."

This is the sort of suspect advice that earns sidelong glances from any New Yorker with a job and debts. What is the angle here? Who figures to gain? Reasonable New York questions from the depth of the average peddler's heart, the heart that knows Christmas is O.K. if you have a credit card that clears the computer.

Last Christmas, before they got the tenement and started writing neatly about love on the walls, four women had reached a certain level of what they considered progress in deliberately becoming poor. They were nuns, who began as the kind you once could safely spot in nun outfits. "Fifteen years ago it was all very nunny," one of them says. But they were dissatisfied and so went and got their own apartment in a Hell's Kitchen walkup.

Their salaries as nursing nuns over at St. Clark's Hospital might total $60,000 a year in money value, but the four agreed to take only $9,000 total for their fulltime work. For four adults this is poverty by the federal standard. The problem is the women are not interested in federal standards of poverty; they care about the standards of a very strange and strong-willed Italian, Giovanni Francesco Bernadone, who shamed some of the materialist preoccupations of Christians seven centuries ago. Since then his image has been sainted and rather unfairly idyllicized into a man called Francis of Assisi.

This man did weird things like throwing away family belongings and squatting with the lepers and with the beggars on the steps of St. Peter's in Rome. Today, this would be like curling up on a bus terminal bench with a shopping-bag lady, which is what two of these nuns were doing last summer when they were puzzling out what their poverty vow should mean in the modern vale of tears, commercial jingles and packaged charity.

•

So they got the tenement building on West 40th Street near the bus terminal, which was no great loss for the owner, the Archdiocese of New York, since the building was a breezy rattrap. There are six nuns now, handsomely plain women who behave like antidotes to the Cosmo girl. They sleep on floor pallets at the top of the tenement and read and pray alone and together beginning at 5:30 every morning. Four go to work as nurses and the two others run the tenement as a haven for shopping-bag ladies, feeding and cleaning them up, talking to them during a two-week respite from the streets, watching over them through a safe night's sleep.

As "the ladies" (the nuns hate welfare words like "clients") lumber into the tenement with their shopping bags every afternoon, the scene seems more Fellini than Francis.

A shriveled, spunky woman named Ida who has no teeth and who has a misleading witch's grin and whiskers is stretched out with a blanket on the couch, cozy and chatty as a little girl at her counterpane, with her feet cradled in the lap of Holly, a quiet young woman recuperating from bad foot sores, who is leafing through People magazine. A woman in a wool cap sits silent with her hands on her face, and another bears an unchanging expression of crankiness, as if life were one long line at the motor vehicle bureau.

"You're not Eddie Cantor's Ida?" asks Gloria, a stub of a woman who looks dressed by Carson McCullers, in sneakers, and a flouncy satin dress. Ida's chisel chin flails the air: "Oh, honey, I wish I was. 'Ida, sweet as apple ci-hi-

hi-der.''" They are socializing before supper, a humble inviting buffet of stew, fresh cornbread and apple pie, the works of a volunteer, Jerry Williams, who runs the kitchen on Mondays.

•

Everything is charity at the tenement, now known as the Dwelling Place, at 409 West 40th Street. The ladies are clothed in castoffs and fed with canned-food donations. The tools and materials for renovating much of the building were written off by Bill Straight, a local hardware dealer. Volunteer aides come in as individuals and from organizations like "Dignity," a charity-oriented group of Roman Catholic male homosexuals.

All six nuns are busy with the ladies at night, and the one sort of volunteer they urgently need is a nightwatch person to ease some of the exhaustion of having a nun on duty around the clock. They have beds for twenty-three ladies, but let the overflow sleep in chairs. They know the ropes of the welfare bureaucracy and try to help the ladies straighten out their government doles.

•

But the nuns keep no records and have no success tale to tell beyond offering a note of temporary community and affection to the ladies. Sister Ann Regina says the experience has made the nuns' vows "truer," and she shrewdly knows the thing to avoid now is letting the place become enlarged and institutionalized. "It all has to do with being spent and given," Sister Regina says, a description that in a way equates the nuns with the ladies.

"One night in the living room, we were all together having a good time and one of the ladies was babbling to herself," Sister Regina says. "Another lady said across to her, 'Hey, no matter what you're talking about, we love you.'"

That statement, of course, is as strange as some of the things written on the walls of the tenement.

[12/13/77]

A Touch of Humbug

It is not easy being good for goodness' sake. "You should forgive my language," said Santa Claus. "But I think the Mayor should get those Krishna Santas the hell off the streets."

Such talk from a red-suited man with more of a glare than a twinkle in his eye was not so much heresy as confirmation of the Dickens perspective: We must be human before we can be even momentarily joyous.

This Santa, a surrogate of the Volunteers of America named Bob McKean, was manning his chimney post on the north side of Rockefeller Plaza the other night and telling how the Christmas begging business had been cheapened, in his eyes, by the rival Santas of the Hare Krishna sect.

"Ho, ho, ho. Ho, ho, Hare!" the nearby Krishna man was shouting, blending two traditions in his jolliness and attracting considerable attention by giving away free candy as he begged.

The Krishna Santa had three round dabs of rouge on his cheeks and nose that gave him mostly a wooden-soldier look. On the other hand, Mr. McKean's outfit included a white hairnet holding his beard in place, so they were a draw on the authenticity scale. But the Krishna Santa was free to work the crowd, while Mr. McKean had to stay by his chimney where, it should be noted, he was tireless in being friendly toward the children nudged into his clutch by parents. Dispatching one tot with vaguely happy promises, Santa eyed his rival.

"These clowns are taking the spirit from Christmas," he declared. "Anyone can put on a Santa outfit and solicit."

He kept working hard, though, and three shy young brothers eventually calmed him down to the point where he wished a lingering adult all the best.

•

Whatever else is in the air, the burnished-coin smell of competition wafts about the city at Christmastide.

Down on Broome Street, the caged turkeys in Cocozziello's sixty-four-year-old live-poultry shop made sounds that were less traditional gobble than vague cooings and murmurings. It was as if they grasped the complaint of one of the family proprietors, Armando, that frozen fowl termed "butterballs" were proving more popular at pervasive places named Grand Union and A&P.

Unhappy with what supermarkets have done to his business, Mr. Cocozziello told of the horse-and-wagon boom times of his father when the poultry moved through in a nervous profitable parade. He lives in the building like a good Dickensian shopkeeper, but don't count on throwing open your window Christmas morning and hailing an urchin to fetch you a fat goose from Cocozziello's. "No, we don't stock geese anymore," he said. "Those pinfeathers are murder."

•

Travel with us, now, to a modest home in Astoria, Queens, where little Elizabeth Fuldi wept and wept as her mother explained what a strike meant the other night when the musicians' silence at the New York City Ballet deprived the ten-year-old girl of her dream of dancing the featured princess role in "The Nutcracker" at Lincoln Center. Hard feelings were understandable, and her mother, Nohemy, consoled her.

"She has been crying, 'Oh, Mommy, Mommy, I can't believe it! Why have they done this to me?' " Mrs. Fuldi related. The mother said there could be no Christmas for Elizabeth until the strike ended and the dance went on.

"I explain to her that they want more money, and that this is the season to push," Mrs. Fuldi said.

•

Walter B. Wriston oversees great amounts of money as chairman of Citibank, but, as his many friends can testify, this hardly qualifies him as a modern-day Scrooge. Yet this is the view Sol Sitzer takes of him as he stands at the bar in Jax 3 Ring Circus on East 53rd Street and fights an eviction order that he and his nearly naked female dancers be gone within the next week or so.

"Get rid of those massage parlors!" Mr. Wriston is reliably reported to have demanded of subordinates when construction started on the new Citibank headquarters across the street. In Mr. Sitzer's telling, it was as if Mr. Wriston was denying an extra lump of coal to lesser businessmen chilled by life and needing momentary warmth.

Actually, Citibank, which has been buying up the block to weed out the fleshly enterprises, does not own Mr. Sitzer's building, not yet. But he contends the pressure to get out is clearly tracked to the powerful Mr. Wriston.

"I bank at Citibank," Mr. Sitzer said over the thumping music in his topless bar. He contended that Citibank executives used to drop by until the trouble. Much of the crowd this night was gray-suited and businesslike, but there was no way of knowing where they were from. The owner spoke of a $100,000 debt he has on the place, and he was so nervous that he had no eye for the six young women who sat separately on tabletops and writhed only inches from smiling seated drinkers.

It was a different sort of sugarplum dance and the scene seemed more heh, heh, heh than ho, ho, ho. But Mr. Sitzer said that it was not vile, whatever Mr. Wriston feels, and that the fight was dispiriting for him and his customers, some of whom carried Christmas presents for their loved ones.

•

A Christmas pilgrim numbed by the season's complicated clash of unhappiness and pleasure repaired to St. Patrick's Cathedral last Wednesday evening.

The créche was up but empty. The religious-articles

store was crowded, but most visitors knelt quietly in pews. Up front at the altar, a priest celebrating mass took up the scripture and repeated a familiar promise:

"The Lord is coming and will not delay. He will bring every living thing to light."

[12/16/76]

The Falling Conqueror

The Chicken Little factor had become enor·
mous from all the weekend weather fore·
casting so that by the time the first flakes hit, they seemed a
pleasant dusting on all the accumulations of fallen sky
invoked down on us by hot-combed weathermen.

But by 10 A.M., the snow was taking hold of the city
sideways, leaving all the people waiting for the Q-8 bus on
Sutphin Boulevard and Archer Avenue in Queens hunker-
ing bitterly and breathing into their own clothing in the
doorway of Henry's liquor store.

"Ladies and gentlemen, excuse me," a lean, poorly
dressed man said, moving like a squirrel from Henry's,
clutching a bagged bottle like a fresh acorn. Across the
slippery sidewalk the man kept carefully in step with his
different drummer, and the envy of the watching bus people
could only be estimated as they stayed wretchedly to their
appointed rounds.

The man with the fresh bottle got into a waiting car,
which immediately lurched off like a motor launch into the
churning traffic. By the time the Q-8 finally came, the man
with the bottle was way ahead of the crowd in Henry's
doorway in coping with the second great storm of this
winter.

•

All over the city, the imperative of going through the
motions was enormously complicated and profitless. Pictur-
esque futility was the best that could be had, a mood
summarized a few doors down from Henry's in the outdoor
bin of the Jamaica and West Indian Fruit Market, where

bright tangelos and honey grapefruits were rimmed in white still life by the snow.

Around the corner, Looney & Burke's bar had five whisky drinkers up front, all of them staring warm and wet out the little patch of a window at the snow raking down through the green skeleton of the abandoned subway el. All down the boulevard, separate necessities brought different groups of strangers together through the snow.

At the OTB parlor near Hillside Avenue, people with cash in hand were willing to bet that somewhere out there horses were running. "You want to put him with For Your Pleasure," a sleepy-faced man advised a woman in a rain bonnet as she slogged through handicapper's fineprint in the racing form.

Through the snow, the black hole of the row of Sutphin Boulevard bureaucracies—the Motor Vehicle Bureau—had enough clerks at work to keep all its circular lines and sublines moving, and the public chattered sheeplike holding bent license plates and spindled forms.

•

A block farther on, the strangest wintry silence could be witnessed indoors, for the morning lot of unemployment recipients were dutifully at their bureaucracy in long, correct lines, tightly holding yellow records that obviously were needed for another round of checks. Through long minutes the lines stayed virtually silent, and the people seemed uniformly passive, young and old, black and white together. The man from Henry's was needed here.

In from Queens, the great veils of snow wrapped around the sparse lunch-hour crowd on Brooklyn's Court Street, and their passage was a great Platonic shadow show for those on the warm side of the long, evenly steamed windows of the Chock Full O' Nuts. The waitresses, normally aloof as this chain goes, were standing about in two's and three's, laughing a bit more, it seemed, ladling extra bits of shrimp into the 55-cent cardboard bowls of seafood chowder.

Wiping a peekhole in the window steam, you could see

three heavy women laughing as they slid and stepped by, and outside the laughter of the woman in the middle could be heard above the wind. They went into Lamston's and ordered ten breasts of fried chicken at the takeout counter, but the counter had mostly legs. "The storm got the chicken man all fouled up," the counterman explained.

Lawyers were everywhere, half-coated like different trees in a storm-blown forest. A Kunstler-looking type moved past with his gray mane freeze-dried and snow napping into his fur collar; a well-tailored woman with a legal briefcase bent into a doorway on Remsen Street for a minute and said one word to no one: "Reprieve."

•

Down below the deepening snow, in one of the tunnels of the city, an afternoon Dyre Avenue express had its whole nature altered by the storm. Heading north under Lexington Avenue, this express train was suddenly changed to a local at 14th Street, crossing the track switch in darkness and moving to a platform jammed with angry passengers. They packed aboard like the drifts above, and instantly panic threatened as someone lost a shoe and a woman who had been standing stylishly in ski clothes was dumped onto a seated man trying to read Virginia Woolf.

"They revert to animals!" declared one man, frozen in a leaning tower of flesh.

"They were animals when they got on," his hard-pressed companion interjected.

By the Bronx, the coming and going mass had mostly popped out of the cars and there, in the snow at Alexander Avenue and 138th Street, a wall of eerily beautiful color was visible—a gray-red stone twenty stories high composed from the towers of the Mitchel public houses slicing through the snow torrent. A woman stepped out from the gray-red wall and in an instant her Afro hairdo was handsomely highlighted in white and she moved forward, taking this second snowstorm in bent stride.

[2/7/78]

Signs of Spring

The woman stood out like a disheveled robin under the sad marquee of the Strand Hotel, a transient place on West 43rd Street, and as good a spot as any to sense the first sign of spring in the city.

The woman startled a passing man-child by asking, "Hey, honey, want to go out tonight?" The wording of the proposition had a charm reminiscent of the 1940's movie code. If the woman had been wearing a suit with shoulder pads and her hair across one eye instead of one of those Times-Square-Fellini outfits, the man-child might have paused.

He moved on by, but tried to keep the spirit of the new season he sensed in the air by plagiarizing a fine urban cartoonist, Mark Stamaty, and telling the woman, "No, thank you, I have to wash my hair tonight."

•

Spring is a time to do something about the city's rocks. Dr. Alfred Jones, a clinical psychologist on Central Park West, is horrified at what the graffiti vandals do to the rocks and walls of the park, spraying fluorescent ego-droppings on them.

For five years, he has mixed a batch of "rock-colored" paint and gone over and painted out the graffiti.

"I've been making mental notes lately as I walk, seeing what needs touching up," Dr. Jones says. Soon he will be stirring a fresh batch of rock paint for that annual moment, as a Middle English lyric puts it, "when spray beginneth to springe."

Spring is a fresh flowing of the city's commercial juices. At Gimbels' cosmetics section, some old women and a few younger ones gather round a counter to get free dabs of something called Line Tamer, a new concoction that, at $18 a quarter-ounce, promises to get rid of wrinkles for periods of several hours at a time, long enough to indulge a dream.

Hope is thrust forward with closed eyes as an old woman leans to receive the ministrations of the saleswoman. Tall, black and youthfully beautiful, the saleswoman gently handles the old lady's face, powdery white as a bun, while the others watch for a miracle.

Up the street at Macy's, there is an acre of such preening—twenty counters for women and six for men where all sorts of sniffing and dabbing and mirror-watching goes on. One beautifying section has hydraulic chairs that can be cranked back, and a woman is being worked on there in a scene that suggests old paintings of early barber surgery.

•

Of all the urban signs of spring, the saddest is the misplaced Saturnalia that takes place among some of the youngsters attracted by the St. Patrick's Day parade. Yesterday, you could see a number of them carrying their own beer and wine, drinking it blocks away from the parade, as they passed through the bus and commuter-railroad terminals from the suburbs. One young man in dungaree-and-down-vest uniform carried an entire case of Lowenbrau up from the Long Island Rail Road asking where the parade was.

•

Some New Yorkers will get out of their cars to look for spring. There are people out by the Rockaways who take a drive to avoid winter cabin fever. They stop by the shore at the Cross Bay bridge, staying in their cars and thinking about the ocean, themselves and other passing phenomena. They try to park facing the meager winter sun to let it flood through the windshield onto their faces, and you can see some of them tilt their heads back like cats to let the sunlight stroke under their chins.

Last weekend, they began venturing out of their cars in noticeable numbers and going down to the water's edge in person. One of them saw a man with a green bucket clamming, and walked over. They exchanged silence and quick glances as impassively as midtown pedestrians—a good reminder that the city had not turned into New England during the winter.

Along the shore dead beach grass seemed to have been threshed beautifully by the months of winter tides and on top of it you could see another sign of spring, the first strewing of fresh plastic wrappings from a fast-food store down the road.

•

Spring in the city is a consumer warning from NORML, the organization of marijuana proponents, that the latest crops of Mexican pot have been sprayed with the herbicides paraquat and 2, 4-D. Not only is the marijuana dangerous, the warning notes, it is also yellowish. "Since good-quality marijuana is also often gold in color, the potential for confusion is obvious."

The sobering words are a good grafting of two concerns of some concrete-bound city dwellers, ecology and grass, and their hopes that spring be heavy, far-out, not silent.

•

Spring in the city is the sound of a power saw, distant and unrecognized at first, as it bites into the decades-old sycamore in the backyard of Paul Gilbert's apartment house on Macdougal Street. He goes to the window. "I haven't been that distraught since my divorce," he says. "They were mutilating a tree that is the heart of greenery for the building, as much a part of my apartment as the furniture."

He quickly flings forth stinging phone calls and actually gets through to the director of the New York Botanical Garden in the Bronx, who expresses shock and promises to come by some time. More impressively, he gets through to the building agent and minutes later the sawing is stopped, with ten limbs gone from the tree.

Spring is Mr. Gilbert's feeling of moderate success as he looks out his window. But spring in the city can also be a doubling back on life, and two days later, when Mr. Gilbert is out, the rest of the tree limbs are cut off. "Dear God," he says, well out of the winter now and depressed.

[3/18/78]

A Holy Place

The women were silent and out of sight in a draped section at the back of the bus as the men from the diamond district got aboard for the commuters' ride home to the suburbs.

It was 6:30 in the evening at Fifth Avenue and West 47th Street and one of the men already was reading the books of Moses and the weekly commentary, moving his lips and nodding intently up front opposite the bus driver, Bernard Lichter.

The commuters, Hasidic Jews with thick beards and long black coats and round hats, chatted in groups around the bus seats, angling toward one another like figures in a dark Rembrandt.

Friesel Mates, the Mayor of their destination, New Square village in Rockland County, had closed his travel agency in time for the homebound bus and he greeted friends and neighbors as they settled down. Everything was in order. There was a shush of brakes being released and the bus moved out on the private nightly run from the diamond district, a seventy-five-minute routine now for eighteen years.

Mr. Lichter handled the wheel easily. On the panel behind him, where you might expect to see a fire extinguisher, the protective ark containing the sacred Torah scroll was bolted and covered with a blue curtain, a small handsome fixture that made the bus a holy place as it cut across town to the Lincoln Tunnel.

"Can't you get any closer, Bernie?" Samuel A. Weissmandl, the Mayor's administrative assistant, was kidding the driver who was so close behind a public transit bus creeping into the tunnel that you could study the napes of the necks of the back row travelers ahead.

"You know you could walk home, Sam," Bernie replied. Sam smiled.

•

A New Square resident, Isaac Rottenberg, sat opposite Sam, periodically telling him a tale of woe. The town tax assessors had revised upward their estimate of the value of his home. He thought they were foolish and wanted to fight them. Patiently, Sam listened to his problem and told him the correct way for trying to resist.

"But you must remember, if you don't bother to file a grievance form right now and then you try to fight it in court, the lawyer will tell you no, no chance, because of the form." Sam stressed this as the traffic eased outward through New Jersey.

•

The bus ride was serving its purpose of community solidarity. A little government business, a little business business, some kidding and small talk and, at the proper juncture, as the greenery thickened to the north, the mincha, the afternoon prayer required of the fervently orthodox Hasidim. Twelve hours earlier, it was the shachris, the morning prayer, intoned in the bus from across the centuries. Breakfast, simple and quick, followed.

This way, the Hasidim honored their God as they made the round trip from the sanctuary of New Square. By material suburban standards, it is a rather humble place where they feel safer and happier in their special religious and cultural enclave.

•

Morris Spitzer, a diamond merchant who at fifty years of age has gray fighting the red in his beard, looked very relaxed on the evening ride. The hum and rumble of the bus made people in conversation lean closer, and Mr. Spitzer spoke of his past.

He came to this country from Hungary, freed from a

Nazi death camp at the end of the war. His is a great family tradition of watchmakers and jewelers and his snowy bearded, eighty-year-old father, Benjamin, still does a bit of his fine hand work up in New Square.

Eighteen years ago, when Morris Spitzer had a jewelry shop on Delancey Street, he became frightened about the increasingly threatened atmosphere of his home neighborhood in Williamsburg. He took a little country vacation in New Square, just then being incorporated by the Hasidim, and he felt such a relief that he never moved back to Brooklyn.

As the bus once again carries him on this treasured exodus, he proudly notes that his seven children and his twenty grandchildren all reside in New Square, hardly tempted to disperse to more secular places. "If you gave them gold, they wouldn't move," he says as the bus races north past bands of shopping malls and woods.

Mr. Spitzer spends his day on West 47th Street, a member of the diamond club of wholesalers, and he loves his work. "It's very exciting," he says, his beard framing high cheekbones and a steady gaze. "It requires a lot of knowledge. I have to know the stones. I have to know the cutters. And my customers. The diamond business works only on reputation. In diamonds, you need peace of mind. One little mistake and a fortune is lost."

There is no difficulty, he says, in the daily transition from prayers to diamonds and back again, from midtown commerce to exurban peace. "I know exactly what I work for," he says. "I know my children are safe, physically and spiritually."

•

A candle is lit on the bus and the men pray mincha, together yet each alone. An older man shuts his eyes tightly and presses his fist to the window and his forehead to his fist as if the bus itself were some sort of spiritual conductor. A short man, eyes closed, arms folded, rocks in a davening reverie. Behind the curtain segregating the few women travelers, a baby cries briefly. Sam, the helpful village bureaucrat, removes the village hall beeper signal from his belt, puts on the gartel, a thin black cincture, and prays.

The bus is soon in New Square, and the men are greeted by children from their large families. The children seem particularly innocent in the dusk as they watch and walk with their fathers, the long black coats stark against the green lawns, and go home together for supper.

[6/16/77]

A Day at Orchard Beach

Barefooted and facing away from the urban pueblos of Co-op City, the ten-speed-bike couple carry their bicycles onto the beach and feel yesterday's warmth in the morning sand.

There is some jagged beer-bottle glass over by the pavilion, but the Orchard Beach cleanup crews are wending their way back to it and by the time the families arrive in numbers this precious, durable cusp of the Bronx is resurrected again, tough as a vacant lot or a pirate's cove.

The first of the families arrive in a car crammed with vittles and children, and in the clear air of the morning the woman of the household uses the word "nigger" endearingly.

"There's your typical nigger," the black woman, attractive in a yellow outfit, says, gesturing in mock despair to her husband as he unloads a cornucopia on the parking-lot walkway. "Drops us and runs."

One of the older children smiles. The husband replies with a sunglass stare of satisfaction and goes off alone to park the car, leaving his beloveds to trek down to the sand with all manner of hampers, coolers, blankets, chairs, hats and lotions.

•

On the beach, the ten-speed couple have chained their bikes to a metal trashbasket down by the tide and they poke their ankles into the water, touching and talking. They are not just white people. They are city-white people, bleached from winter, coltish and vulnerable in the hot sun. Even though the sand is almost deserted, they seem searching for privacy.

Off the south end of the quarter-mile pavement bordering the beach, a scattering of men, most of them of Hispanic origin, have gone out on the rock jetty with fishing gear and settled quietly, ignoring a warning sign: "Peligro. No vaja las rocas." The men are right; the rocks look comfortable, not dangerous, particularly in comparison with parts of the Bronx mainland.

Orchard Beach is not where most city-dwellers go to be touched by the ocean, but it gets its tens of thousands every hot weekend day, a sometimes idyllically integrated crowd of the lower middle class and the poor, turning their backs on the city and being spared the rigamarole of getting to more distant, more stylish beaches.

Early last Monday, there is a faint burnt almond smell over the sand from the city dump not too far away on the horizon, but this peels away along with the mist that made the water glassy. The morning tide has raked the lower beach into soothing striations. If you crop your view a bit, eliminating the "Peligro" sign, and keep City Island's boat pilings in the background beyond the reed grass and fluted sand and fishermen, Orchard Beach looks like some of New England.

There is the whirr of a fishing line being cast, the plunk of the lure into the water, the caw of a dump gull. But then there is a jet plane, curving down toward Queens, sighing like a great crowd. And two joggers bob past, looking smug in their mania for immortality.

•

The first lifeguard arrives and climbs a gray wooden tower chair, opening out an orange and green umbrella that glows rich as a lawyer's shingle. He hunkers down under it, all mustache and sunglasses and passivity. Further along, a second lifeguard settles in like a raccoon, fidgeting with all sorts of sacks and vials, hanging his radio just so on the chair.

It is tuned to a disco song, "Come On and Dance with

Me," which already seems to have that special summer music virtue of shimmering well across beach blankets.

The arriving human mix is going well. Numerous blankets are being carefully fluttered to the sand and anchored with socks and shoes.

Back in the picnic area, large families, including separate black, Italian and Latin groups within the same stretch of tree shade, are laying claim to double-table spreads, putting down table cloths and raising the first barbecue smoke of the day. In the direct sun, two older Jewish couples, tan and thriving, talk in a semicircle of folding chairs they have carried with them.

Five police officers arrive to open the day's precinct outpost. Four are in uniform and the fifth might prove convincing in his undercover beach mufti, for though he wears a dated looking football jersey, it covers a summer-looking beer belly. Two of the officers soon emerge on motor-scooters and putt away on their rounds.

"Mama! Mama, call Ella," a teen-aged girl shouts furiously to her mother, and Ella, a younger child, has to retreat to the picnic as the older sister and two friends roam off in great sophistication.

By 11 A.M., all sorts of foods are on the fire, and bodies are dipping into the ocean, and forty handball courts are popping with sweaty contests over by the parking lot.

That song blares again. "I can make your dreams come true . . ." and a mint-fresh young woman comes prancing along on platform-espadrilles that give her the nubile posture of a roadster hood ornament. "Come On and Dance with Me."

The ten-speed couple cannot be located easily because so many people have arrived and flopped down. The couple are found, flat out by the chained bikes, lightly touching, murmuring, risking their city-white legs as the sun pours onto Orchard Beach.

[6/1/78]

Requiem for Mike

There is no such thing as a tavern in grief. But Reif's bar, a temptingly dingy and odiferous working-class place on East 92d Street had to put up a sign after the police told what had happened to Mike Russek.

The sign said, "Mike the Polack, alias Mike the Window Washer—Mike Russek—died at his trade and has no family. He will be laid out on his birthday, Jan. 4."

All the regular drinkers pushed a dollar bill or two across to Bob Reif, who was close to Mike, and they said a word to Theresa Reif, Bob's mother, who knew Mike at her place for over thirty years. She had watched him clean and mop up through the rich Sunday morning brew smell of a bar at rest. She had watched him sit alone in the back room with his wine and club soda, watching cartoons and sit-coms on his own little TV set. Once in a while she saw him privately sobbing—a very small, obviously necessary part of his life of being pleasant and meaning no harm.

He died in a better part of town, forty-five blocks due south. It was there his barrel-chested strut and waved greeting, accented by the bucket, squeegee and chamois tucked under his arm, were known to most good shop-keepers, residents and service workers in this fancy-apartment neighborhood.

Mario Marsala, Mike's close friend and a doorman at 10 Mitchell Place, near 49th Street, was crossing First Avenue and saw the police cars and ambulance outside No. 865, a red brick tower, where he knew Mike was washing windows.

"He landed on his back," Mr. Marsala said. "Eleven stories. Everything was broken. The cops couldn't find any relatives. He was a simple man, good company. I really liked the little guy."

The doorman was recalling this in the little basement service kitchen of his building where he would cook a special evening meal for Mike and himself every day after Mike finished the window washing.

"The last one was pork chops with a white wine sauce and small potatoes," Mr. Marsala said. "Sometimes I'd put a little placecard for laughs—'Mike the King'—and he liked that."

Mike Russek was always striking up friendships from small talk and going on and telling strange stories, often about pet animals he loved on some farm long ago. Usually his mother in the story would cook the pet for food. His friends were not sure what to believe in the stories, but they listened and talked to him, and most put credence in the one about someone who, Mike said, struck him on the side of the head with a rock and left him a little funny so he had to leave school.

Mr. Marsala had to do the final identification of Mike's body through a little window at the morgue, and he knew that the only thing left was to see that Mike, who died poor at age fifty-five, got a decent funeral, and a burial better than Potter's Field. He went uptown—a journey from one lone hamlet to another by Manhattan's way of life—and met Bob Reif, and they went to see Mike's furnished room. It had large holy pictures all over, and they found pay stubs showing how little Mike had made for decades of washing windows with the same company.

They said it was good he had quit the company a few weeks before he died. He enlisted his own regular customers who liked him and finally made a better dollar, they said. The two friends said the company was spiteful enough to demand that Mike turn in his bucket and safety belt, and so he began wearing a used, thirteen-year-old belt up on the windows.

280

"I told him, 'Don't use that belt,' " said Tony Pinto, a butcher at First and 51st, where Mike did clean-up delivery jobs. "But does he listen?"

Mike was wearing the old belt the day he fell the eleven stories into a backyard near a tree. His friends say that talking about the belt is no help, that Mike is gone as certainly as he lived.

"It's hard to say why you liked him so," Tony Pinto said. "He was a simple guy, never stopped talking. Generous—he gave us that little flower pot in the window."

At closing, Tony would pour Mike a parting glass of wine. "He'd tell you to be quiet, the plant is sleeping in the window."

While Bob Reif printed Mike's obituary over the bar uptown, Mario Marsala made the rounds of the service help, shopkeepers and affluent apartment dwellers downtown. There were residents who had never given him a tip all those years, but there were others who nearly loved him and had given him clothes and wine and money. A few of these chipped in with heavy checks, one for $100 and another for $200.

The generous places, it should be noted, were 225 East 46th, 405 East 54th, 1 Beekman Place, No. 10 Mitchell and Reif's bar. Mario Marsala supplied the grave—the last slip left in his aunt's plot at old St. Raymond's in the Bronx. And while the people at Donovan's funeral parlor uptown had quietly cut some prices to help, the money began coming in so strongly that Mario and Bob began upgrading Mike's funeral.

"We went from a wooden casket to one of those shiny steel jobs," Mario said. "And I told them to put on all the candles for the mass. Mike would like that."

They used up the money and forgot about flowers, but Mario confidently ordered two big sprays, one for across the casket. "I knew someone would come through, and sure enough Jackie O'Brian from penthouse D at 225 East 46th came over the night before the funeral and gave me $50. Another good guy."

There was more money, too, from Reif's bar to go with the penthouse grief, and both of the floral pieces said, "To Mike. From your friends."

[1/17/78]

Night Life

The two pregnant giraffes looked beautiful. Not just because they were giraffes and stood there like soaring patchwork fantasies, and were containing images of themselves. But because it was becoming night in the Bronx Zoo and all the humans had been cleared out except for a favored few who could witness the great contrived gathering of life even more clearly in the dusk and in the absence of most human babble.

"Hello, everybody," James G. Doherty, the mammal curator, greeted the giraffes and some less exotic creatures after letting himself into their house with his private key. Silence and a great stare from on high. For whatever the rest of the world can tell about giraffe labor, Mr. Doherty guessed maternity was days or weeks away and so he said good night and withdrew.

The other species waited in the gloaming. Mr. Doherty, a member of the zoo's more or less permanent collection of bipeds, lives on the grounds with his wife and two children, and on the way home in the evening he takes a final look at life and life looks back with some magnificent glistening glances.

•

On this evening, across from the owl cage, a group of humans was having a postwork party in the administration building—the staff of the zoo, with just a taste of wine for each, celebrating the fact that the zoo's magazine had become a national publication.

Other than that, it was an ordinary night beginning at the zoo. By 6 P.M., an hour after the visitors were gently herded out through the gates in the ultimate step in zoo-keeping, the gibbons were flaked out sleepily like small furry boulders on the lake island they share with the pelicans.

The great machinery of the zoo was working normally. The water and air temperatures in the reptile house were automatically monitored with a nighttime alarm set to go off in the family home of one of the curators living on the 252-acre grounds. The incubators containing the bird eggs in their great variety of colors and sizes were heating and rotating according to plan.

In short, the generations were proceeding, and on some far more complicated levels than outsiders might suspect. For example, it is one kind of pride for Joseph Bell, the chief ornithologist, to note that the handsome white-cheeked touraco had not been snatched from the wild but was born of second-generation zoo birds. But beyond that, in more than twenty years' residency at the zoo, Mr. Bell, whose uncle had preceded him as a zoo worker and resident, raised his own small brood. And his son, Kevin, who roamed the hills and cages as a boy, now is curator of the Lincoln Park Zoo in Chicago. The generations were proceeding.

•

Mr. Bell is very relaxed and informative as he makes some evening rounds. "Everything sounds different at night," he says. The wolves sound off, of course, and some times a lion does. Over at the elk pasture, the great antlered Roosevelt chief is rounding up his herd and an incongruous bark is heard. It is from the sea lion house, over the hill, and it takes a minute of adjustment for an observer, much the way the tip of an apartment house out in the South Bronx is momentarily puzzling on the woody horizon.

It is no simple thing, letting nature take its course at night, according to the zoo director, William G. Conway, who also lives on the grounds and keeps a walkie-talkie watch on things. Sometimes traps have to be put out for animal invaders, including gray and red foxes that raid the silently sleeping water fowl. (There are legitimately resident red foxes, too, in the zoo, who live among the bear dens but are shy of daytime visitors. This evening several are stretched out on the rocks of the den, handsome as frozen flame in the dusk, with red coats tipped in white at the tail.)

•

Sometimes the simplest of creatures are most troublesome—dogs and cats gone feral in the South Bronx slums, trying to enter the zoo for a nighttime snack. Even the most well-controlled of jungles, such as the zoo, has life and death decisions going on. When Mr. Doherty enters what amounts to the backstage area at the House of Darkness, a beautifully eerie building full of bats, flying foxes and other night life, he casually steps on a darting roach that has no official business there. But off to the side a large package of live crickets is spared, a chirping mass scheduled to sustain, on the morrow, some of life's more featured creatures, flapping and crawling about now under glass.

The House of Darkness, of course, is man's marvelous trick on the vampires and other creatures that stay up all night. During human daytime, the lights are kept extremely dim in this building and thus the denizens think it's night and so stay awake, flying and scampering about for visitors. Then at 10 P.M. sharp, when they normally would be stepping out of their nests anywhere else, the fluorescent lights automatically go on in the House of Darkness, and this reverse sunrise sends everyone to cover and sleep.

The bats are not awakened until 10 A.M. when the lights are turned back down to a haunting dimness. This is four and a half hours after the 5:30 morning shift of commissary workers arrives to stock the coffee urns, bring in fresh food and prepare for the daylong job of feeding the humans.

[10/4/76]

Sweetness and Light

Seasons's blessings on Peewee Gevenski, an old man on a blue bicycle, happy as a child on this special day as he pedals down to the state dock to kibitz and watch all the fishermen—no-nonsense old-timers and whisky-laced amateurs—launch themselves into the new scallop season.

Everyone seems to find an excuse to stop by the sea on opening day of the scallop season.

"There's Sobatka, the dogcatcher," Peewee says as a houndless truck pulls up to the dock with a happy-looking man at the wheel who is peering at the early boats coming back at mid-morning, heavy with the first bushels of scallops.

"Hey, Sobatka!" Peewee cackles. "There's no wild dogs in the ocean. What ya doin' here?"

But blessings on Sobatka, too, and all free-roaming humans and dogs this day. Everyone knows Peconic Bay scallops are such sweet things in life that it is hard to resist a peek at the first catches to be dredged up after six months of official amnesty and tender growth on the bay bottom.

•

The third Monday in September is always a splendid moment on the North Fork of Long Island. The summer people have gone back to the vertical world. The farms are left warm and open by the roadsides, with fields glistening like well-used palettes daubed with corn-yellow, pumpkin-orange, cabbage leaf-green. And the Peconic Bay scallop is once again as vulnerable as virtue, plucked from the sea in shells that seem mythologically ribbed.

"Look at them, Peewee," Ray Adamiak says, leaning on the dock rail. "Everybody's happy. You can see the mood. They're all coming in with loads of scallops. They're all happy."

Mr. Adamiak is a retired merchant mariner who hasn't left land lately, but there's no way he will miss watching from shore as the scallop season opens.

In contrast to colder days to come, this first day—a shimmering blue and gold prize of bay and beach, white-tufted sky and sun-laden breeze—brings out far more than the tough professional baymen. There also are boatloads of amateurs—some on vacation, others faking sick days—who make an annual ritual of their craving for the small tender eye of these sea creatures.

•

Among the amateurs, a few are deerhunter tipsy, but most are serious enough to have obtained a $7.50 state license and a $90 metal dredging net to drag behind their outboard boats. The scallops are bumped up into the net by metal rings that drag the bottom, and some heavy lifting by hand gets the nets of shellfish into the boat. Scallopers were out at dawn, under the watch of two state environmental officers, Frederick Pradon and Henry Jackson, in their white launch, Osprey. Many return by 10:30 in the morning, delighted with their legal limit of 10 bushels a day.

"The first day, with all the extra guys—what we call 'bluebird' fishermen—always reminds me of a gold rush," Officer Pradon says. "People are running around happy, earning fresh money after the summer."

Peewee casts a hungry eye on the catch of John Corwin and George Atkinson, two dispatchers from the Riverhead Fire Department who save vacation time for the scallop season. They crank their motorboat out of the water onto a car-trailer backed down the state's concrete ramp built into the bay. Their 20 bushels gleam fresh and wet, some of the delicate fluted shellfish coming ashore in the clutch of starfish.

"Now comes the hard part, shelling them." says George Atkinson, a salty looking fireman in overall boots.

•

The season's opening is a matter of socializing as much as foraging. "You see them out there tugging at their beer, making noise," says John Karzenski, unloading his catch from a 14-foot outboard boat. Adventurous in his retirement, he went out alone with a single can of beer for breakfast and a second-hand dredge and came back a happy man, his sneakers wet, his boat awash in shellfish. It beats sitting on a bench on the Grand Concourse.

Up at the dock, Peewee is fantasizing beyond the shucking. "You ever taste raw scallop?" he says, squinting under the bill of his red baseball cap. "Nothing sweeter than raw scallop."

"Or stewed scallop," Ray Adamiak says, joining the reverie. "Or scallop broiled quick with nothing added. Or battered up and deep fried."

Taste buds weeping, Peewee confesses how vicarious his pursuit of the scallop has become in recent years. "In the '20's we used to go out sail-powered and get them all day with a chain of dredges, not just one. But now, hell, I don't think I take more than five bushels a year. I make sure I have my license, though."

•

Across the creek from the launching ramp, a family of geese is at home in the reeds, preening in the sun. A few rod-and-reel fishermen sit on the pilings, dallying a line for snappers, eyeing the scallopers coming back from the bay fruitful and satisfied. Against the ocean horizon, Peewee's blue bike and red hat mark the day as a pristine event.

"Enjoy this day, Peewee," Ray Adamiak advises. "There won't be many more like it."

But that seems arguable to Peewee. "What you talkin' about?" he says, watching the scallops come in Peconic fresh. "There's always more scallop days." He seems right, leaning against his bike. To beg for another third Monday in September is not to seek immortality, but only to enjoy mortality in its sweet cycle.

[9/20/79]

8

And Yet
A Little While

Waiting for
the Blossoms

To the credit of everyone at Calvary Hospital, when a TV news reporter recently
tried one of those how-does-it-feel type questions on a
terminally ill woman, the woman carefully deflected the
inquiry. As the lens zoomed in, she refused to yield a
melodramatic squib on something so important as her own
life and death.

Calvary is an uncommon place of special strengths in the
Bronx where all the patients have cancer and all have been
certified as terminally ill by their physicians. It is a world
near the end of the world for an ever-changing population of
150 patients who average fifty-five days of life in their final
place of care.

There are remissions at times for perhaps one out of ten
who go home, but finally they come back to Calvary. There
is an operating room, but only for procedures like a
tracheostomy to make final breaths easier. There is a quick-
footed code-blue cardiac-revival process, but mainly for a
stricken visitor or worker, not for patients. There is no need
for an emergency room, but there are handy pantries that
accommodate family dinner parties by candlelight.

For the believer, Calvary is reassurance at the final
crossing. For the nonbeliever, it is the last attempt at
decency. It is carefully labored consideration from some
humans who have more time to live. It is pain killing of the
best sort invented so far. It is, in its bright new wedge-
shaped building, a heroic design to capture great gulps of
daylight or night sky through the 6-foot-square window in

each patient's private room. It is more light through the window walls of the community day rooms, and more light flooding the newest terrace garden waiting to bloom in the Bronx, any day now.

The garden contains 1,000 daffodil bulbs, planted last fall when the hospital moved to the new seven-story building on Eastchester Road in the East Bronx. Calvary moved from its sixty-three-year-old base on Macombs Road in a decaying area of the West Bronx, where the old garden had become forbidding to the patients.

"I want an explosion of color," Lorraine Tregde, the executive director, says, craving the first blooms for her people. This call to the spring sun somewhere on its way immediately transcends everything else in the Bronx, the weedy contentions of Charlotte Street, the money-rich grass of Yankee Stadium awaiting the recreation of another season.

A visitor must hope the little man wearing a beret and sitting in a wheelchair watching television has time enough to see the daffodils come. That's as good as any goal at Calvary. Then the professional voyeur could better ask: How does it feel to see daffodils?

The little man in the beret smiling hello is dying, but he looks up as if he knows the same secret about everyone else. There are no profound questions that come to mind from his look, rather a reminder that life is a series of details to be cherished. To someone from outside Calvary, it is refreshing to discover that a patient is as free to get a beer or a glass of wine from the pantry at any time as to visit the chapel downstairs where the candles burn. There, the image of the risen Christ on the wall seems to beckon not so much in glory but more grayly, more believably, in relief at finishing with death.

The crowd in the mural watching Christ's death depicts relatives of Calvary patients, a ragged string of faces that show anger as much as sadness, and that is the human truth at Calvary, Miss Tregde says.

•

Upstairs, the subject is pain as Dr. James E. Cimino, the medical director, chats by one of the long, low, triangular nurses' stations, which are ingeniously designed to be always reassuringly visible from any open doorway of any of the fifty patient rooms on each floor. He will not speculate why, but the doctor is fascinated by the finding that an average of one of five in Calvary's cancer-ridden population never needs narcotics, and an additional four or five out of ten cut back their pain-killers to almost nothing in the final two weeks of life.

These nuances are part of the hospital's special purpose of being totally attentive to the terminal cancer patient. The doctor feels other, more general hospitals can be so distracted by more promising cases that the final days of a cancer victim become a dismal, forgotten priority, a revealing indignity.

Calvary was founded eighty years ago on Perry Street in Greenwich Village by a fireman's widow who discovered a new purpose in caring for people written off as terminal. It was run by nuns in recent years, but now the Roman Catholic archdiocese has mostly a lay staff in charge. The staff has a very small turnover for a hospital, about 1 percent a month. Dr. Cimino says they carry on the nuns' tradition of compassion, changing dressings hourly if necessary for cleanliness and morale, trying to see the person through the final ravages of disease.

Only saints and psychotics are happy as death closes in, Dr. Cimino says. "You die as you've lived," he says. "If you were paranoid in life, you'll be paranoid when you're dying. If you faced reality in life, that's likely the way you'll be in dying."

Two to three people die each day at Calvary, finding the limit to time that we all know is here. There is no shortage of replacements for the 150 beds, just as there will be none for the final 50 beds due to open later this year, some time after the first new daffodils come to bloom at Calvary.

[3/6/79]

Courage, My Love

The streets leading to the library in the slum are lined with broken glass and empty buildings with charred window hollows that suggest a jack-o-lantern mockery of the people still coming for the books.

Life—the library's reason for being and the all-encompassing category of its volumes—has been driven farther and farther away from the red brick building on Southern Boulevard in the South Bronx. And the readers who venture to it past the Bruckner Expressway and other chaotic shoals of Hunts Point find the library unexpectedly shut at times because the hours and staff have been cut by half.

The other morning, there seemed more activity down the boulevard at Bloom's Furniture ("Welfare Welcome"/ "Su Credito Es Bueno Aquí") than at the library. But if you stayed a while, the library's hold on life became clear as moss on a rock, and the people who work and read there seemed part of a word ministry echoing the isolated monasteries of the Middle Ages.

Gregory Rivera has invested fifteen of his twenty-nine years in behalf of books in the South Bronx, his home neighborhood. The son of an elevator operator, Mr. Rivera began as a library page soon after his first childhood escape to Tara as a GWTW reader. Now he is involved full-time in liaison for the library system, charged with searching out groups of potential readers in the increasingly deserted neighborhoods of the South Bronx.

"It's becoming harder and harder," he says. "I spent a lot of time arranging a lecture on the Tiana Indians and their history in Puerto Rico, and only eleven people showed up."

His own experience seems to shore up his optimism. "More than the books of the library, it was the people I came in contact with who motivated me," he says.

•

Carmen Reyes first came to the library two decades ago with her children, and revealed to them the fairy-tale joys of Perez and Martina, something of a local classic in the sizable Hispanic section. Now she is a grandmother and senior clerk at the Hunts Point library who has seen young troublemakers return years later as established parents proud of their days at the library.

"The library even gave them heat for their bodies, I would say," Mrs. Reyes said, noting the rough South Bronx winters. She has seen the daily circulation of 1,000 or more books cut in half since the area's more-crowded days of past Jewish settlement.

"But this library already is becoming something special," she said. "It has the best Hispanic collection in the city and people are starting to come from all over to use it."

Over in the biography stacks, Osualdo Melendez selects "The Diary of Anne Frank," but the fifteen-year-old's special literary flair already is displayed on his belt, where he has stenciled a message to no one in particular: "Courage My Love."

With his faint beard and hunter's hat proclaiming the name "Duke," he could easily be taking an aimless, finger-popping stroll down Southern Boulevard. But he says he discovered the library five years ago: "Hey, great, I think. I use it to study, and I like the science fiction and the girls you can meet here."

•

All such motives are welcome to Sylvia P. Bean, the chief librarian wise enough to respond to questions about the library by taking a visitor on a tour of the neighborhood. Walking and watching, she has great stretches of burnt-out streets to herself, and is sad. She brightens in pointing to a bit of rehabilitated housing at 163rd and Simpson; she saddens in spotting fresh desertion over on Hunts Point

Avenue. But Colin Graham, once a happy child at the library and now a strapping twenty-year-old student at Brooklyn Polytech, arrives just in time with a greeting.

His Caribbean lilt is deeper than Miss Bean's but she put her own to charming advantage earlier in greeting Jerome Marshman, the gray-haired proprietor of the bakery-restaurant that has been open on Hunts Point Avenue for close to thirty years. Besides making the bread and rolls for his pastrami sandwiches, he makes collages and paintings, and they are displayed at Miss Bean's library.

The more interesting lives at the Southern Boulevard library are not on the shelves. There is, for example, Luis Prez, a forty-three-year-old guard at the front door, who appreciates the opportunity to bring magazines and books home to his wife, Carmen, but misses his old job in a corrugated box factory where he made twice the $6,700 a year he gets at the library.

•

There is the young children's librarian, Christine Behrmann, thankful for the trip to work from Manhattan every day because of the special nature of her readers.

"I hate to say it, but the kids are much nicer here than in middle-class neighborhoods," she said. "I think it's because here you either get the good kid or no one at all."

There is Christopher Maass, a twenty-two-year-old dropout from City College. "I have lived here from day one," he says in the midst of distributing the new community newspaper he started. At the moment, he wants help from the library with his campaign to organize various fragmented block associations, and with his effort to encourage the poetry of Pedro Torres, a twelve-year-old soul he has discovered in making his street rounds.

And there is Betty Miller, a clerk who knew so many local faces until recent years, when she was burned out of one nearby apartment, saw a second one wither, and so moved away.

[10/20/76]

Eroica

Paralyzed from the neck down for years and years in his room and linked to breath by machinery and to hope by Beethoven, R. Marshall Loftus took the sipping-straw-like steering mechanism of his new battery-powered wheelchair in his lips and gently huffed and puffed a course out of doors two months ago.

This was the first time he had been outside the Brooklyn Veterans Hospital in twenty-two years.

The event was mighty, Beethoven mighty, as Mr. Loftus steered himself by mouth among the grass and the trees near the Narrows passage to the ocean, taking in the salt breeze in measured, humming breaths of his girdle-type respirator. His body was inert in the chair and the one proof of animation was the gray-haired, blue-eyed, vulnerably grinning head of R. Marshall Loftus carried along like the pontiff of a one-man religion that had maintained faith in himself and his own resurrection.

Wonderfully, the man was ambulatory, pastoral and, he recalls, incredulous at what he had done with himself.

"Oh, wow, when I was first motorized I couldn't believe at the end of each day I really had been up and out and driving myself around," Mr. Loftus says, enlisting the aid of a visitor to plug his chair's recharging cord into the hospital wall, casual as a suggestion for a bracing cocktail. "Now I feel no surprise, like it was just a long delay and I was meant to be out there."

•

He was a twenty-six-year-old wholesale ice cream salesman when, on Aug. 30, 1952, he was stricken in one of the last great polio plagues before the Salk vaccine was perfected. At first, the issue was life and death, crushing pain and inability to breathe, survival in an iron chamber with, he says, his willpower reduced to the barest minimum.

"I definitely refused to die. I mean really," he says. "Not from fear, but just stubborn refusal. This was not going to be the end. I felt I had more to do."

What he had to do mainly for all the years since was to lie alone on his back and not become desperate. "What it takes is the ability to be both extroverted and introverted. In other words, when I'm alone—I can't explain how—I'm able to entertain myself no matter what, even all the years when we couldn't have our own televisions and radios."

And what he had to do through those years, he concedes, was to pester people for bits of improvement in his life, the most wondrous bit being, of course, the E. & J. Model 30 powered wheelchair adapted to breath controls by Paul Fried, a former space program engineer who is the hospital's biomedical engineer.

Before that, though, there was Mr. Loftus's fight to wear his own clothes at the hospital as an exception to the policy of most patients' going about in uniform robes.

"Those days when they didn't understand why I wanted my own clothing," he says, "that was not a good time."

But there is more humor than bitterness in the retelling in which he first discovers that some mental patients and drug addicts are allowed their own clothes and, with this wedge, he pesters officials.

"They gave in, but then they come around and say, 'No, the clothes have to be fireproof.' Fireproof! I'm making the point how dehumanizing it is and they're talking about fireproofing."

Something of a science literature buff, he read about the carcinogenic danger of fireproofing and soon he was triumphant. The memory prompts a kind word for the hospital and a big red-faced grin from Mr. Loftus as he lies resplendent in a denim pants and jacket whose blue-washed tones match his eyes.

In similar bureaucracy-fighting fashion, Mr. Loftus has the distinction of being the only patient with a private telephone line, which is connected to a Paul Fried panel contraption facing Mr. Loftus in bed. His only bit of useful motor ability below the neck is to move his right hand an inch or two up and down, like a slow telegrapher, and this is the key for signaling panel controls that run the telephone, TV, radio, nurse call, lamp and stereo over by the window where he keeps Beethoven, Brahms, and Chopin cassettes stacked up like hypodermics for his soul.

"In this weather, I really can't get enough of the Pastorale," he says of the symphony the deafened Beethoven concocted from imagination, memory and affection. Mr. Loftus does not allow himself sentimental music. "Why dwell in the past?"

The alternative he prefers to classical is rock music, and thus the fifty-one-year-old man is happily pelted late at night, and he can celebrate Linda Ronstadt as easily as Beethoven.

He reads science and Eastern philosophers when he has volunteers to turn pages for him. He made sure the hospital got a 40-foot extension cord so he could stay outside longer by plugging back into the hospital. He is ruddy and ebullient from the sunshine and as he lies there, other patients—fully capable of normal mobility—stand around wanly in bathrobes as if envious of Mr. Loftus and his vitality.

For the first twenty years, his goals were to get out of the bed, then out of the hospital. Now he wants to get off the grounds to the rest of the city if he can get some sort of aid. "I am going to do what I want to do," he says.

"Some day I will be there at Lincoln Center," he says, "in my wheelchair in a side aisle, plugged into an outlet for their vacuum cleaners and hearing it all—the ballets and symphonies, the symphonies most of all." With the sipping-straw mechanism hanging just beyond the defiant curl of his lip, what Mr. Loftus said seemed more vow than fantasy.

[3/28/77]

Click:

After Rosemary Cashman, mother of nine (including a fine Flatbush balance of a nurse, an F.B.I. agent and a seminarian), warns about her husband setting up his slide projector, she quietly leaves the room.

Her husband, Sgt. John J. Cashman of the New York City Police Department, smiles and puts a large wheel of slides onto the projector. "She's a wonderful girl, my wife," he says. "She has a friend, a nun, who was in Hawaii and got me Lindbergh."

The lights are dimmed, the projector whirrs to life and one after another, as Jack Cashman clicks the trigger, his favorite pictures slide past onto the wall: shot after shot of tombstones and graves, grim granites and lachrymose limestones, from Daniel Boone's stone in Frankfurt, Ky., to Tallulah Bankhead's stone in Kent County, Md., from James Whitcomb Riley in Indianapolis to Lydia E. Pinkham in Lynn, Mass.

These are as candid as snapshots can get. The sun slants onto names chiseled into stone after stone on the surface of the earth.

Click: We are in Princeton, N.J., at John O'Hara's grave. "I got John when I was down there picking up Grover Cleveland," Mr. Cashman says, hitting the trigger.

Click: John Dillinger's stone is heavily chipped by lurid souvenir hunters.

Click: J. Edgar Hoover's headstone doesn't look much better. "Yeah, isn't that awful, the lousy upkeep?" Jack says, "I got to write to the F.B.I. guys down there and tell them to shape it up."

He gets some of his slides by writing to cemetery officials, history buffs and other policemen around the country. He knows of no cemetery addict precisely like himself, with wheels of slides. But, in a pinch, he knows one cop always tries to help another cop. "I got Millard Fillmore from a Buffalo cop. Good guy, he got out of his radio car for me up there."

Click: "There's Bill." Buffalo Bill, William F. Cody, Lookout Mountain, Colo.

Click: "There's Margaret—she was run over, you know." Margaret Mitchell, Atlanta, Ga.

In the manufactured light, the two-dimensional color shafts of the final places of people past cut across the room, one by one (with the exceptions of Eng and Chang Bunker, the famous Siamese twins resting unsundered in White Plains, N.C.).

•

In his fifty years of life, Mr. Cashman has visited dozens of cemeteries, and when he wants to get away from the considerable life in his own home, he still packs a sandwich and heads over to Greenwood, the classic rural cemetery near his Flatbush house. For decades he has stone-hopped and hobnobbed there. "I tell Rosemary, 'At least I'm not in a gin mill,'" he says.

On a drizzly afternoon walk, before hefting his wheels of slides, Jack Cashman stops fondly at a Greenwood headstone depicting a little schoolboy in a sailor outfit, chiseled life-size, innocent and happy. His name is carved below: "Frankie." And under it: "Yet a Little While." He is 102 years gone.

"Isn't Frankie something?" Jack Cashman says, patting the limestone lad's shoulder and book strap.

As a boy, Jack lived next-door to Greenwood, near Fifth Avenue and 25th Street, and got a job mowing the grass. "I was a go-for for the gravediggers—I don't know how many sandwiches and beers I carried into this place—and the

303

gravediggers would tell me all their stories." These were gothic tales updated—the World War II sailor who happened by one night and lent his peacoat to a pale and beautiful woman he found confused at the gate. Returning the next day to meet her, he found only his peacoat on a young girl's tombstone. "Believe that and I got a dozen more," Jack says, laughing in the graveyard.

Jack is fascinated by Greenwood's wonderful graves. The 109-year-old grave of John Matthews, who is depicted life-size in stone, sleeping under a handsome shed roof, was cleaned recently and Jack is upset that this further eroded the soothing murals placed under the roof in sight of the stone Mr. Matthews. They depict the deceased as he lived—sitting and thinking and inventing the soda fountain, which provided the man fortune enough for an eye-catching grave.

•

But Jack Cashman himself is at least as interesting as the headstones he favors, particularly in the tense of speech he slips into in his hobby, a kind of pluperfect present. "I'm not here," he says, speaking of the future interment plans of himself. "I'm over in St. John's in Queens where my parents are. That's where I'll be going. Nothing much in the way of famous people there. A lot of gangsters."

He could do better, for Jack Cashman is so well known locally for loving Greenwood that a woman in the neighborhood made him a gift of a plot, all legal, full deed and fathom deep. But Jack is a family man, a patriarch, and knows where he belongs.

"Hey!" he shouts, coming into the Cashmans' three-story wood house, an inviting, rambling structure on Marlborough Road. "Who's home? Where is everybody? They're here all right," he says, enjoying his family's scattered presence, going up to get the projector out. "They're hiding from my slides."

He has a complete set of Presidents and their wives on one wheel. Click: "There's Dolly." The Madisons, Montpelier, Vt.

Stone after stone, wheel after wheel, they slide past as Jack Cashman pleases, strangely random and eclectic, the way life is.

Click: Joey Gallo. Click: DeWitt Clinton. Click: Cole Porter.

Click: Nelson Rockefeller. "There's Nelson."

Click:

[5/26/79]

Q101

As the city's buses go, the Q101 carries the most troubled riders. These are the relatives and loved ones of an island of accused criminals who can't make bail—quiet bus passengers who make the round trip between freedom and Rikers Island prison, grasping shopping bags of treats for the accused and holding the hands of small children spawned into a world they did not make, a world filled with crime and streaked with retribution.

The children take the 50-cent bus ride like any other, chatting, swinging their legs, looking out at all that's passing new in the world. But the adults seem to be looking somewhere else, caught up with lives waiting in a state of suspension in the defendants' pens across the Hazen Street bridge on Rikers Island.

As the accused hope or not for justice, mothers and lovers, siblings and offspring join in the curbside routine at Queens Boulevard and Jackson Avenue where the subway lets them off from other neighborhoods of the city. They are mostly women and children, and they make the bus ride poignant as the Q101 moves on its northernmost cut through the clean, striving-class neighborhood running along Steinway Street. The single inviting word on the sign in Amorelli's real-estate window at 22d Avenue—"HOMES"—touches the mood in the jouncing bus with the world's universal yearning for a warm and secure abode.

•

In its way, Rikers Island is a part of that yearning, a place where society claims a greater edge of security by penning thousands of New Yorkers accused of criminal harm against thousands of victimized New Yorkers. The Hazen Street bridge is a very special thread in the city social fabric, promising security to the optimists in one community and symbolizing eventual release to the optimists in the other.

And so the Q101 moves at a lumbering pace back and forth between the packed and pretty houses of Queens and the dense and ugly Rikers housing.

One morning Richard A. Ochetti gets on the Q101. He is a very polite man in a gray suit and summer straw-hat, carrying a big envelope of paperwork, a different-looking sort from the rest of the bus group. He is a thirty-six-year-old senior trial attorney with the Legal Aid Society, building another workday around the Manhattan-to-Queens, E train-to-Q101 wheels of city justice.

Mr. Ochetti has had to make these trips, which expend a lawyer's entire workday including lunch hour, ever since the Legal Aid Society won a "victory" in suing against the conditions of rabble and bazaar suffered by defendants and their lawyers at the old Tombs jailhouse next to the main criminal courtroom in downtown Manhattan. The society won its point, but in lieu of the next-door chaos of the Tombs, defense lawyers now have the long maze to Rikers Island if they need face-to-face discussions with their clients.

Life adjusts a bit to this legalistic bulge in the city's great Skinner box; a few lawyers car-pool over when they can time their visits together. But Dick Ochetti is Legal Aid and settles for the E train and Q101 which, he hopes, occasionally impresses a spiritless defendant. "To come all this way lets him know I'm interested in his case and what he has to say," says the lawyer as the Q101 starts and stops its way toward the island.

•

In his eight years a a public defender, Mr. Ochetti says he has come absolutely to love his work. He is a lawyer who is a pleasure to travel with on the bus. Refreshingly, he doesn't imply he knows the inside track on all about him, and he does not offer romantic rhetoric about the presumption of innocence. He talks of outside preparation as the key to a worthy court performance, and he neatly lays out the Rikers routine—which window clerk is most helpful, which island visitor-van routes are the most direct in reaching his clients—as if it were an important part of his brief. The people on the island and on the bus could do worse.

When he wins a case, of course, there is no big fee or celebration. "Actually," he says, "the nicest thing a defendant ever said to me after acquittal was, 'Thank you, I never won anything before.' I'm sure he was telling the truth. The fellow was a miserable specimen."

•

The correction workers in the reception center do a reasonable job of organizing, searching and shuttling all the visitors. The junk-food wall of vending machines, the baby cries, the anxiety of waiting in plastic chairs all seem no worse than a bus terminal passage.

Mr. Ochetti has papers ready to visit two accused as rapists, a gunshot-case defendant, and a fourth man whose charges are compounded by possible psychiatric problems.

In three hours on the island, he reports good case-productive conversations with the first two men. The third cannot be found immediately; he may have opted to work out in the prison gym rather than see his lawyer. And for the fourth, Mr. Ochetti is told he is too late—it is after 3 P.M., when Rikers defendants must settle toward the evening routine, and so goodbye.

Mr. Ochetti knows he always can and must return another day. He catches a van back to the reception center. Then he gets on the line with the women and children waiting for the Q101 bus, and he goes back across the Hazen Street bridge to the rest of the city.

[7/10/79]

Esther Mollov

IN MEMORIAM

Esther Shulamit Mollov lived from April 24, 1962, until Feb. 5, 1978, and two days before she died she told her mother how angry she was that everything was ending for her.

There really seems no way to know who Esther was, but her mother has insisted we try. "Why shouldn't an ordinary person be memorialized?" Mrs. Mollov asks.

A visit to her house on 81st Avenue in Queens—a talk with her mother, a glimpse of Esther's room with the bed made neatly, a picture of her as a five-year-old smiling simply amid brilliant azaleas in the backyard—and all we have done is to confirm how we missed her. But the mother, whose grief is keen and controlled, presses the challenge. As she talks, the same backyard azalea bush can be seen out the window, abloom, fiery red, alive beyond Esther.

•

Esther was an excellent student, and in the ten months of her terminal illness with lymph cancer, the fifteen-year-old fought hard to pick up her studies at Jamaica High School. The quality cited by teachers after her death, Mrs. Mollov says, was Esther's talent for asking questions, for poking at points of a lesson, for wanting to push toward the heart of a matter.

This clearly is a great comfort to Mrs. Mollov, and she recalls this same refusal to be sidetracked when the girl was ill. "Esther never referred to her illness," Mrs. Mollov says. "She resented being treated as an illness instead of a person, and would say so."

In her brief high school career, Esther was an honor student, quite proud that she had been selected to write the Hebrew essay for the school's foreign-language magazine. When she was a sixth-grader at the Yeshiva of Central Queens, the girl had won a boroughwide essay contest on Soviet Jewry. The following year, she won the school's oratorical contest for her presentation of Elie Wiesel's speech "Against Despair." When she graduated, she entered the Prozdor program of the Jewish Theological Seminary of America.

For all these reasons and more, the Mollovs went to Israel after Esther's death—her mother, her father, Norman, and her older brother, Ben—and planted a grove of trees in her memory. "We wanted it to be something living for those who are," her mother says.

•

Through the months of Esther's illness, the daughter and her family went through a gray-to-black spectrum of emotion. From a minor symptom, a stomachache, the disease bloomed in the girl, and the prescribed treatment of steroids changed her radically. "She had two psychotic episodes from the treatment—she just went plain crazy," her mother said. "She lost her hair. She went blind as the cancers spread everywhere."

But the madness would pass, and Mrs. Mollov would again see evidence of her daughter's special quality. "She would ask me, 'I can go home if I'm blind, right?' That was Esther. In ten months she confronted more trouble than most people have in three lifetimes." But the daughter sought ways to prevail, and the mother is grateful for that memory.

Somewhere in those ten months, Mrs. Mollov says, she looked about her and made the most comforting discovery of Esther's brief life. "I suddenly realized how many people were involved, trying to help."

The range was enormous, Mrs. Mollov says, stretching from Esther's lifelong next-door buddy, Meg Lovejoy, who never missed a day's visit when Esther was out of the hospital, to Sol Nichtern, a psychiatrist with Jewish Child Care. "He fixed it so Esther could reach him at any time, even call him up when she was raving," Mrs. Mollov says. "He would call us two or three times a day." In the process of death, the mother says, she met a number of medical professionals who seemed intent on retreating from a lost cause. "But here was a doctor who realized his role was in helping the family."

•

Mrs. Mollov thinks she discovered that the ordinary good people of the world are legion, both as individuals and as members of Esther's school and religious associations. She found that some of Esther's classmates regularly visited her on Friday evenings, walking, not riding to the hospital and up to the sixth-floor room, in accordance with Sabbath strictures. They would say the Tillim, the prayer for the sick, and then, the mother says, have a gossip session that Esther always cherished. Here, says the mother, is the real memorial for her daughter.

At the same time, the Mollovs found different circles of friends organizing themselves into ever-present, never-intrusive sources of help. One group, led by Dave and Esther Andron, would be in daily touch and always able to sense what relief was needed at the hospital. The family's oldest friends, Selma and Gabe Block, made their house a second home for the family, with meals and quiet conversation. This, too, the mother counts as Esther's memorial.

"One of my friends would sit all day with Esther and tell her about her own career," Mrs. Mollov says, and the girl loved this vicarious touch of life. So many teen-agers came by, and when, in the aftermath, Mrs. Mollov checked further she found that their parents had reminded the youngsters of the value of responding to Esther. So all this, the mother says, is a memorial for Esther.

"When Esther died, she was sane and knew everything," her mother says. The funeral was on the day the city struggled out from the huge early February snowstorm last year. Cars could not move, but scores of people showed up at the funeral home, and the weather became part of the occasion. "All nature cries out for Esther," a rabbi said.

Recalling all this, Mrs. Mollov turns to the window and the azaleas where Esther once stood and smiled. She knows the importance of Esther, her daughter. The mother speaks again of the need for somehow memorializing "someone who is not known."

[5/12/79]

Billy Pulls His Weight

At age thirty-seven, Billy Conklin has the kind of honest child's presence that could interrupt the Pope, as he did once.

Everybody was supposed to be reverentially quiet as John XXIII came into a Vatican room for an audience. But Billy Conklin, hardly retarded socially, went over and said, "Hello John." The Pope, who stood about as tall as Billy, embraced him and said, "Questo é il regno dei cieli"—of such is the kingdom of heaven.

Years later, Billy Conklin's kingdom remains the earth, and it is not bad as he roams it. He was one of the first retarded persons in the city to be taught systematically to ride the subways and buses alone—a special virtue of the city that is widely used now by the moderately retarded.

His mother, Jessie, saw his resources when others didn't, back in the days when people tended to generalize pessimistically about the "mongoloid" retarded even more than they do now. She shopped around carefully and got Billy a job in an eyeglass shop on Nassau Street as a messenger.

She stayed on the job with him one week while he put his firm memory to work getting down the twists and turns of his job and its neighborhood. Then he was left on his own each work day, and for the last fourteen years he has made the trip back and forth from the Conklin home in Bay Ridge, Brooklyn. Abe Schwartz, his employer at Crystal Opticians, says there is no one like Billy. He says he is always helpful and on time and once when he was late he somehow managed to get a note from the subway conductor explaining the train was delayed.

•

Billy's father also says there is no one like Billy, that he'll always surprise you. He taught Billy to ride a bike in the dark, when there were not so many people on the streets to watch. That was years ago and the whole Conklin family has since become far less defensive, to put it mildly, about Billy. The father remembers when Billy's I.Q. was measured at forty-six and he sees now it is measured at seventy-one, so he is not that interested in the prescriptions of experts.

Billy gives a very plain and direct interview, walking on his lunch hour down Nassau Street and over to another eyeglass shop on Broadway run by his friend, Artie Gustafson. Billy stops and points to a visitor's pad. "Artie needs more business," he says. "Take that down, Times."

Billy stops to buy some hot-dogs, take-out, and carries them up to Artie's place of lenses and little boxes and polishing machinery. Artie, a gray-haired fatherly man, is busy and laughs at Billy's generous idea of promoting more business. Artie chats with Billy and does a little work, like every lunch hour. He helps Billy do lengthy crossword puzzles, nonsensically but happily. He gets Billy onto one of his favorite subjects, the Mets.

"The Mets," Billy says. "The Mets should get rid of Koosman," he says flatly of a hard-luck pitcher. "Take that down, Times." He watches as you do.

Last week Billy had to go to Surrogate Court, and it was like the Vatican all over again because he suddenly decided to speak up to the judge. At Artie's place, Billy remembers word for word what he said: "I love my folks. I have a good home. That's the story of my life."

Artie likes that and Billy nods a little in proud emphasis, showing the retarded person's special unguarded smile.

The Surrogate Court can boggle the most sophisticated mind, and Billy's father found it annoying to be there at all. It seems there is something in the law that requires the parents of a retarded person to go before the surrogate and be declared legal guardians of their offspring after the eighteenth birthday.

It was a formality of five minutes, the father said, but if overlooked, as often happens, it can prove costly later in estate management. A lawyer, of course, was required for the brief mission through the court, and a typical fee for this runs up to $400.

After this experience it is only natural that Billy's father should have introduced a bill in the State Senate to change this, proposing that the burden be reversed with an affidavit procedure—and no lawyer's fee—that continues the parents as guardians unless someone successfully challenges this natural right in court. Billy's father is State Senator William T. Conklin, a nonlawyer who got into politics years ago in large part because of Billy, when the Conklins realized there was no great public awareness of the problem.

•

The Conklins helped organize the Guild for Exceptional Children in their local neighborhood and Mr. Conklin went on as a legislative lobbyist for the retarded and finally got elected to the Senate on his second try. He is the legislative expert in this field, serving now as deputy leader to the Republican majority. While he can be as foxy and partisan as any politician on some issues, he is feisty on retardation, making sure the Legislature has more than forty retarded persons working in the capital as messengers and clerks, and pushing for the pioneer legislation requiring birth tests for PKU, the brain-damage disease.

The Senator's only regret about Billy seems to be that for the first four years the family took the traditional closet approach, wanting to believe the broken-hearted relatives' advice that of course he was normal, he just needed extra carrots or milk or something. Billy's first subway mission alone was a day of intense anxiety for the Conklins, but the recollection years later by the Senator is in terms of a great moment in the life of everyone.

Billy has never missed a transfer. "I take 'M' to DeKalb and take 'N'—no more Sea Beach—to 59th Street. RR to 77th Street and I walk home." Billy turns suddenly to Artie. "I met Artie's sister on the train. Artie, what's her name?"

"Mildred," Artie says.

"Mildred," Billy says. "Take that down."

[12/17/77]